D0281052

For the Popular Culture Collective

and the friends I have danced with on this journey.

We were never being boring.

From Revolution
to Revelation

Generation X, Popular Memory and Cultural Studies

TARA BRABAZON

ASHGATE

Published by
Ashgate Publishing Limited
Gower House
Croft Road
Aldershot
Hants GU11 3HR
England

Ashgate Publishing Company
Suite 420
101 Cherry Street
Burlington, VT 05401-4405
USA

Ashgate website: http://www.ashgate.com

British Library Cataloguing in Publication Data
Brabazon, Tara
From revolution to revelation : Generation X, popular
memory and cultural studies
1. Generation X 2. Popular culture 3. Young adults 4. Youth
5. Culture - Study and teaching
I. Title
306

Library of Congress Cataloging-in-Publication Data
Brabazon, Tara.
From revolution to revelation : generation X, popular memory and cultural studies /
by Tara Brabazon.
    p. cm.
Includes index.
    ISBN 0-7546-4396-4 (hardback) -- ISBN 0-7546-4397-2 (pbk.)
    1. Generation X. 2. Popular culture. 3. Young adults. 4. Youth. 5. Culture--Study
and teaching. I. Title.

HQ799.5.B72 2004
306--dc22

2004022244

ISBN 0 7546 4396 4 (Hbk)
ISBN 0 7546 4397 2 (Pbk)

Printed and bound in Great Britain by MPG Books Ltd, Bodmin, Cornwall

Contents

Introduction

Changing the dedication

Shall I rewrite or revise
My October Symphony?
Or as an indication
Change the dedication
From revolution to revelation.[1]

        Pet Shop Boys, 'My October Symphony'

Political changes have swirled through the last two decades. It has been a time of decaying economic infrastructure, the decline of the traditional left, the rise of neo-liberal agendas and a birth of a(nother) third way. The Berlin Wall crumbled and shoulder pads slithered back into the style orphanage. Midway through these two decades – in 1990 – the Pet Shop Boys released an anthem to the era, a statement stark in its irony and bright in its boldness. This lyric traced a movement away from credible, authentic, public domain politics to the realm of affect, identity politics and change-fatigue. They also provided a t-shirt slogan that charts the journey of Cultural Studies through these decades: *From Revolution to Revelation*.

Cultural Studies has always worked well with the bubbling present. The delight in ephemera, the ever-morphing wash of images, beats, fabrics and gloss, has created a loyal but stroppy community of scholars and – concurrently – vocally dismissive critics. The great and pervasive absence in the paradigm remains a reflexive theory of its own trajectory, rather than a banal restatement of great men.[2] Raymond Williams, Richard Hoggart and Stuart Hall are no longer names holding content. Theorists summon these ghosts to talk of something else. I desire more than a genuflection to this past: I ask for a critically interpretative cultural history. When Richard Johnson edited *Making Histories* in 1981, it should have been the start of a small but significant specialism in the paradigm, a way to transform the Birmingham Centre for *Contemporary* Cultural Studies into a theory with a past, and a methodology to explore it. However the triumphantly tandem paradigmatic forces within Cultural Studies – textual analysis and ethnography – have not required attendant historiographical handmaidens.

At its exciting, passionate best, Cultural Studies discerns a fashion, fad, cult or theory just in time, and then writes about it as it dies. Cultural Studies scholars grasp at the coat tails of expiring fashions, mediating between the High Street and the Op Shop. Popular culture is fast in its production and audiences are swift to judgement. Theorists are left with discarded, shiny fabrics and endless remixes of songs no longer in the charts. Such an (un)fashionable phenomenon is best revealed through youth subcultural theory, which has peppered the politics and resistive metaphors of Cultural Studies. The fame of the best scholarship – from the Birmingham Centre and the Manchester Institute for Popular Culture – is deserved because the resident scholars wrote about punks and ravers with immediacy and punch. The postgraduate students were dancing and thinking, watching and writing. While there has been remarkable, committed and significant scholarship produced around the world beyond these centres, both these sites of study are iconographic and remembered because of the intense relationship between popular culture, politics, place and time. These scholars took a photograph so affective in its application – so sensual in its sociology – that the research has been remembered even after the books are no longer in print and the theorists have moved on to other projects.

What happens when the strobe is turned off, the bar closed, the colostomy bag belt unhooked, and the sweaty, smiley bandana discarded? There is something tragic about visiting youthful ghost towns. To read about the Roxy Club and the Paradise Garage of 1978 – or the 1991 Hacienda – in the present is a dislocating, nostalgic experience. For those of us who have never experienced a centred subculture (tautology or paradox?) in this way, how are we to grasp our time, while mobilizing the past in a coherent, considered fashion?

This project is the task of *From Revolution to Revelation*. To rewrite Greil Marcus, I am interested in the dustbin of Cultural Studies, the discarded remnant of political struggles and theoretical hopes that were not realized. I rummage through (un)popular theories, rediscovering Popular Memory Studies as it was sketched by Richard Johnson and others in the late 1970s and early 1980s. Such a paradigm offers extraordinary potential, particularly as a way to understand the first (post) youth culture, sometimes (and retrospectively) termed Generation X. Those born between 1961 and 1981 have endured many (post) youth cultural labels, from slackers to the chemical/blank generation and baby busters. Yet there has been no systematic study of the literacies and popular culture that are the basis of – and for – this imagined and imagining collectivity. There is a reason for this intellectual blind spot. There is a long-standing mistrust of popular culture, and not only within universities.[3] While Cultural Studies writers have attacked this suspicion,

2

Graeme Turner has recognized that this defence has become a "default investment in the popular".[4] *From Revolution to Revelation* does not defend or accept popular culture – thereby shutting down interpretative space – but watches it morph and change as it twists through time. I document the disappearances of history, showing how popular memory – like the Hacienda – can be (re)built, even after the building itself has been destroyed.

The affiliation between Generation X and Cultural Studies is not randomly selected. It was left to Grossberg to remind us that Cultural Studies is

> the Generation X of the academic world ... Like the post baby-boom generation that is referenced in this odd phrase ... everyone is talking about it but no one seems to know what it is. Lots of people are suddenly claiming to do it while others, nervous about its rather sudden success, are attacking it.[5]

Such a realization is brilliantly revealed and well captured, but needs further research and clarification. *From Revolution to Revelation* takes up Grossberg's challenge, following the bread-crumbed trail of popular memory that snakes through both Cultural Studies and Generation X. Importantly, this study traverses the world, from the United States to the United Kingdom, Canada, Australia and New Zealand, and through the Asian and Pacific region. It is a study of movement, and is in a state of tussled motion. Popular culture and popular memory do not stop at national borders, but slice – energetically and passionately – through rhythmic and looped time. Investigating this range of mobile local allegiances is necessary in an era where transatlantic 'theory' has become a replacement for historical specificity. Popular culture is promiscuous, and flirts between capitalist markets.

From Revolution to Revelation executes a simple project: to investigate how Generation X and popular culture dance through popular memory. To take this topic seriously (and yet mischievously at the same time) is to rethink the political and theoretical nature of Cultural Studies as a research and teaching enterprise, and as a method of writing in the public domain. The style of prose is part of the argument. This is not a dry textbook with bullet-pointed questions at the conclusion of a chapter. There are enough of these streaming from publishers. The consequences of these books to Cultural Studies and how they crumble the complexity of the paradigm is best observed through publishing catalogues. Monitor the following advertizement for *Cultural Studies – the basics*, which was released in 2002.

> This is a book for anyone who wants an unfussy, authoritative critical introduction to cultural studies. It equips you with all you need to know about theorists of

cultural studies: what they say, how they differ from one another and what are the strengths and weaknesses of each position. It provides biographical information on major theorists plus assessments of key texts. The book is designed to be used and read by students who face the pressures of essay deadlines, examinations and dissertations.[6]

An outstanding higher degree could be written about language choice and style within these catalogues. They reveal the great problems in both the monograph market and universities. I keep this paragraph above my desk at work, to remind me how *not* to teach first year students. The use of completely disparate adjectives – unfussy, authoritative and critical – is meant to summon the three key markets: students, librarians and academics. It is disturbing, even at the level of advertizing, that any book blurb could claim to provide "all you need to know about theories of cultural studies", while servicing students facing "the pressures" of scholarly protocols and assignments. The impact on the field of this simplification and codification suffocates innovation and creativity. It also denies the importance of radical interdisciplinarity. Cultural Studies imports new theories, political goals and agendas. It must be dynamic, energetic and exciting.

From Revolution to Revelation is not a first year textbook for the "unfussy" reader who wants to slam down a couple of paragraphs on the "strengths and weakness" of cultural studies. Because of its topic, my writing moves between style journalism and academic explication, dense theory and performative panache, intense interrogation and playful parody. To do any less is not accepting the challenges that popular memory provides for scholarly writing.

This book is organized into two parts. The first section establishes a research framework by 'Building the Hacienda.' The aim is to construct – carefully and precisely – a methodological journey from youth culture theory to Popular Memory Studies, moving through the Cultural Studies and historical paradigms. Each shard of the debate – about (post) youth, cultural politics, truth and ideology – is required to create a workable model for popular memory. The second section, 'Sound and Vision' applies this framework. There is attention to dancing, film and music. The topics capture the obsessions and redundancies of popular culture to ask the (seemingly) easiest of questions: why do we remember, and why do we forget? Dancing is an appropriate metaphor, method and trope of this research. Intense, mobile and fleeting in its commitments, dancing – like popular memory – hovers at the edge of logic, reason and verifiable evidence.

I write of popular memory to summon a (post) youth culture, commodified readerships who – like all the youth cultural imaginings in

Cultural Studies – challenge the political certainties of our lives. Further, I suggest that popular memory allows the writing of a cultural history not only by academics, but by the style lifers of an era: journalists, dancers and fans. Steve Redhead's work on the *Repetitive Beat Generation*[7] explores the dance writing emerging during and after the post-Acid House era. These authors were also ethnographers. Writers like Irvine Welsh documented a culture in a diffident, awkward – but appropriate – fashion, plugging (while revealing) the intellectual gap caused through the decline of governmental funding for humanities research and teaching. These fiction writers jotted their prose at speed, with eerie similarities to the Stencilled Occasional Papers from the Birmingham Centre. They were locked into their cultural moment – just like the scholars within the Manchester Institute for Popular Culture – writing bristling, fervent theory to critique the Criminal Justice and Public Order Act of 1994, the law that criminalized a generation through their fondness for dance culture and 'repetitive beats'.

Critical passion, and passionate criticism, is important. The popular culture featured in this book is my culture. I have lived with, and loved, these rhythms, images, fashions and styles. My words sizzle and syncopate with the rhythms and energies of sound and vision. The prose meanders through fan and intellectual spheres, opening critical languages for the study of popular culture and weaving Popular Memory Studies into the research cloth of contemporary Cultural Studies. I am interested in what happens when texts move through time and space, and the snail trail of this movement that glistens through contemporary life. I care about these texts and what happens to them. The label of Generation X offers an incubator, a safe, warm space where the textual eggs of an earlier time may hatch to live beyond the rarefied environment of transitory marketing imperatives. This book does not fuel the pyre of accelerated culture,[8] but slows the speeding clock, walking a step behind bustling urbanity, and picking up the discarded artefacts of once fashionable objects and sounds. While claiming the space of a fan, I am not only textually critical, but historically aware. So much of Cultural Studies has told the story about how *they* got *there*. I show how *we* got *here*.

Notes

1   Pet Shop Boys, "My October Symphony", *Behaviour* (Parlophone, 1990).
2   The great exception to this statement is Graeme Turner's *British Cultural Studies* (London: Routledge, 1996). Published through two editions in 1990 and 1996, it has rightly become a standard textbook of the field. Importantly, he provides a subtle history and consideration of the relationship between the 'centres' of British

Cultural Studies, including John Hartley and John Fiske's work in Cardiff and the role and place of the Open University's courses.

3   One of the most evocative and spirited defences of popular culture is Adrian Martin's *Phantasms* (Harmondsworth: Penguin, 1994). This book reveals wide-ranging scholarship and evocative writing, providing a powerful bridge between Cultural Studies and cultural journalism.

4   G. Turner, "Tabloidization, journalism and the possibility of critique", *International Journal of Cultural Studies*, Vol. 2, No. 1, April 1999, p. 61.

5   L. Grossberg, "Cultural Studies: what's in a name?", B. Aubrey Fisher Memorial Lecture, published by the Department of Communication, University of Utah, Salt Lake City, Utah, October 1993, p. 1.

6   Publisher's description, *Cultural Studies – the basics*, by Jeff Lewis, Media, Communication & Cultural Studies, *SAGE Publications Catalogue*, London, 2004, p. 20.

7   S. Redhead, *Repetitive Beat Generation* (Edinburgh: Rebel Inc, 2000).

8   In many ways, *From Revolution to Revelation* is a companion volume to Steve Redhead's two books on Paul Virilio published by Edinburgh University Press in 2004: *Paul Virilio – Theorist for an Accelerated Culture* and *The Paul Virilio Reader*. While these books summon a theory of speed and accelerated culture, I present a paradigm of popular memory, pause and deceleration.

Section One
Building the Hacienda

Chapter one

The archaeology of X: making a (post) youth culture

I'm applauded, then forgotten.
It was summer.
Now it's autumn.[1]

'Crystal', New Order

Contemporary popular music, at its belly-button revealing best, is gleaming in its disappointments. Nice girls with strong abdominal muscles and weak politics are hurting feminism as much as the ears. With voices so frail, they could not pull a skin off a rice pudding let alone reveal the inconsistencies of the patriarchy. Their naivety, while carefully groomed, renders them as sharp as a wet cornflake. J. Lo's hipsters have not taken us to the Promised Land. Women's trousers are now so revealing that hipsters have become vaginasters. Brazilians are as compulsory to contemporary women's fashions as text messaging is to David Beckham.

Once upon a time, in a mythic era known as the 1980s, women and their fashions were different. There was colour and shape, humour and energy. Bring back Tina Turner, with the wild hair, gravel voice and punch-drunk autobiography, or Debbie Harry's seething sexuality and x-ray eyes, or Cyndi Lauper's rainbow wardrobe and piercing laugh. Pat Benatar's eyeliner fetish and addiction to hair products transformed femininity, as much as love, into a battlefield.

Popular culture in the new millennium is safe, punctuated by grating canned laughter. *Big Brother* was telecast but, unlike the Orwellian vision, it left out the irony and fear. We are all complicit in an invasion of the private sphere. The more complicated and frightening that war, surveillance and poverty has become, the more underwear is revealed above women's hipster-vaginasters. This simple relationship between sex and politics may have worked when Jesus was playing fullback for Jerusalem – or at least the 1950s – but it now appears too obvious. Marilyn Monroe died in the nude. Britney Spears lived in her virginity and then got married in Las Vegas. Annulment ensued, as did therapy and a second marriage. Yawn. We have – indeed – heard it all before.

This chapter investigates youth culture and the invention (and decline) of Generation X. As an urban archaeology, these words dig through the dustbin of the post-war period. The aim is to discover the spaces of political change that are left to us and why young people could never deliver on the promises of resistance and social justice after the Second World War.

Vintage youth

> I smell youth.
> Vintage youth.[2]
>> Pet Shop Boys, *It couldn't happen here.*

Youth is a crossroads culture, occupying spaces and colonizing times. Images of youth are 'handled' by the media, with opinion polls and marketing surveys monitoring what the young people are thinking, wearing and voting. Youth audiences are carolled and controlled by such surveys. Streetwise cred is summoned through buying into – not selling out of – popular culture such as film, magazines, fashion, music and television. There is a reason for this interest: youth is the potter's clay of capitalism and endlessly malleable. As Lawrence Grossberg confirmed,

> Youth is a saturation point of hegemonic techniques of normalization, disciplinization, and the institutionalization of difference.[3]

To define a particular age group at a specific time as 'youth' is shorthand for institutions that maintain control over young people. While Hebdige argues that "youth is present only when its presence is a problem",[4] youth is also dismissed when not required as a market.

Youth is far more than a description of an age group, or a stage in a rite of passage. Youth was present at its own making,[5] and that making arose in the post-war world. During the 1950s and 1960s, youth was a marketing focus. The making of youth culture was not an amorphous result of ill-defined social changes, but determined by an economic system that required niche markets to continue and increase the rate and role of consumption. To stress the label of youth – or woman or black or gay – to the detriment of other social variables simplifies consumption patterns and decentres the paradoxes and ambiguity of identity.

Consumption is a trace of how communities, collectives and grou produce meaning. Youth during the 1950s and 1960s became a metaphor for social change, with the consumer boom and an identifiable teenage market assisting the formation of this 'revolution'. It was the 1980s that offered a break in this narrative. Steve Redhead provided one explanation for this rupture: "it is not ... so much that youth culture died in the 1980s; more that its position as a subject of conflicting historical discourses in specific cultural formations is radically shifting".[6] As a result of structural unemployment, youth were no longer required as a market. They were therefore unmade. While the mods and rockers were (over)invested with radical or revolutionary potential, the (post) youth of the 1980s, through their style-lifing, were a travesty or betrayal of the 'authentic' political moments of 1968 and 1976. If political change is found only in a masculinist, heterosexual, productive public domain, then style-lifing is demeaned as an ephemeral, trivial waste.

If style becomes a force for revelation, not revolution, then a new locomotive of history is tracked. Consciousness – not class struggle – is the best political outcome to expect in these dark times. This shift between different models of change initiates innovative understandings of consumption, politics and the public sphere. Collectivity and community can emerge in the present, but are summoned through popular culture and shared literacy. That these new definitions and potentials remain irrelevant or discounted within New Labo(u)r and progressivist social forces demonstrates the power of the (post) neo-liberal rhetoric of individuality, families and religion. Homology, as a sociological concept to understand the alignment and replication of social formations, was not appropriate to handle the political realities after 1979 – post-Thatcher and Reagan.[7] That is why Baby Boomers always appear more radical than their children.

The 1980s signalled the popularization of newness: new theories, styles and cultures. Concurrently, rigid economic policies focused legislative attention on youth. Markers on the passage to adulthood altered during these years. As Abbott and Wallace realized, "what is the point of socializing someone for manual work, when industry is in decline: or socializing young women into the role of mothers when they may not have children?"[8] Without steady employment, a mortgage and family responsibilities (post)youth never made it into adulthood as defined by the standards of preceding decades.

Although the life cycle model – of school, stable work, marriage and family – has corroded, the 'youth as problem' mantra endures, despite the major shifts in social conditions. If young people were not framed as moving through a stage of incompleteness or transition in their 'adolescence', then guidance would not be required from familial, scholastic, medical, legal and psychological 'experts' to assist the passage into adulthood. Positioning youth as a time of adversity results in any difficulty being framed as 'a problem of youth', rather than a dilemma of adults, patriarchal or homophobic family structures, economically rationalized educational systems or the capitalist mode of production. The 'problems of youth', as erected through the life cycle paradigm, inevitably evaporate once the young person 'matures'. Too often – and only half jokingly – this system could be tracked through a four-tiered system:

1.   Construct youth as a time of problems.
2.   Provide solutions (training, counselling) to the problems.
3.   Stop looking for these problems after the age of 25.
4.   The problems disappear.

I am being simplistic and ironic here, but (too) many studies of youth culture shadow this exact mode of analysis. Publications such as *Adolescence, Youth and Society, Youth and Policy* and *Youth* are dominated by articles applying such a system, detailing the horrors of teenage suicide, anorexia nervosa and bulimia, dissolving family structures and premarital sex. The blandness and 'impartiality' of these articles make their argument seem 'scientific' and 'serious'. These studies are rarely contextualized. The 'sample' for the 'scientific' study was (too) often 200 American college students. These results are then extrapolated to fill out the entire category of youth. Michael Stefanko, in a 1984 *Adolescence* article, reviewed the 'major conclusions' of the journal. He discovered two crucial 'findings'.

Adolescents were ill-equipped to face the increasing opportunities for intimate contact.[9]

Few differences were found between social classes and ethnic groups. There were differences between the attitudes of males and females, with female attitudes seeming to have changed the most and the fastest.[10]

The journal's approach and methodology requires an obvious, overt and clear split between youth and adulthood and this division is confirmed through 'scientific' extrapolation. The political difficulty in 'managing' questions of race and ethnicity, as they are relevant far beyond an age-based study, meant that these terms remain both volatile and under researched. It appears easier for writers to view, judge and evaluate the changes to young women. Feminist theory has provided a smoother graft to youth studies than post-colonialism.

There are consequences for investing distinct stages of life with assumed meanings and consciousness – outside of history and beyond politics. The serious and trivial are cut up and deposited in the categories of either adult or youth. For example, Frank Fasick pronounced,

> Youth culture is a twentieth-century phenomenon that appears to act as a mechanism by which adolescents who find themselves playing dependent roles at home and at school can develop a sense of autonomy. This culture is constructed, for the most part, of such transitory and trivial matters as those dealing with clothes, music, sport, and dating that have little carry over to adult life.[11]

The workings of popular memory do not obey such vacuum-sealed interpretations of significance and stupidity. Obsessive fixations on trivial matters – such as hair styling products, music and sport – do spill beyond the age of 25. As Andrew remarked in *Peter's Friends*, the Generation X equivalent of *The Big Chill*, "adults are just children with debts, that's all".[12] Youth is not a halfway house between childhood and adulthood. Increasingly age and ageing are socially inscribed and dynamic. Being seventy years of age is not the same in the 2000s as it was in the 1920s. Neither is being seventeen. Adults do not cannibalize their past, nor do they arrive at the age of twenty five as an ideological clean skin.

If the veneer of these studies of 'youth as problem' is stripped away, what remains? The texts of popular culture, whether they are songs or discarded plastic bags containing glue resin, hint at a blissful amalgam of intoxicating pleasure and elaborate socio-economic deferral. The politics of desperation that shadowed young people through the 1980s and the 1990s resulted in inward attacks on the self, rather than outward assaults on the state. It is a neo-liberal misrepresentation that an individual only creates a myth to his or her advantage: there is a unity and consciousness in powerlessness. The political struggles in the 1960s and 1970s could not be repeated. Youth cultures from the 1980s and 1990s became pastiched cover versions and dub mixes of the 'hit' subcultures from the 1960s and 1970s. Muggings of the mind replaced collective and public rioting.

Youth – like all identity formations – requires a narrative or story. That is why a desire exists from journalists and theorists to clothe (post) youth cultures in beige tones, rather than Trotskyist red. Economic conditions and the demands of casualized and temporary work, university fees or a maxed out credit card rarely supply juicy newspaper scandals (and folk devils) of sex 'n' drugs 'n' rock 'n' roll. For example, Gross and Scott stated,

Down deep, what frustrates today's young people – and those who observe them – is their failure to create an original youth culture. The 1920s had jazz and the Lost Generation, the 1950s created the Beats, the 1960s brought everything embodied in the Summer of Love. But the twentysomething generation has yet to make a substantial cultural statement.[13]

These words were written in 1990. Over a decade later, it could be argued – using the same approach and in an increasingly conservative environment – that no political statement was ever made by those 'twentysomethings'. But a youth culture cannot compete with an imagined 'sixties' that does not exist except through nostalgia. These two critics erected historical phantoms that cannot be equalled or measured because they were fictional imaginings in the first place. Only material traces of radicalism or compliance endure. Rayban sunglasses are the pivotal metaphor for the 1980s and (post) youth culture discussed by Gross and Scott. Shielding the eyes, hiding emotion and conveying voyeuristic intentions, the Raybans were never removed from the collective face of Generation X. Instead of reading 'against the grain' in an attempt to recover 'authentic selves', there is much to be gained by glancing at surfaces and revelling in the superficiality. In *not* looking for a substantial cultural statement – a revolution – the revelation of (post) youth culture on popular memory and popular culture can be revealed through subtle shifts in consciousness.

All communities are imagined and all colonize moments of dreaming. For the New Left, '1968' scores a deep resonance. For the gay community 'Stonewall' reverberates with activist importance. Every community requires a past that is 'owned'. At specific moments, youth are hailed into existence through an overpowering unity against an event, economic agenda or political figure. The rage of the Sex Pistols against the establishment, the screams of young women when the Beatles arrived in America, display not only traces of passion but a desire for change. Just as the French Resistance was created and united from disparate socialist, communist, nationalist and religious strands to stand against Nazism and Vichy, so have youth been collectivized through a single issue, song or idea that overcomes other differences. A youth culture temporarily summons a critical mass of unity that displaces and masks the divisions instigated by class, religion, gender and race. For Dick Hebdige though, one image disturbed him: "the silent crowd, anonymous, unknowable, a stream of atomized individuals intent on minding their own business".[14] This is a (post) youth culture with Raybans impeccably in place, perfect consumers who grasp identity through shopping but make few political demands on a system that subjugates them.

Put bluntly, the new political problem for cultural theorists is how to research not the pulse of a dance floor or graffiti on a wall, but commodified, satiated silence. We need a method to understand a moment when nothing happens, a way to explain why resistance does not emerge and shopping replaces protesting. To understand this present, we must crane our necks to the past, to grasp how we got here. Popular Memory Studies can provide a method for this mode of research, which recognizes that every 'now' has a past and every silence is an answer to an uncomfortable question. By denying the movement into narrative and instead searching for the Greil Marcus-inspired 'Lipstick Traces',[15] a journey is summoned through post-New Times, post-9/11, post-COW (Coalition of the Willing), post-Blair and George W., post-Howard and post-Clark, and post the postmodern.

Cultural Studies has always written about a vanishing youth culture. The Birmingham Centre and the Manchester Institute are the clearest examples of this trend. Few methods are available to monitor this disappearance. One answer is offered in this book: Popular Memory Studies. To write a cultural history of an ageing youth culture is a morbid task: endlessly documenting the vanishing. This is rapid writing, expunging academic words at the speed of the popular culture's emergence and decay. I am more interested in steeping popular culture, slowing the clock and gently watching the subtle circulations of memory. Such an ironic distance raises difficult questions: how do we reconcile the parallel success of Cultural Studies – a radical interventionist paradigm – and the rise of the New Right? More specifically, how do we attune the chronological connection between the arrival of Margaret Thatcher and the most successful book of youth cultural theory: Dick Hebdige's *Subculture: the meaning of style*? In the United States, James Carey saw "the Left … fighting over the English Department while the Right occupies the White House".[16] The New Right successfully reconstituted the parameters of citizenship, moving the language of public discourse from rights to responsibilities. Cultural Studies theorists were able to track this movement, but not intervene or mould the political changes. A reason for this political failure amid academic success needs to be found, so that we can teach and write with honesty, clarity and compassion in a post-Iraq War II environment. Until we can staunchly address our political context, all Cultural Studies will be Terrorist Studies.

The use of *sub*culture as an analytical tool in sociology may provide a constant theoretical reminder that there are larger units of societal organization to consider, such as class. Yet with class politics and class consciousness being sidelined through the 1980s and dismissed in the 1990s, there is a deep, dense discussion to be had – again – about the relationship between subcultural/symbolic politics and real/parliamentary politics. Subcultural theory was effective in showing that politically inert periods – like the 1950s and early 1960s – encased nodes of political challenge. The Teds, Rockers and Mods shredded the interpretation of 'quiet times' or 'grey decades'. The difficulty occurs when these groups are overloaded with political consciousness. They 'represented' far more than they ever actually achieved socially or politically. Youth were assembled into a collective only in the affluent social conditions of the post-war baby boom.

During the 1980s and 1990s, many 'youth cultures' waited to be made. Only temporarily, such as during the rioting in Brixton during 1981 or post-Rodney King Los Angeles, did youth rear their recognized, politicized head. Unity as a 'youth' can never arise like the sun, emerging from within a gathering of young people. The label must come from outside. Thatcher, like Bush the Younger and John Howard, was effective in silencing and depoliticizing political adversaries through claims of a singular nationalism. As proven through Iraq War II, Tony Blair was never as effective at calming and silencing his critics. In muzzling a yet unmade youth, resistance and struggle, even if it was performed via the pen of sociologists, was also quelled. Harris expressed this best: "in real life, the youth of the 1980s in Britain ceased to be the metaphor for change and stylistic innovation and became victims of social and structural change instead".[17] There are problems with victim-based politics. Feminism has taught us this truth. Harris has realized though that young people were no longer the focus for marketing initiatives. To move his argument beyond victimhood and ask why this shift has occurred, we must go back theoretically and politically.

Enter the X

Alexander Laurence: Since you have turned thirty, what has happened?
Douglas Coupland: After you turn thirty, people begin to talk behind your back.[18]

Early 1990s popular culture captured a dark, deep despair. Irvine Welsh is pointed in his memory of this time: "you're either right outside society or you're exploited".[19] He argues that those in regular employment, frightened of losing their weekly paycheque, have no mental space to consider alternatives. Those 'outside' the system, while being materially disadvantaged, actually have the privilege of thinking critically about their surroundings. There is a generational rub to his hypothesis. Baby boomer is now synonymous with the establishment, the dominant culture, while Generation

X is – dialectically – the other.[20]   Obviously, such simple generational divisions are neither accurate nor particularly useful, but they provide an entry point into social and semiotic transformations. New phrases and ideas exploded from the early 1990s: date rape, dumbing down, hate crimes, cross-addictions, co-dependence and self love. Whatever went wrong – economically, sexually or politically – seems to either encircle or be caused by Generation X and their apathy. To make matters worse, the popular cultural icons of the era were incredibly articulate. Instead of Sting's da do do do, da da da da, Tracy Chapman documented a poignancy of vision, of fast cars and no plans.[21] Alanis Morissette screamed the greatest revenge (to the bastard who dumped me) song in "You Oughta Know".[22] This righteous rage was a long way from Sting's calming yoga and emotionally generous tantric sex. The flashy style – of stilettos and dancing around the handbag – was locked into the 1980s. From the 1990s, it appeared that Laura Ashley had taken out a patent fabric over the entire planet. We now live in a time when wearing beige is a political statement. The language of beige is festering into camel and tan. Yak will be next. Concurrently and thankfully, the humour and reflexivity of those watching fashion also increased. That fash-mag-slag Patsy made the world *Absolutely Fabulous* through her cocaine cough. From such a popular cultural environment, authentic youth subcultures became as real as Ali G. Street credibility involved little more than a bomber jacket, excessive gold jewellery and yelling 'Yo!' at every opportunity. The era of pogoing, gobbing, safety pins and a Mohawk – that is symbolic violence – seemed breathtakingly distant from 'bling bling'.   Blunt anger has been replaced by clever but innocuous commentary. All the world is a talk show and the men and women are merely guests.

Consumerism has always summoned ambivalent politics. Credit cards and the consumer debt that results from them, refer not only to a temporary abeyance or deficiency of funds, but a gulf between expectations of needs and capacity to pay for them. Credit cards also mask inequalities and create a complex muddling of rich and poor. Alice Rawsthorn also recognized this peculiar tendency for credit card-based consumer spending at a time of unemployment.

> What makes this ethos of conspicuous consumption so difficult to entertain is that the official figures on soaring consumer expenditure sit so oddly with the other official figures – those which paint a picture of a Britain in which years of prolonged unemployment and depleted benefits have taken their toll on the disposable incomes of so high a proportion of the population.[23]

While the rules of this credit card Never Never Land are profoundly odd, arising in a time of both unemployment and hyper-consumerism, similar contradictions were observed in George Orwell's Britain. His *Road to Wigan Pier* presented the tragedies of poverty, unemployment and disease that proliferated in industrialized Britain during the 1930s. In one section of the book, he outlined the diet of the unemployed and discovered that it included white bread, margarine, corned beef, tea and potatoes. Instead of eating cheaper, healthier food, the working class of industrial Wigan were consuming poor quality, over-priced victuals. Orwell argued through the reasoning for this decision.

> The peculiar evil is this, that the less money you have, the less inclined you feel to spend it on wholesome food ... When you are unemployed, which is to say when you are underfed, harassed, bored and miserable, you don't want to eat dull wholesome food ... Unemployment is an endless misery that has got to be constantly palliated.[24]

From the 1980s, bad shopping replaced bad eating as the tonic to the nation. But Orwell's words demonstrate that the documentary *Super Size Me* has a cause, origin and reason.[25] The obesity epidemic – like all questions of lifestyle – has a context. With a fear of terrorism, unemployment, underemployment, divorce and the next bill, bad eating is placating the citizenry, smoothing over the disappointments of life with sweet, tasty, satisfying fast food. With a massive growth of a dependency culture on American Express and Mastercard, the connection between autonomy, pleasure and consumption only lasts until the arrival of the next bank statement. The joy of bad food continues until the next weigh-in and measurement. In the meantime, the fridge is full and the takeaways are open. Orwell's study of Wigan is still incredibly relevant and holds an application beyond his imagining.

Remarkable, dense transformations have taken place in the economic fabric of many nations in the last twenty five years. Cultural Studies writers, youth studies scholars and sociologists have shifted their gaze. Sheila Allison discovered for example a major change in the topics discussed in the magazine *Youth Studies Australia* between 1986 and 1996.

> The first 1986 issue of the Bulletin of the National Clearinghouse for Youth Studies (no wonder we changed the title!) carried six papers on youth unemployment. While that topic hasn't gone away, one of the main topics of this issue, rave, was not yet heard of, nor was the technology for making it happen. Some things change slowly, some are fast.[26]

This shift in emphasis was not only a movement from seriousness to triviality, or unemployment to dancing. During this period, the phrase Generation X gained both publicity and currency. The social category of 'youth' was attended by new intonations, inflections, beats and ideas.

As a term, Generation X has been mobilized three times in the last forty years. Firstly, it was a 1960s collection of interviews with young people, compiled by Charles Hamblett and Jane Deverson. Then it became the name of a punk group featuring Billy Idol. Finally in 1992, the 30-year-old Canadian author Douglas Coupland wrote *Generation X: Tales for an accelerated culture*. It was a post-yuppie treatise, anti-materialism and pro-apathy and irresponsibility. It attacked the filofax lifestyle of appointments never kept and telephone numbers never dialled. Coupland recorded the tales of the jaded, the nothing-to-lose, casualized, consumerist citizenry. The book's strange form and gems of consciousness created a sensibility, rather than offering a 'reflection' of the authentic baby buster *mentalitae*. The text contained moments of hailed understanding that constructed a foundation for consciousness, the making of a collective. A journalist from *The Modern Review* articulated the basis for this affiliation.

> Generation X knows too well what it is up to ... burdened by too much history. And ... Generation X's preoccupations – disconnection, lassitude, the unremitting despair of a visit to the launderette – make it genuinely saleable, an authentically over-the-counterculture.[27]

In being 'burdened with too much history', twentysomethings had a past that was too big to grasp and wildly dissociative. Since the success of Coupland's book, Xers were present at their own making (appropriately) invented by a fiction writer. This popular cultural creation – while a marketer's dream – had a cost. By writing and inventing Xers as bored, listless, over-educated, underemployed media sophisticates, we lose something: the popular memories that constructed 'the us' before the label was used. Complexity and diversity are always lost at the moment identity is categorized and commodified. How do we (con)textualize torn movie tickets, sweat on a dance floor, fingerless gloves and a pair of Raybans? Grasping meaning from these memories is difficult, as there is no Xer historical methodology. Generation X does not have a past: they were invented by Douglas Coupland in 1992.

Douglas Coupland's *Generation X* was not meant to be an explosive best-seller, but it captured real cultural movement and social change. The casualized, transitory workforce that Coupland fictionalized has 'managed' profound economic and social consequences that are yet to be fully evident to the rest of the population. This group first confronted post-Fordism, underemployment and media(ted) identity. The desire to impose 1960s life paths and trajectories – of birth, school, marriage, family, death – over all of society was becoming inadequate, inappropriate and politically misguided. Vanessa Walker presented the depressing pathway:

> Compared with baby boomers who plodded away at their lifetime careers and trod the well-worn path of school, marriage, birth of first child and entry into home ownership, the report [from the Committee for Economic Development of Australia] predicts Gen-Xers could end up lonely, broke and still renting.[28]

There is a desire by conservative governments to re-establish and reinforce the 'normal' passage of life. There are reasons for these precise determinations of life patterns and values. Neo-Conservative policies only function if 'we' agree on the shape and trajectories of identity. Alterations in this pattern are seen to lead to loneliness, rather than the social alternatives of independence and self reliance. The monogamous, home-owning heterosexual couple raising children is an incredibly recent – and increasingly redundant – cultural formation. The notion of 'choosing' to not repeat this life narrative is beyond Walker's reasoning. Generation X is not lost, but found – through popular culture and consumerism. This is a generation that understands, densely and clearly, that marriage is not a medication for loneliness. Mortgages and employment do not guarantee social stability. A sizeable group of the population has already silently stepped off the heteronormative, consumerist and suburban treadmill. As always, earlier structures still offer nostalgic appeal. Peter Costello, a Conservative Australian treasurer, sold his 2004 budget with an initiative to increase the rate of childbirth and 'build' families. He suggested that Australians (or Generation X and Y in actuality) have "one [child] for your husband, one for your wife, one for your country".[29] Such a crass ideology validates and entwines marriage, monogamy, heterosexuality and the nation state. In such a context, determinations of 'resistance' or 'social change' are not easy to track, locate or even define. To place this (un)popular culture in context, it is necessary to enter the sphere of representation.

If there is a single defining motif of the X space, then it is an intense and passionate relationship with popular culture. As for Princess Leia, Obi Wan Kenobi provides the only hope. *Fight Club* rules can be cited. Jay and Silent Bob can be parodied. This popular culture weaves distant times and places. Brian Wilson invented California, Oasis summoned Manchester and silverchair created Newcastle. While MTV may be the perdition of a generation, it freeze-dried new meanings, images and ideas, a life lived in the moment and out of the ordinary. It was a bower bird culture, attracted to the shiny, bright and unusual objects in the world. To misquote Paul Simon, Generation X ended up living in a cartoon, in a cartoon graveyard.[30]

Xer films are filled with mantras: choose life – you are not the content of your wallet – may the force be with you. These sloganized truths slice through the inconsistencies and fill up gaps in daily life. The entertainment discourse forms a language and iconography to understand the paradoxes, unfairness and inequality emerging through a (supposedly) liberal democracy. Hollywood's history, as Mark Carnes suggests, "is so morally unambiguous".[31] Popular culture allows audiences to make sense of their lives, when the structures and truths of families, governments and the workplace contradict experiences. Film, television and popular music have a transformative impact on cultural groups, creating enthusiastic audiences who are able to mark out and claim their differences. Generation Xers possess a media literacy which allows a celebration of an investment in the images that is not linked to the real. For this process to work, an ironic stance must be maintained.

(Ironically) alongside the irony is a profound desire for authenticity. Best embodied by Kevin Smith's films, the director is able to combine black humour, a desire for faith and a dark reflexivity. Smith actually plays the character of Silent Bob, with long coat, expressive hand gestures and no dialogue. Like a Charlie Chaplin on Mogadon, Bob had (only) one monologue in the New Jersey trilogy of films. It offered the perfect amalgam of irony, lost innocence and nostalgia.

I went through something like what you're talking about. Couple of years ago, with this chick named Amy … So there's me and Amy, and we're all inseparable, right? Just big time in love. And then about four months down the road, the idiot gear kicks in, and I ask about the ex-boyfriend – which, as we all know, is a really dumb move. But you know how it is – you don't want to know, but you just have to … stupid guy bullshit. Anyway, she starts telling me all about him – how they fell in love, how they dated for a couple of years, how they lived together, her mother likes me better, blah, blah, blah – and I'm okay. But then she drops the bomb on me, and the bomb is this. It seems that a couple of times, while they were going out he brought some people to bed with them – ménage a trios, I believe it's called. Now this just blows my mind. I mean, I'm not used to that sort of thing, right? I was raised Catholic, for God's sake … So I get weirded out, and just start blasting her, right? I don't know how to deal with what I'm feeling. But I figure the best way is if I call her a slut and tell her that she was used. I mean, I'm out for blood. I want to hurt this girl now. That's when I look her straight in the eye and tell her it's over. I walk ... It was a mistake. I wasn't disgusted with her, I was afraid.[32]

This is a moment of astounding, gritty truth. Heterosexual masculinity is unsettled. The man who has – literally – been silent for three movies presents a truth so provocative that he reverts back to a Shakespearean soliloquy for effect. The space between image and reality – film and viewer – is pierced, probed and poisoned through such words.

Kevin Smith's finest filmic moment is the script that followed *Chasing Amy*: *Dogma*. A highly controversial tale, it links the bible, *Star Wars* and John Hughes' films in a suffocating embrace. It is a theoretical film, a story of metaphysical speculation and excessive humour. The story continues the tale of Jay and Silent Bob, who travel to Illinois because of John Hughes, the director of proto-Xer classics like *Ferris Bueller's Day Off*, *Sixteen Candles* and *Breakfast Club*. Jay explains their need to move to Illinois.

See, all these movies take place in a town called Shermer, in Illinois – where all the honeys are top-shelf, but all the dudes are whiny pussies. Except Judd Nelson – he was harsh. But best of all, there was no one dealing, man. Then it hits me – we could live like phat-rats if we were the blunt-connection in Shermer, Illinois. So we collected some money we were owed and caught a bus. But you know what ... we found out when we got here? There is no Shermer in Illinois ... Movies are bullshit.[33]

This text is Applied Cultural Studies 101: watching a film that tells its viewers that they are watching nonsense. Films are fake and require a fakery to convey this information.

Through such films, it is obvious that Generation X cannot be understood or theorized using conventional approaches from youth culture or subcultural theory. Like Silent Bob, we cannot expect Xer popular culture to reveal or reflect the values of a generation. Instead, he simply stands there, bemused but not terribly interested. Films and popular culture generally, do not provide us with an easy 'representation' of post-boomer generations. Instead, these texts are actively negating a coherently performed self, hailing an audience with references to other films, other fictions and other views of the world. Popular culture is inadequate, but provides an iconographic database that builds a banal, superficial, but satisfying literacy. This is a method of reading and understanding inequality that rarely unsettles social structures. It creates revelation without revolution.

Such ironic authenticity is also the basis of the post-*Simpsons* animation. Programmes like *South Park* play with essentialist versions of childhood and the religious right's desire to 'protect' the young. The distinction between childhood-youth-adulthood is difficult to determine. Age is determined in, through and by consumption. As Marian Quigley realized,

> The practice of transgenerational address … provides new opportunities for communication between adults and the young at media sites such as the *South Park* programme. Media is enabling the erosion of the child/youth/adult boundaries, allowing for the realization that the path to citizenship is a continuum bound up with the dependence upon interaction with media texts.[34]

Media literacy has reached such a point that an audience realizes that lifestyles cannot be bought and sold. The images alone must satisfy. Cooking programmes dominate during an era where food has been McDonaldized. Gardening shows offer a suburban, mortgaged dream denied to many. Life is not a Pepsi commercial and happiness is not found through catalogue shopping. We can (only) look.

The main question to ask is with regard to consciousness: how does such popular culture provide knowledge about the self? Music, film and television do not offer moments of resistance: they frequently reinforce disempowerment or discouragement. But those transitory connections of beat and ear, music and memory may create identification, leading to the building of a community. The *may* is significant here. It is always conceptually easy to analyse an historical moment when something happens, like the era of punk or the Prague Spring. Yet to modify Marx, the history of all hitherto existing societies is not a history of spectacular youth subcultures. (Post) youth cultures are silent consumers who build literacies, not capital. Dancing to music or watching a film must not be celebrated as intrinsically resistive because it creates pleasure. The politics of consumption – of buying and selling – requires more attention and critique than this. But it is a tactic for bad times.

Cappuccino politics

> I think Starbucks has patented a new configuration of the water molecule, like a Kurt Vonnegut novel, or something. This molecule allows their coffee to remain liquid at temperatures over 212 degrees Fahrenheit. How do they get their coffee so hot? It takes hours to cool off – it's so hot it's undrinkable – and by the time

it's cool, you're sick of waiting for it to cool and that 'coffee moment' has passed.[35]

Douglas Coupland

Join the revolution. We have nothing to lose but our Visas.[36]

Jason Cohen and Michael Krugman

Something is seriously wrong with coffee culture. During the 1980s, the wine tossers drove us mad with discussions of shiraz and old oak, the south side of the hill and corked taint. Coffee has become the new cabernet, just like Ikea has become the new Laura Ashley. We have down-marketed our consumerism and suburbanized our interests. The consequences of this Cappuccino politics and chattering around the cheeseboards are yet to be fully realized. Because politics was so nasty – so adversarial through the 1990s and 2000s – popular culture became a retreat and a hope.

Books like *Trainspotting* and films like *Shallow Grave* appear to have no history. Hits from nowhere, there was little record of the litzine world that spawned them, created by Rebel Inc and Clocktower Press. Actually these chemical generation writers – or Britlit – were created in the space of an historical lie. The active forgetting and rewriting of the Miners' Strike, the Cold War, the (first) Iraq conflict and the nuclear threat were necessary for John Major's survival and the rise of bland Blairism. The gap between the actual events and current political ideologies and policies required a radical and rapid rewriting of the past. Truth, opinion, fiction and fact were courted in both history books and newspapers. In such an environment the success of working class writers was remarkable. Irvine Welsh became a celebrity and books such as Toni Davidson's *Intoxication* and Sarah Champion's *Disco Biscuits* unearthed a market for stimulant-based writing. It was popular culture written through the strobe and pricked a pulsating political nerve. The bizarre celebration of consumerist choices, the notion that mobile phone ring tones and belly-button piercings actually matter, was attacked ruthlessly in Welsh's writing. Besides his fiction, Welsh has also strongly intervened in the cultural system that is using and abusing the disempowered for commodified ends.

The point is that while a well-funded cultural system exists to spew out ruling-class culture, any culture, art and history promoted outside of this system relies largely on concerned maverick groups or individuals. The society is only 'liberal' or 'pluralist' to the extent that it tolerates these different voices which are generally

let in to spice up the mainstream only when it becomes intolerably bland. In the
meantime, we lose so much of our culture.[37]

Within Welsh's reckoning, women, the working class and black communities
are only of use to the powerful by freshening up consumerist items. The
centre – the dominant and the strong – takes what it wants from the
periphery. Cultural symbols are appropriated, without consequences or cost to
the dominant culture.

In Australia, this cultural conflict was of a distinct order. Through the
1990s, a generational lit war took place. Cultural Studies was at the
forefront of the pecking order. Mark Davis published *Gangland* in 1997 and
was attacked by forces of the establishment rarely seen outside of
Conservative Party branch meetings. He argued that "there is a group of
figures, born somewhere between the late 1930s and early 1950s, who now
dominate the media, who set the tone of debate on popular social issues
from feminism to education to multiculturalism".[38] In locating this
defensive orthodoxy in journalism and publishing, Mark Davis asserted
that Australia presented few spaces for writers under fifty years of age.
Young writers only occupy the function of translators – explaining what
the young people are wearing and why.

Debates about religion and politics no longer fill the airwaves. Seemingly, it
is assumed that we are all Christian and Conservative. Cutting through such
assumptions, popular culture is the arsenal of generational attack. It is in the
universities – and through Cultural Studies – that many of these debates about
value, morality, politics and ethics are rehearsed. In this intellectually dirty war,
Cultural Studies has become equated with difficult, elitist theory, rather than
the study of culture.

> Not one essay here shows the slightest interest in the academic debate about the
> pure theory of 'Cultural Studies' presently preoccupying too many cultural
> commentators here and overseas.[39]

Abusing 'theory' is an excuse to avoid the 'real' discussion about cultural
value and critical literacy, but there is no awareness of how this statement
corrodes critical thinking. It is impossible to access 'real culture' or 'the
real society' without a theory – or an interpretation – of the world, just like
Nigella Lawson does not cook 'real food' for 'real people'. No objective
truth can be magically typed at the keyboard. All citizens – let alone all
writers – have a theory of the world, an approach or framework that
determines how their view coalesces into a reality. Every discipline, from

25

medicine to engineering and law, requires theories of how and why a truth is formed. The notion that we all – intrinsically – *know* culture without mediation through experience is untenable in the politicized, binarized post-September 11 environment.

Cultural Studies through the 1990s made many conceptual mistakes. Perhaps the greatest miscalculation was the commercial appeal of Neo-Conservatism. There was too little theorizing of the political economy and too little attention to history. There was too little radical interdisciplinarity, with assumed synergies between literature and sociology. Lawrence Grossberg – unfortunately – was wrong when he stated that "Cultural Studies is radically contextual".[40] The 1990s showed that he was incorrect. Too many Cultural Studies textbooks, readers and edited collections recycled the old paradigms about youth and resistance, television and its audience, film and the gaze. It not only got boring, but unsatisfying. Politically, we become the McDead, recycling over-used words and consuming barely edible knowledge bytes. While the New Times project tracked post-Fordist remakings of subjectivity, new life stories were being told through headphones and on dance floors. New theories are needed to track this beat. Popular Memory Studies returns the clock to Cultural Studies. So let us return and rewrite the script, but not in a nostalgic search for when I was younger – so much younger than today. Silence the nostalgic soundtrack. Cue the gritty drum 'n' bass. Switch on the strobe.

Forgotten something?

You can't remember what you chose to forget.

Douglas Coupland.[41]

Consumerism does not prepare us for unhappiness. Whole episodes of *Oprah* are filled with the dense longing for something more, a life beyond mobile phones, headache tablets and ill-fitting trousers. For Oprah's entourage, remembering spirituality and learning meditation is a transitory mechanism to erase what they have chosen to forget. The point of growing older is to learn to deal with the two Ls: less and loss. Most of us own more compact discs than we can hear in a lifetime. I have a nasty habit of buying a new bottle of body lotion for every special occasion. My bathroom is filled with over-brimming, luscious cream that will never be used. Life teaches us that there is a point where plenty of stuff is actually too much. Generally accompanying this realization is the knowledge that the micro-moments of intense happiness are transitory. The more happiness we feel, the greater the loss that will cut into our selves when the joy is over. Douglas Coupland has been able to capture this realization:

> New Order saturates the warming car. Erik and Jamie have returned to a future they can live with: spare, secular, coherent and rational – a future reflecting their almost puritanical belief that excess is its own punishment.[42]

The 1990s was the decade that paid for the excesses of the 1980s. The entire period lacked unity and was frayed with ill-kept textures and fibres. Bill Clinton's indiscretions bounced along with heroin chic, over-priced models and over-the-counter culture. Through the acceleration of fashion time, it was no longer possible to claim an image or moment as representative of anything more than a micro-trauma or political filament.

We have all become ageing Baby Janes, wandering around the cultural landscape and applying the polyfiller principle to make-up. Ageing has become pathologized, a disease to be cured. Supposedly, the aim of plastic surgery is to ensure we have a butt like J. Lo, are as thin as the Hilton sisters and – through Botox injections – have a face as expressionless as a cadaver. It may be just me, but the new goals of beauty seem dangerously modelled on medical experiments. Andrew Blaikie has asked

> Why is it that this babyboomer, born in the middle of the twentieth century – a potential pensioner – wishes to remain forever young or, at least, non-aged, and what may be the implications assuming I am typical of my generation.[43]

I have never understood the fear of ageing. Each wrinkle represents a tragedy confronted or a difficulty overcome. Lined, roughened hands signify a life of work, struggle and survival. To deny these changes – to erase (or hide) the lines in the mirror is to live a life that disrespects a journey made and struggles surmounted. Boomers, with baseball caps backwards and bodies anaesthetized underneath the surgical knife, have not developed the vocabularies of ageing. Time is not an enemy to be battled against. It is neither predictable in its application nor precise in its movements. Placing plastic wrap over our faces may preserve the skin, but important experiences and ideas are decaying below the shiny, suffocating surface.

There is no moat between memory and history. The destruction of our lives – our experience – and the crushing homogenization of 'everyday life' has been masked through the hyped-up, hyperconsumerism of capitalism. Plastic surgery is a metaphor for denying history, experience, discomfort and change. As long as we can choose the ring tone of our mobile phone, all is right with the world. What happens when our experiences are different from the knowledge passed to us by authority figures? Good Guys and Bad Guys no longer wear white and black hats. They look the same. Both use violence. Both justify the use of violence through religion. We simply cannot appropriate and apply these stories of the powerful. Every history and memory enfolds a theory of time. In our present, our notion of time is neither objective nor predictable. It is invented, catastrophic and combustible. Our memories of difference are the only negation left to us – the only lucid 'No' to be offered to a dominant culture. In this context, memory is a political lever, neither safe nor nostalgic. Private memories can be used for public struggles. They establish a connection with the past and a recognition that life can be – and has been – lived differently. Dave Hickey – Boomer rock critic (surely tautological) – has not recognized the function of memory for those displaced from history.

> Two nights ago, I was talking with some local artists about things that used to be cool and weren't anymore – things that we missed. These artists were mostly kids, so they missed some really stupid stuff, I thought, like Adam Ant and giant shoulder-pads in women's clothes.[44]

These ordinary moments have extraordinary revelatory power. Disempowered groups – like Gen Xers, women or black communities – will invariably utilize the dustbin of history to grant meaning, substance and shape to their lives. Those in power claim parliament, radio stations and newspaper editorships. Those outside of the structures are left with Adam Ant, big shoulder pads, water stained taffeta, pastel handbags and styling mousse. These are talismans of struggles lost. Disempowered groups become tourists through their own past, disenfranchized and disoriented. That is why popular culture is so important. It is a catalogue of memory, a record of feelings, sensations and experiences.

The aim for those of us interested in popular memory is to let popular culture fill cycles of meaning and build consciousness. Generation X is a first, significant community to monitor the link between history, popular culture and popular memory. The resultant images and narratives are like teeth of an old piano: some white, some black and some missing. Through the absences and inaccuracies, such a project provides space for dialogues, dissonance and difference. Before we can go forward – or even occupy our present effectively – we must settle accounts with Cultural Studies. The next chapter asks what the paradigm gained from the investment in youth culture and the deficits left in the political account.

Notes

1   New Order, "Crystal", words and music by B. Sumner, P. Hook, S. Morris and G. Gilbert, *Get Ready* (London: London Records, 2001), track one.

2   Joss Ackland, *It couldn't happen here* (Video Collection Int. Ltd., 1997).

3   L. Grossberg, "I'd rather feel bad than not feel anything at all", *Enclitic*, Vol. 8, 1984, p. 107.

4   D. Hebdige, *Hiding in the light* (London: Routledge, 1988), p. 17.

5   The inflection in this phrase about youth has its origin in E.P. Thompson's statement about 'making' class in *The Making of the English Working Class* (Harmondsworth: Penguin, 1968). In his 'Preface' to the 1963 edition, he explained that the word 'making' is important, "because it is a study in an active process, which owes as much to agency as to conditioning. The working class did not rise like the sun at an appointed time. It was present at its own making", p. 8.

6   S. Redhead, *The end of the century party* (Manchester: Manchester University Press, 1990), p. 41.

7   Australia and New Zealand were delayed in this neo-liberal restructuring, with a semblance of social democracy surviving through Bob Hawke and David Lange.

8   P. Abbott and C. Wallace, *Gender, Power and Sexuality* (Houndmills: Macmillan, 1991), p. 10.

9   M. Stefanko, "Trends in adolescent research", *Adolescence*, Vol. 19, No. 73, 1984, p. 5.

10   *ibid.*, p. 9.

11   F. Fasick, "Parents, peers, youth culture and autonomy in adolescence", *Adolescence*, Vol. 19, No. 74, Spring 1984, p. 15.

12   Andrew, played by Kenneth Branagh, in *Peter's Friends* (Renaissance Films, 1993).

13   D. Gross and S. Scott, "Proceeding with caution", *Time*, July 16, 1990, p. 62.

14   D. Hebdige, *Hiding in the Light* (London: Routledge, 1988), p. 20.

15   G. Marcus, *Lipstick Traces* (London: Secker and Warburg, 1989).

16   J. Carey, "Political correctness and Cultural Studies", *Journal of Communication*, Vol. 42, No. 1, Spring 1992, p. 62.

17   D. Harris, *From class struggle to the politics of pleasure* (London: Routledge, 1992), p. 93.

18   A. Laurence and D. Coupland, "Interview with Douglas Coupland", http://www.altx.com/int2/douglas.coupland.html, accessed on June 15, 2004.

19   I. Welsh, "Post-punk junk", in S. Redhead, *Repetitive Beat Generation* (Edinburgh: Rebel Inc, 2000), p. 144.

20   To observe the fine presentation of this argument and the consequences of it, please refer to Paul Dawson's "Grunge Lit; Marketing Generation X", *Meanjin*, Vol. 56, No. 1, 1997, pp. 119-125.

21 T. Chapman, "Fast car", *Tracy Chapman* (Elektra/Asylum, 1988), track two.

22 A. Morissette, "You oughta know", *Jagged little pill* (Maverick, 1995), track two.

23 A. Rawsthorn, "Never, never, land", *Marxism Today*, January 1987, p. 3.

24 G. Orwell, *The Road to Wigan Pier* (London: Victor Gollancz, 1937), pp. 85-86.

25 *Super Size Me* (The Con, 2004).

26 S. Allison, "NCYS Transitions", *Youth Studies Australia*, Vol. 15, No. 2, June 1996, p. 2.

27 K. Eshun, "Generation E", *The Modern Review*, Vol. 1, Issue 16, August-September 1994, p. 4.

28 V. Walker, "Baulking about my generation", *The Weekend Australian*, February 16-17, 2004, p. 21.

29 K. Hughes, "Three-child policy strikes a chord", *7news on Seven*, May 12, 2004, http://seven.com.au/news/feder_budget/81101, accessed on July 1, 2004.

30 P. Simon, "You can call me Al", *Graceland* (Warner Brothers, 1987), track six.

31 M. Carnes, "Introduction", from M. Carnes (ed.), *Past Imperfect: History according to the movies* (London: Cassell, 1996), p. 9.

32 K. Smith, *Clerks and Chasing Amy: Two Screenplays* (New York: Hyperion, 1997), pp. 285-6.

33 K. Smith, *Dogma* (New York: Grove Press, 1999), p. 39.

34 M. Quigley, "The politics of animation: South Park", *Metro Magazine*, No. 124/125, 2000, p. 52.

35 D. Coupland, *Microserfs* (New York: Regan Books, 1995), p. 51.

36 J. Cohen and M. Krugman, *Generation Ecch!* (New York: Fireside, 1994), p. 201.

37 I. Welsh, "Foreword", in P. Vasili, *The first black footballer* (London: Frank Cass, 1998), p. xii.

38 M. Davis, *Gangland* (Sydney: Allen and Unwin, 1997), p. 22.

39 D. Headon, J. Hooton, D. Horne, "Introduction", *The abundant culture: meaning and significance in everyday Australia* (St. Leonards: Allen and Unwin, 1995), p. xvi.

40 L. Grossberg, "Cultural Studies and/in new worlds", *Critical Studies in Mass Communication*, Vol. 10, No. 1, March 1993, p. 2.

41 D. Coupland, *Polaroids from the dead* (New York: Reganbooks, 1996), p. 45.

42 *ibid.*, p. 50.

43 A. Blaikie, *Ageing and popular culture* (Cambridge: Cambridge University Press, 1999), p. viii.

44 D. Hickey, *Air Guitar* (Los Angeles: Art Issues Press, 1997), p. 9.

Chapter two

Settling accounts with Birmingham

There is no sadder sight than the fortysomething ex-Leftie, the thirtysomething ex-Punk, the twentysomething ex-Stylist, burying their disappointments in their search across the surface of popular culture for pure sensation.[1]

Simon Frith and Jon Savage

Academics, like all other groups in a culture, build altars of meaning based on nostalgia, curiosity and, at times, irrational defence. Particular universities, scholars, books or historical moments extend a tenuous, but taut, grip on the consciousness. Cultural Studies scholars are no exception to this rule and actually accentuate the principle. The Birmingham Centre for Contemporary Cultural Studies no longer exists. It has not existed for two decades. Very few students were trained within its tutorial rooms.[2] Most academics teach more students in one year than the Centre's staff met in five. Through much of its history, postgraduates were the focus of their attention. Many of the staff and students that passed through the corridors of the Centre became – at least in academic-speak – famous. Careers were made by and through an association with this powerhouse in the field.

I am not – remotely – interested in constructing another history of the great men and (very) few women who 'built' contemporary Cultural Studies. These books are myriad and retell the same tale with a genuflection at the start and end of proceedings. I am not one of those kneeling writers and *From Revolution to Revelation* is not one of those respectful tomes. It is important to be intellectually generous to those who came before us, but also to create precisely aimed and critical interpretation of earlier knowledges. I was not born when the Centre was formed and was in kindergarten when Stuart Hall was its leader. I never studied in England – being both Australian and from a working family meant that I had to earn a living: there was no opportunity for a pilgrimage, scholarly or otherwise. I only once visited Birmingham's then Department of Cultural Studies as a Masters student and met the gracious Richard Johnson. By the start of the 1990s, he realized – perhaps more poignantly than any other scholar – that the Centre (or then Department) of Cultural Studies at Birmingham no longer had a theoretical function or political role in the present. It had become a memory text visited by young and enthusiastic intellectual tourists like me. Such a realization was intensified through the actions and statements of (ex)members of the Centre who worked there during the 1970s 'boom years'. I have no 'authentic' or 'real' knowledge of the Birmingham Centre. I have read, researched and explored its insights and influences through the gauze of both time and space. This is an ideal position in which to assess its influence, not in terms of a 'real contribution' but as a site of popular memory. I investigate the function of the Birmingham Centre in the present research and teaching environment, particularly as the Department of Cultural Studies has been closed by the policies of a Labour-led government. This chapter goes on a tour of Cultural Studies sites, to show how the ventriloquist puppet of youth spoke for their theoretical Masters. I provide a context to the Birmingham Centre's research on youth, rather than applying their theories and maxims to every nation and every time.

The popular memory of Birmingham has erased or displaced many other remarkable centres of Cultural Studies. The victors of history always do. American, Australian, New Zealand, Canadian or Hong Kong sites for the study of culture lack the gleam of credibility and the dust of authenticity. Any subsequent centre will always be deficient in the sparkle and passion of 'the original'. That is the nature of popular memory: the present can never be as interesting, important or special as a glorified past. Such a moment of commemoration emerged at the first 'big' Cultural Studies conference, held in Urbana, Illinois from April 4 to April 9, 1990. This conference in itself has become awash with memory: who was there? Who was not invited? What is forgotten is the (now) ironic title of the conference: 'Cultural Studies now and in the future.' Neither the 'Now,' nor the 'Future' was terribly relevant to the participants. They were building the field in the United States and (so appropriately) like *The Great Gatsby*, they were "borne back ceaselessly into the past".[3] The (former) members of the Birmingham Centre were given a platform to create a myth, summon a dreaming and write a history. Also, when the 'other' papers – or the papers from 'the others' – did not gel with their narrative, a seething directive from the Imperial core emerged. Ponder this statement from Angela McRobbie in the concluding paper of the conference and book:

> But what has worried me recently in Cultural Studies is when the theoretical detours become literary and textual excursions and when I begin to lose a sense of why the object of study is constituted as the object of study in the first place. Why do it? What is the point? Who is it for? On my first reading of many of the

32

papers [at this conference] I was gripped by panic. Where have I been for the last five years? Much of this kind of Cultural Studies does not at all tally with what I teach, with what I find useful in understanding the everyday world and everyday culture around me.[4]

She was particularly concerned that "lived experience"[5] was only considered in one of the papers in the collection. Invariably lived experience is in the eye – and the pen – of the beholder. At this conference, the organizers booked Stuart Hall to offer the definitive lived experience of the Centre, even though he was only one of many leaders at Birmingham.[6] Within the popular memory of Cultural Studies though, he stands alone. While he enjoyed the "moment of self-reflection on Cultural Studies as a practice", there were some moments in the presentation that were disturbing. He spoke "autobiographically", not to claim "the authority of authenticity", but to "take a position in relation to the 'grand narrative'".[7] This he accomplishes with panache, as the keeper of the political flame. Of course he claims authority. Of course he summons authenticity. Popular memory does not require intention. There are always parts of the authentic, the real or the lived that are forgotten or decentred. Hall, for example, in this same presentation stated that feminism "crapped on the table of Cultural Studies".[8] Very often – in fact, every time – when I have reminded senior academics in the field of this statement, they demand to see the reference. They had 'forgotten' that such a maxim was uttered, because of its political consequences. As the only full-time female staff member in my Cultural Studies department and fighting for the right of women to even enter the dining room of academic life let alone cast ablutions/aspersions, such a statement has remained in my mind. Heroes cannot make mistakes such as this.

Cultural Studies does not require another history of the Birmingham Centre. Neither does *From Revolution to Revelation*. Instead, what is needed is a popular memory of the Centre, showing how their studies of youth culture have had major consequences on the way in which we now (do not) think about time, space and history. Simply teaching the narrative and assumptions of the Centre is no longer enough. We live in a time that does not respect alternative memories, particularly relatively radical ones. That is why no centre – not the Manchester Institute for Popular Culture (MIPC), Murdoch University in Perth, Canterbury University in Christchurch, University of Queensland in Brisbane, or even the University of Illinois – could claim the mantle of Cultural Studies. The Birmingham Centre has died, but like all deaths it has been exaggerated. As the paradigm has aged, it is ironic that its most famous studies have been of youth. Like all Dorian Grays, there is a portrait of (post) youth in the attic.

The archaeological constitution of youth within Cultural Studies in the last forty years has revealed two major conjunctural moments. Both these transformations revolve around women: Margaret Thatcher and Angela McRobbie. When McRobbie published her "Settling Accounts with Subcultures" in a 1980 *Screen Education*,[9] she emphasized an absence that, in retrospect, appears blatantly obvious. The 'classic' sociological works conducted by Cohen and Willis not only emphasized spectacular subcultures to the detriment of 'normal youth,' but relegated women to the roles of mothers and girlfriends. McRobbie also highlighted the contradictions arising through a discussion of class and gender in relation to youth. Although she did not probe issues of 'deviance' and sexuality, her articulate attack effectively pinpointed the major weakness of the Birmingham paradigm. McRobbie chose her time correctly: Willis, Cohen, Hebdige and others had, for too long, refused to ask the most preliminary feminist question: What about women? They rebuffed the exploration of any youth group beyond spectacular male behaviour in working class urban communities in England.[10]

Concurrently, the installation of a Conservative Government and the radical economic shifts of Thatcher's first administration made the study of youth seem secondary or trivial. Only with Blair's ascendancy could a Wilson-like Cool Britannia again be summoned. There is a contextual linkage between the rise of Thatcher and a decline in the investigation of youth. The political fights of the 1980s were so brutal – through the miners' strike and the long death of industry in the north of England – that no group, including young people, could offer a far-reaching alternative agenda. Consumerism had become too pervasive and hyper-individualism blocked a desire for collective sense making. This new context meant that youth were not performing the resistive function that had been written for them in various books associated with the Centre, such as *Policing the Crisis*[11] and *Resistance through Rituals*.[12] There were no mods or rockers, no punks and safety pins, to perform resistive signifying potential against the capitalist mode of production. Instead, the yuppies with their filofaxes performed a style-lifing that left most of the fortysomething (ex)lefties retracting into the subcultural case studies that fitted their politics. Even McRobbie, in the preface to her 1991 collection of essays, nostalgically remembered the days of punk.

> Long after the moment of punk style had passed, a wider subcultural field had installed itself in the dreary blighted heartland of the West Midlands producing a

sense of a 'continuous present.' This was so forceful and so captivating that it gathered people up in an endless whirl of events, which blocked out the depressed economic present by creating a local utopia, a Birmingham bohemia.[13]

Although a decade earlier, McRobbie offered an important critique to the 'lived experience' of male sociologists and how such memories restricted their interpretation of young people, she was content to personalize the importance of punk and mention Dick Hebdige's status as occasional doorman at the Shoop disco and Paul Gilroy's DJ-ing work at Digbeth City Hall.[14] The consequence of claiming punk as a 'continuous present' – fifteen years after the music and style were replaced by new wave – was an evocative rhetorical flourish, but does have consequences.

I remain curious when academics stop their popular cultural clocks. McRobbie has every right to claim punk as being extraordinary – revelatory – remarkable. I am certain that it was for her and many others who shared those moments. Experience is an unpredictable theoretical intrusion that, once mobilized, unlocks the dual potential of insight and oppression. We are currently teaching students in Cultural Studies who barely remember the Spice Girls, let alone the Buzzcocks. Experience is a text to be read, a way to affirm differences and/or superiorities that are neither real nor intrinsically relevant.

McRobbie's intervention in the youth culture paradigm was necessary and fundamental to the long-term success of a critically interpretative Cultural Studies. Unfortunately, she was unsuccessful in her feminist challenge. The normalization of youth as a masculine formation re-appeared through the post-Acid House music scenes. The positioning of women in rave culture remained under-theorized. Electronic dance music is still dominated by male DJs, male club owners and male record producers. The spaces provided on the dance floor allowed new modes of femininity, sexuality and pleasure to emerge. The only problem is that few theorists or journalists seem interested in it. Such a lack of interest has a long history.

Subbing for en-ger-land

Although those working in the Birmingham Centre had a diversity of academic interests, their most famous analyses were those conduced on youth (sub)cultures. Howard Sercombe went so far as to term the BCCCS "the theoreticians of youth".[15] This study of youth had a long chronology in sociology before it was 'discovered' by Birmingham. The Chicago School, in the 1920s and 1930s, linked subcultures with gangs and 'delinquent' behaviour. Their focus on the urban environment, utilizing a method of intricate empiricism and a politics of reformism, aimed to create an ordered and stable society. Social plurality was not their goal: 'deviance' was diagnosed as a sign of pathological illness rather than political consciousness. The Birmingham Centre responded to this theoretical model, moving their research from the United States to the United Kingdom and augmenting the study of deviance with an overtly Marxist perspective. Youth subculture became a working class phenomenon, to be demarcated from the middle-class dominated counterculture. The *sub* in *sub*culture referred to the dependent relationship that youth collectives assumed in respect to class cultures.[16] Youth subcultures (per)formed a way to manage (temporarily) the contradictions of class culture. Capitalism – instead of youth – was configured as criminogenic. Deviance was a way to fight alienation. As Phil Cohen argued,

> Mods, Parkers (sic), skinheads, crombies, all represent, in their different ways, an attempt to retrieve some of the socially cohesive elements destroyed in their parent culture and to combine these with elements selected from other class fractions, symbolizing one or other of the options confronting it.[17]

Style became the battleground for class warfare. The methodology for this type of study, which was reliant on homology, (de)generated the history of youth into a linear, narrative, predictable and progressive form.

The archetypal subcultural study from Birmingham remains Dick Hebdige's *Subculture: the meaning of style*. This book provides a model to understand the shape of Birmingham's politics and theory. It was deeply influential, dynamic and popular. It has become the Cultural Studies equivalent of the Rosetta Stone. Decode the text and gain an insight into the language, structures and assumptions of the can(n)on. By the time Hebdige's book was published in 1979, the punk movement had enacted the dispatch of 'Great' Britain with performative panache. When the book was released, punk was already decaying in the cultural refrigerator. His book is a testament to that moment when popular culture became redundant and banal. Hebdige's argument was that "the emergence of such groups has signalled in a spectacular fashion the breakdown of consensus in the post-war period".[18] If, as Hebdige argued, subcultural style and fashion indicated the breakdown of consensus, what can explain the absence of subcultures during Thatcher's administration? Thatcher destroyed consensus, demolished the welfare state and muffled effective socialist critique. Yet Cultural Studies analysts were silent about subcultures during this period. Was it a simple case of epistemological shock?

The 'crisis' of Thatcherism was very different from the wolf that had been cried in *Policing the Crisis*.[19] There were few muggers or mods to slip into the role of youthful Folk Devil. Perhaps the 1980s were so politicized that the ideological scope of the Conservative project did not have to be stressed: it was obvious. Actually, the theoretical problem for Cultural Studies researchers occurred much earlier, when groups such as teds, rockers, mods and punks were overloaded with political consciousness. These subcultures were visible, exciting, passionate and distinct. The intellectual investment in these (frequently) spectacular young men by theorists is understandable, but there have been long-terms costs for framing (symbolic) politics in this way. The Birmingham model was a successful method for interpreting their space and time – and their influence spread. Very few writers have attacked British – and in particular English – Cultural Studies practitioners for their lack of concern with the (former) Empire, particularly in South-East Asia and the Pacific.[20] The 'world' of Birmingham was incredibly small, including jaunts through French theory, German philosophy and Italian prisons, but few touristic journeys through indigenous knowledge systems or dense colonial structures. For too long, there were no colonial cracks in the Cultural Studies Jack. While remarkable work was produced elsewhere, the large scale 'fame' for these other 'centres' was elusive. For example, the Manchester Institute for Popular Culture and Steve Redhead in particular, established a working papers series, instructed a group of passionate and brilliant postgraduate students and researched in a volatile and exciting context for youth culture. The resultant MIPC book series from Ashgate generated an important series of monographs that paralleled Birmingham's affiliation with Hutchinson. The 'fame' of the MIPC has not – and could not – match the Birmingham Centre. A mythic past can never be tarnished. Part of the MIPC's project was to dismiss the existence of 'authentic subcultures,' as they were only generated by authentic subcultural theory. Redhead recognized the profound consequences of this realization.

> [T]he problem for pop and youth culture history is that if subcultural explanations ... can now finally be laid to rest, their contemporary irrelevance throws into the melting pot the accepted theories and histories of the connections between pop, youth and deviance *before* the 1980s as well as after.[21]

In doubting the effectiveness of earlier subcultural resistance and the theories used to interpret these symbolics systems, the role of performative resistance in the present is also questioned. Cultural Studies scholars needed the language of authentic experience, resistance, social justice and political change and they required avatars like youth, women, black or gay communities to promote this function. This symbolic politics was – in retrospect – an easy politics, evocative to write about and teach and creatively malleable.

The Manchester Institute for Popular Culture continued researching youth and culture in a way that owed much to the BCCCS until 1994, when Justin O'Conner replaced Steve Redhead and Derek Wynne in the Directorship. Appropriately, but sadly, cultural policy and urban studies became more important than the politics of popular culture. The repetitive beat of a drum machine was replaced by the swiping of a credit card. For a brief moment – when Manchester was a centre of dance culture – young postgraduates engaged in ethnographic research like the Birmingham Centre. They also produced exciting books, stretching far beyond the Birmingham Centre's interests, including a potent mix of sport, fashion, fandom and music. They were not granted the time or space of the Centre to actually build a long-term legacy. Because of their movement into policy, they never activated the connection between popular memory and (post) youth culture. While the current research in creative industries has walked away from many of the fascinating interdisciplinary potentials of the first MIPC, the Manchester Institute remains historically significant to the archaeology of youth culture, as it was among the first to problematize the linear structure of youth culture and to end the search for the 'new punk'.[22] The goths, casuals, new romantics, Sloane Rangers, gender benders, acid housers and ravers are part of a different history, one that is not progressive or chronological. They cut up and sampled time.

The MIPC narrative demonstrates that quality of work and passionate political commitment is not enough to obtain scholarly fame. Indeed, the MIPC is not the Birmingham Centre. No American, Australian, Canadian, Malaysian or New Zealand 'Centre' is in the race for such notoriety. They could never be. Publishing careers, textbook distributors and teaching templates require Birmingham to hold 'meaning' and 'significance'. Such judgements are not evaluating quality, but the foundation of a burgeoning popular memory.

Trying to say something new about the Birmingham Centre is much like writing about the Beatles. In the search for unused and mistake-ridden out-takes, we all hope to grasp a trace of 'the Cultural Studies moment'. The death of youth culture coincided with the death of the Birmingham Centre. The two were theoretically and politically meshed. The vestige of either is summoned through myth, nostalgia or conference panels. The work of the Birmingham Centre for Contemporary Cultural Studies was brilliantly evocative for its era, but its time is over. For their particular 'crisis,' the BCCCS responded to the policing of the political process with expedience and ideological wit. Now, major (ex)members of the Birmingham Centre are policing the boundaries of Cultural Studies with the same vehemence with which they once engaged in polemic debate.[23] The right of certain pivotal exponents of Cultural Studies to determine the limits of the field inevitably results in a disempowering of current workers and theorists. Maybe not much is left, but it is enough.

Like all fairy tales, we expected the Birmingham Centre – or at least its renamed progeny, the Department of Cultural Studies – to live happily ever after. Third Way renderings of post-fordism, environmentalism, feminism, gay and black politics seemed to provide enough gritty intellectual work to keep the memory alive. Ironically (but actually not) it was Prime Minister Third Way himself – Tony Blair – who oversaw the 'real' death of Birmingham in 2002 as an academic pilgrimage/tourist location. Currently, the United Kingdom's higher education sector and the staff in it, is assessed through a Research Assessment Exercise. Departments and scholars are judged, ranked and assessed. The resultant 'grade' has profound and destructive impacts on many and positive and agreeable consequences on a few. A '5' rating is excellent, a '3a' is suicidal. The Department of Cultural Studies in Birmingham received a 3a. In 2002, the University 'restructured' them out of existence. Current students complained, former staff and students were horrified and the dream – to paraphrase John Lennon – was over. Martin McQuillan, who as head of department at Leeds School of Fine Art, History of Art and Cultural Studies also had to 'manage' a 3a trauma, asked one of the truly important questions:

The future of Cultural Studies has never looked brighter. Cultural Studies seems to have won all the battles it has had to fight. The canon has been complicated, theory is the mainstream across the western humanities, otherness and difference are the watchwords of the academy, interdisciplinarity is everyone's preferred modus operandi. Once, the CCBCS made an intervention into the academy to challenge those who laid claim to dominant culture; now the vocabulary of Cultural Studies is the language of power. This is something we should welcome. It is also something that should worry Cultural Studies greatly. We might pose this dilemma in the form of the question: why at the moment Cultural Studies has achieved a certain intellectual hegemony within the academy should the CCBCS close down?[24]

There reaches a point in every family where graves are no longer visited, when no one actually remembers where Grand-dad Ryan or Great Uncle Phil were buried. There is a time when the box of ageing, sepia-toned photographs no longer reveals faces with names. The family still exists, the lineage continues and the names pass through genealogical charts. But we no longer need the bodies, or their likeness. The Birmingham Centre for Contemporary Cultural Studies stopped being *contemporary* and entered popular memory. Their stories, theories and political struggles were not relevant. The Centre can disappear in fact, because it lives in memory. It is no longer needed.

No future?

> With the public sector, education, the welfare state – all the big, 'safe' institutions – up against the wall, there's nothing good or clever or heroic about going under. When all is said and done, why bother to think 'deeply' when you're not being paid to think deeply?[25]

Dick Hebdige

Hebdige published these words in 1988. His analysis is even more shockingly accurate in the 2000s. When making this statement, the big eighties was still twisting into Hebdige's vista. The 1980s were important because they were years of desire: they offered much – tantalized – teased – licked the lips of power – but delivered on few of its sensual pleasures. That is why Generation Xers remember this time – no matter how unpopular or excessive it may appear – with secret happiness. It was an era of disappointment, but it was a textualized disappointment. Tears for Fears gave us 'Shout,' Julie Burchill wrote novels in new literary languages and Fudge produced great hair gel. Anyone who underestimates the importance of hair products deserves dreadlocks. Inevitably, this attitude is best conveyed – not surprisingly – by a savvy letter writer to *The Face*.

> I've worked since school and all I seem to be doing is running on the spot, chasing dreams that are constantly on the horizon. It seems ironic that my life, and the lives of the people round me, revolves around hedonism and looking good, but what else is there? The Government is so out of touch it makes you sick.[26]

Hair gel and hedonism replaced attacking governmental policies. Yet even from the pages of *The Face*, attention to politics was connected – and tightly – to culture. Theorists in Cultural Studies have not often managed this relationship as well.

By the early 1990s (and really much earlier), the Birmingham Centre's concepts of homology and resistance were not working. The class structure was corroding and corrosive: the political economy transformed so rapidly that the blanket word – globalization – became an explanation/justification for the movements of capital and the loss of jobs. Style journalism, design and popular culture became the avenue for explosive angst and anger.

> We are the first generation since the war who can't envisage doing any better than our parents. The alternatives of the real world are out of reach, the sums of modern living leaves us always in debt, and the future holds no certainties. Abstinence from anything never works unless you actually replace it with something concrete like guilt, religion, or Charlie. What could be better in life than a gram up your nose, Andy Weatherall at the Drum Club, and the knowledge you're not going to make a complete idiot of yourself? Not a lot in John Major's classless, jobless, thankless, hopeless heaven. Time to get the mirror out.[27]

The great tragedy of Hills' statements is the realization not only that 'we' will not live as well as our parents, but that our parents did not actually live that well. The scrimping, the catalogue shopping, the food coupons and day-old bread are not the foundation of a consumerist utopia. Proto-Boomers did not own a lot – they led small lives – and were satisfied. In other words, they were fodder for the capitalist mill. Unfortunately, we are worse off than our parents and grandparents. We actually believe that styling mousse and attention to accessorizing will make us happy. We deserve what is happening to us.

Notes

1   S. Frith and J. Savage, "Pearls and swine: the intellectuals and the mass media", *New Left Review*, No. 198, March/April 1993, p. 116.
2   It is significant to remember that for much of its early history, the Birmingham Centre only taught postgraduate students.
3   F. Scott Fitzgerald, *The Great Gatsby* (Sydney: Modern Publishing Group, 1990), p. 154.

⁴ A. McRobbie, "Post-Marxism and Cultural Studies", in L. Grossberg, C. Nelson and P. Treichler (ed.), *Cultural Studies* (New York: Routledge, 1991), p. 721.

⁵ *ibid.*

⁶ A thumb-nail chronological outline of the Centre shows that it was formulated at the University of Birmingham in 1964 with Richard Hoggart as its first Director. Stuart Hall then assumed the leadership, to be followed by Richard Johnson in 1979. Jorge Lorrain took on the directorship and had to deal with pressure to rejoin the Department of English. The Centre then transformed into the Department of Cultural Studies and offered undergraduate programmes. In 2002, the Department was closed by the University, in response to a poor rating in the Research Assessment Exercise.

⁷ S. Hall, "Cultural Studies and its theoretical legacies", Grossberg et al., *op. cit.*, p. 277.

⁸ *ibid.*, p. 277.

⁹ A. McRobbie, "Settling accounts with subculture", *Screen Education*, Vol. 34, 1980, pp. 37-49.

¹⁰ While McRobbie's critique was timely, there is no doubt that the nature of her commentary shut down analytical space surrounding youth. One of the major reasons why youth culture was *not* an issue in the 1980s was the effectiveness of McRobbie's article. It must have been extremely difficult for men educated in the subcultural paradigm to follow through with their work in the light of McRobbie's comments. The date of McRobbie's article in *Screen Education* (1980) in many ways signalled a death of the study of youth culture. Certain 'taken for granted' categories and interests could no longer be justified.

¹¹ S. Hall et. al., *Policing the Crisis: Mugging, the State and Law and Order* (London: Macmillan, 1978).

¹² S. Hall and T. Jefferson (eds), *Resistance through Rituals* (London: Hutchinson, 1976).

¹³ A. McRobbie, "Introduction", *Feminism and Youth Culture* (Houndmills: Macmillan, 1991), p. xvi.

¹⁴ *ibid.* McRobbie is right to use experiential ideology, but is wrong to be reliant on it. While she critiqued the 'authentic voice' of male sociologists in their examination of street corners and 'deviant' behaviour, it was an obvious contradiction in her argument to then relate her experiences with the punk movement in Birmingham.

¹⁵ H. Sercombe, "Youth theory: Marx or Foucault", *Youth Studies Australia*, Vol. 11, No. 3, Spring 1992, p. 52.

¹⁶ A example of this distinction is found in Phil Cohen's work, where he argued that "I do not think the middle class produces subcultures for subcultures are produced by a dominated culture not for a dominant culture", in "Subcultural

conflict and working class community", *Working Papers in Cultural Studies*, No. 2, 1972, p. 30.

[17] *ibid.*, p. 23.

[18] D. Hebdige, *Subculture: the meaning of style* (London: Routledge, 1987: 1979), p. 17.

[19] For Hall et al. in *Policing the Crisis*, "the 'mugger' was ... a Folk Devil; his form and shape accurately reflected the content of the fears and anxieties of those who first imagined, and then actually discovered him: young, black, bred in, or arising from the 'breakdown of social order' in the city; threatening the traditional peace of the streets, the security of movement of the ordinary respectable citizen", p. 161.

[20] For example, Meaghan Morris commented in a question time at the Urbana, Illinois conference, "I'm restless about the map of Cultural Studies being constructed at this conference, about what's not on the map, rather than what is. We've talked about local and global relations in a world where Japan, South Korea, Hong Kong, Taiwan, Singapore and Indonesia simply don't exist", from "Question time", in Grossberg, et al., p. 476.

[21] S. Redhead, "The politics of ecstasy" in S. Redhead (ed.), *Rave Off* (Aldershot: Avebury, 1993), p. 24.

[22] For a record of the Centre's early work, please refer to Steve Redhead's *Unpopular cultures* (Manchester: Manchester University Press, 1995), particularly pages 103-108.

[23] For example, Stuart Hall, at the 1990 Cultural Studies Conference at Illinois, asked "Does it follow that Cultural Studies is not a policed area? That it is whatever people do, if they choose to call or locate themselves within the project and practice of Cultural Studies? I am not happy with that formulation", from "Cultural Studies and its theoretical legacies", in Grossberg et al., *op. cit.*, p. 278. The repercussions of Hall's pronouncement are obvious. Who has the right to determine that one subject area or theoretical framework is Cultural Studies and another arena or paradigm is not? Such an arbitrary distinction articulates more about the way in which power is distributed in Cultural Studies than about the intrinsic 'worth' of the project.

[24] M. McQuillan, "Pennies for your thoughts", *The Times Higher Education Supplement*, August 16, 2002, p. 15.

[25] D. Hebdige, *Hiding in the light* (London: Comedia, 1988) p. 167.

[26] C. Miller, "Letter", *The Face*, Vol. 2, No. 52, January 1993, p. 52.

[27] G. Hills, "Wonderland UK", *The Face*, Vol. 2, No. 52, January 1993, p. 52.

Chapter three

Thank you for the history lesson

Picture this scene. Two heavyweight scholars meet at the 'Media Wars' seminar at the Queensland University of Technology Australia in November 1998. Keith Windschuttle and John Hartley battled out the nature of truth, politics and history. Unfortunately, the former has a tendency to repeat the same three points wherever and whenever he speaks. At this venue, Windschuttle attacked Hartley using the blunt instrument of historical narrative, punching out a potted chronology of journalism in Western culture. Not surprisingly, at the denouement of this tale, Hartley responded, "Thank you for the history lesson".[1]

Such a story captures the major tales to be tracked in this chapter. After settling accounts with Cultural Studies and Generation X, we now theorize and forge a graft to history. I explore the lessons of history – or more precisely historiography – for contemporary Cultural Studies. Research in (post)youth and popular memory requires a concise linking of Cultural Studies and history. This interdisciplinary work is arduous, challenging and under-written. Historians and Cultural Studies practitioners have clashed throughout the last twenty five years. Even more often, they completely ignore each other's articles, journals and monographs. While the last chapter gave a history to theories of youth, this section gifts a clock to Cultural Studies.

Licking the lipstick trace

> Someday soon, presumably, another E.H. Carr will announce that the more cultural historical studies becomes and the more historical Cultural Studies becomes the better for both.[2]
>
> Lynn Hunt

Tara Brabazon is no E.H. Carr and this chapter is not an appendix to *What is History?*[3] for the 2000s. My task is far more tentative and questioning. In offering a paradigm for a new cultural history, I hope a border dialogue will (re)commence between history and Cultural Studies that is advantageous to both intellectual terrains. With Keith Windschuttle's ruthless separation of traditional history and 'trendy' Cultural Studies, few students are encouraged to be trained in both disciplines. In arguing for a cultural past as much as a cultural future, the dialogue between history and Cultural Studies changes, shifting understandings of text, context, truth and politics.

Windschuttle commenced an attack on Cultural Studies through his 1994 book, *The Killing of History: how a discipline is being murdered by literary critics and social theorists*. The title is severe: the text is even more relentless. He decried "a breed of literary critics, literary theorists and social theorists who have moved in and begun writing their own versions of history".[4] For Windschuttle, these theorists perpetuate a sacrilege: that there is no overt distinction between fiction and non-fiction. While he clings to historical facts and objectivity, his book features only one reference to the Annales School, two to Ferdinand Braudel and thirteen citations to Christianity. Actually, the Annales School received as many references as The Faerie Queene.

Although published in 1994, Windschuttle is shadow boxing intellectual phantoms of an earlier decade. Many of his criticisms about Cultural Studies and history are found in the writings of the mid-1980s. Lesley Johnson, for example, described all history as "a fabrication, formed always within the concerns of the present, by the politics of the present".[5] She framed popular culture as a site of struggle. Particularly, she argued that women's history is excluded from nationalized narratives. Through such modes of argument, all of Windschuttle's buttons were pushed. But Johnson's work was written in 1986 and Cultural Studies has changed enormously since that time, particularly influenced through the expansion of the field in the United States and Canada.

(Too) many historians are seething about Cultural Studies. Much of this hostility has to do with the awkward dance between truth and ideology in the paradigm. Attendant to this disquiet is the jurisdiction and function of 'theory', For example, Lawrence Grossberg described one of his texts as "a book with too many arguments and not enough evidence, but it may be forgiven in a world with too much evidence and not enough argument".[6] Theory always intervenes between historian and fact. Sources never reflect a society. Instead they mask, repress, but most significantly represent a version of the past. Windschuttle is not simply a crazy, conservative historian bitter at his younger, trendier rivals in Cultural Studies. His words are part of a movement of abuse, ridicule and dismissal against progressive – and occasionally radical – scholarship. He is an artillery-laden historian in a cultural war being fought within Australia, the United States and the United Kingdom.[7] Such a battle picks off such phrases as dumbing down, political correctness and femocrats. Cultural Studies is frequently the target of these attacks because it performs the crisis of purpose within the contemporary University. Straddling the humanities and social sciences, theorists demonstrate that unified, coherent and elite notions of culture are no longer working (for some). As Wark realized, the Australian Cultural Studies project "brought together people whose roots were in feminism, multiculturalism, Aboriginal cultural activism and much else besides. It was a vast and amorphous movement".[8] The significance of collecting these alternative narratives and theorizing them through a politicized interpretative matrix created new ways to 'do' knowledge.

With historians and Cultural Studies practitioners frequently occupying disconnected discourses, the aim of my work in this book is to offer an interdisciplinary translation between two paradigms. Translation is the correct word. The differences between history and Cultural Studies relate to ontology, methodology and approach, but the two subject areas are partitioned through the use of idiosyncratic languages. The disparate terminologies convey distinct applications of knowledge. While textual analysis probes signs, codes, ideologies and discourses, investigations of historical sources aim to generate verification. The line between fact and fiction is not as clear as Keith Windschuttle would wish. The point at which an evidential representation has enough credibility to enter the realm of fact is highly debateable. How many footnotes are enough? The historical chronicle – one fact after another – is a mask of the selection process which validates an individual statistic, quotation and viewpoint over others. Marcus has described chronology as "the way history is cheapened and restricted".[9] Every moment that passes sees the destruction of alternative views, trajectories and source material. The notion that historians make a past built on factual evidence is delusional at best and politically blind at worst. The disappearances of history, the source material that does not survive through time, result in a profound narrowing of past realities. To not acknowledge such losses is either complacent or complicit.

Epistemological discussions that detail the nature of history have existed since the discipline had a name. The impact of women's history and social history has certainly changed the way historical methods are constituted.[10] Concurrently though, the historical discipline has also separated into distinct threads, with social history distanced from the 'credible' political or diplomatic histories. The hierarchy of historical research has allowed the main sources of evidence to remain parliamentary papers, newspapers, journals of political organizations and diaries. Similarly, the research strategies through which these 'conventional' sources are being accessed display little knowingness of contested subjectivities, multiple readerships or the complex text/context relationship.[11]   Instead of asking E.H. Carr's old question 'What is History?', it is time to rephrase the problem. Greil Marcus has captured the tone of this new enigmatic question.

> What is history, anyway? Is history simply a matter of events that leave behind those things that can be weighed and measured: new institutions, new rulers, new winners, new losers, or is history also a matter of those things that seem to leave nothing behind, nothing but the mystery of spectral connections between people long separated by place and time. If the language they are speaking, the impulse they are voicing, has its own language, might it not tell a very different story from the one we've been hearing all our lives?[12]

Historians protect the boundary of their discipline by not admitting this type of lipstick trace. Such tentative questions – rather than definitive answers – peek through the counterfactual history movement: those scholars who write the 'what if ...' alternative trajectories of the past.[13]   In maintaining a solid, clear, jargon-free writing style, credible historians avoid the theoretical enthusiasms (and double-speak) that are pervasive in Cultural Studies. In recording an era that is not the present, historians do not consider themselves writers of fiction. Indeed they are not: they are writers of empowered fictions. The real becomes a product that is shaped ideologically and politically.[14] Historical facts cannot be verified, but only checked against other subjective accounts. Historians have access to representations of the past, not the past.[15]

Questions of fact frequently spill into debates about language and interpretation. We need to ask more subtle questions about how knowledge is formed and why gaps and silences exist in the historical record.[16] Notions of evidence, truth and verification must shift to incorporate new sources, visions and versions. Flicking through government reports does not display the truth of the events that took place on the colonial frontier. These documents demonstrate how indigenous peoples were 'managed' by the empowered, not understood by the citizenry. Greil Marcus presented the consequences of this type of 'evidence' for the marginalized and dispossessed:

> There are people who act and speak but whose gestures and words do not translate out of their moments – and this exclusion, the sweep of the broom of this dustbin, is a movement that in its way is far more violent than any toppling of statues.[17]

To ignore the alternatives – to blandly place faith in the written document over the popular cultural trace – is to perpetuate an inequality and oppression that is wide in its magnitude and dense in its consequences. Women, as much as indigenous and black communities, gays and lesbians, the working class and youth, have been sliced from time, space and historical evidence.[18] To construct a history of the ephemeral – the shadows cast by 'authoritative' source material – requires a range of interpretative techniques that are beyond the parameters of both history and Cultural Studies, but requires a nuanced dialogue between the two.[19] Through changing the genre, mode and modality, a new type of interpretation can emerge.

History is inserted within a discursive space that is structured by the binary opposition of fact and fiction. Once that division is problematized, then the search for a determining truth is undermined. The status of 'facts' will always be problematic. An historian's task is to consider what the past means in – and to – the present. The desire for certainty is understandable: with the end of Platonic absolutes, the Nietzscherian death of God, the Foucauldian death of Man and the Kristevan death of Woman, an affirmation of the resolute status of a fact is a way to make sense of a chaotic social reality. Actually, there is no singular truth to be recovered or lived experience to be revealed: only lived ideology can be explored.

Such subtle realizations are rare in the politically destructive environment of the last twenty years. Allan Bloom's *The closing of the American mind*, published in 1987, battled the cold war in the academy. Believing that "America tells one story: the unbroken, ineluctable progress of freedom and equality",[20] he attacks all those who fragment this simple narrative, such as feminists,[21] musicians, film makers and those teaching other nation's histories. The desire to separate history from talk, gossip or popular culture has a political function.[22] The disempowered lose a mechanism to talk back to the oppressor. This function of history is rarely articulated: it is a way of speaking, teaching or reading, a selection criteria for source material or methodological assumptions perpetuated through the result of special training. History is not the study of the past: it is an analysis of material traces that have survived from past cultures and experiences.

The historical profession has altered radically and rapidly since the 1960s. The influence of E.P. Thompson and George Rude initiated much interest in a history from below and a muddying of the base/superstructure model of social and economic relations. The way in which material conditions are examined complicates Marxist paradigms, but also grants the Annales School interpretative validity. In their exploration of the serial, functional and structural approaches to society, as applied by Ferdinand Braudel's history of the Mediterranean world,[23] the Annalists widened our understanding of time. Also, while being situated in the social sciences, the School was open to new methods and approaches. Through this mode of tiered analysis, theories of culture were not relegated to a 'reflection' of social reality. It was a poignant and powerful critique. Masuzawa articulated the confusion arising from this loss of linear or singular time.

> We thought we were quite accustomed to living in terms of beginning, middle, and end, and we thought we always travelled in a passage of time as smartly arranged as the pages between two hard covers, but now it looks like we are traversing a bad infinity, which is worse still, strangely convoluted.[24]

This temporal confusion subverts any claims for an historical origin or endpoint. Instead, possibilities arise that produce contingent, intertextual histories. Lipstick traces from the past provide a tantalizing taste of another way of living and another way of thinking.

Pulping the past

The nexus through which academics engage with/in history and Cultural Studies has been tortured and conflictual. Cultural Studies has (too often) maintained separate literary and sociological strands. Raymond Williams recognized that a strong potential existed for a dialogue between history, culture and sociology.[25] The dissociation and cleft between history and Cultural Studies does have an origin and specified location: *History Workshop*, 1978. Richard Johnson, the resident historian of the Birmingham Centre, engaged in an Althusser-fuelled critique of the 'authentic', experiential history of E.P. Thompson. Johnson clearly recognized the split that was fracturing the English (rather than British) humanities.

> We are really speaking now of two co-existing traditions in this country, which also ... represent disciplinary boundaries (history as against sociology or philosophy) and even intellectual generations (pre-and post-1968 in their formation.) These clearly have the greatest difficulty in speaking intelligibly to the other.[26]

The tone of the debate erupting from Johnson's critique verified his argument. The resultant commentaries were rude, aggressive and reliant on the 'I-know-Marx-better-that-you-know-Marx' school of historiography. Johnson attempted to accomplish a single goal: to show historians that "theory is a moment in the historian's method – the moment of forming questions rather than testing them, a moment always provisional in status, always subject to the ultimate control of 'grand facts',"[27] While Thompson listened to the poor Stockinger, Luddite and the handloom weavers, Johnson suggested that Althusser would have read their lives critically, not searched for the authentic voice. Richard Johnson wrote the words that most historians and cultural analysts knew: after perusing 880 pages of E.P. Thompson's *The Making of the English Working Class*, readers learnt much about 'human agency' and the 'human spirit', but "we still want (and need) to know how these things came to be".[28] Critiquing E.P. Thompson anywhere, at any point during the 1970s, was brave. Questioning Thompson in the journal-mecca of Socialist and Feminist Historians was a profoundly symbolic act.

If Johnson had wished, in classic Gramscian fashion, to transform his 'good sense' into 'commonsense', then the tone and approach of his questioning was perhaps misplaced. The response to his article was so fierce that this piece ended for over ten years any serious theoretical work that connected history and Cultural Studies. In response to Johnson's 'attack', culturalist historians waged a defence of history. Two examples, one from Tim Putnam and the other from Robert Shenton, exhibit the vulgarity of the response.

> We must resist 'critiques' which make 'theory' a law unto itself. Richard Johnson has, unfortunately, given us such a critique.[29]

> The brilliance of Thompson's and Genovese's work is that they show us that even in the darkest hour the 'culture' of the oppressed survives. Are we now to denigrate it in the name of 'theory'?[30]

These two excerpts and other critiques of Johnson within *History Workshop*, illustrate that the parameters of history were strictly patrolled. Those attempting to offer alternatives and interdisciplinary options were slammed down as 'theorists' or engaging in 'critique' rather than 'creation', Richard Johnson, in response to the force of the (too frequently) personal attack could only state that "the truth is the article did not merit this kind of attention".[31] The 'truth' is that the critique within *History Workshop* had little to do with Johnson, Thompson or even cultural history. Instead it was the result of an intellectual demarcation dispute – who has the right to write about 'experience' and 'politics' within history. The venom of the Johnson debate was only brought to a close when Gareth Stedman Jones, displaying customary intellectual generosity, wrote that

The vocabulary of anathema, heresy and inquisition should not be the terms in which socialists address each other ... Let us therefore, disagree with Richard Johnson's arguments if we wish to, but let us confront the real issues involved and not hide self-righteously behind the masques of fake Marxisms.[32]

While the attack on Johnson was stopped (at least within the pages of academic journals), this interchange also ended much of the intellectually generous and open discussions of theory, politics, culture and history. Cultural Studies and history splintered in approach and practitioners, with each sphere performing caricatures of the other. By 1980, Johnson could only remark, "I find it hard ... to think of myself as a 'historian' now, though perhaps historian-of-the-contemporary is a rough approximation in some contexts."[33] Johnson's journey away from history and towards Cultural Studies is understandable, particularly considering the extent of personal assault waged against him by historians.[34] Importantly, through the 1990s and 2000s, Johnson continued researching popular memory, finding an effective outlet in folklore studies.[35] By 2004, he and his colleagues at Nottingham Trent University developed a book titled *The Practice of Cultural Studies*.[36] This text continues to promote his belief in interdisciplinarity, while much of Cultural Studies totters at the edge of the disciplinary moat.

This debate in *History Workshop* was to have lasting consequences, made worse when the great Thompson stated in print that "What Richard Johnson is not interested in – what scarcely seems to enter the door of the Birmingham Centre for Cultural Studies – is any consideration of the politics."[37] This direct and completely inaccurate attack on Cultural Studies allowed Thompson to win a polemical battle – as he so often did – but to lose the political war. Shutting down the space of dialogue between Cultural Studies and history was disastrous and had profound theoretical and intellectual consequences through the conservatism of the 1980s and 1990s. Richard Evans realized by 1999 that "drawing up the disciplinary drawbridge has never been a good idea for historians".[38] As will be postulated at the end of this chapter, other options have arisen from this preliminary and courageous interdisciplinary critique by Johnson.

Through the conflict and personal attacks, the Birmingham Centre – and Richard Johnson – did build a foundation for a productive link between history and Cultural Studies. The 1982 text *Making Histories: studies in history writing and politics*, is one of the most under-cited texts published during the Centre's era of influence. This text works through the importance of the Annales School, George Rude's history of the crowd and E.P. Thompson's research. Their thesis – that history and politics enact a constant dialogue – is actualized through a careful investigation of the British left, humanism and class. Most significantly for the purposes of *From Revolution to Revelation*, they formulated one of the clearest sketches of popular memory, confirming the patrolled borders of academic history and the potential of research beyond these scholarly confines.

Cultural Studies, being built on and through interdisciplinarity, has been more open to alternative methodologies than the historical discipline.[39] As Hall recalled during his time as Head of the BCCCS, "we did the rounds of the disciplines".[40] This intellectual pillaging resulted in the formulation of a Cultural History Group in 1973, which was featured in the ninth edition of the *Working Papers in Cultural Studies*.[41] From this promising beginning, Cultural History was practically effaced: only one paper in the Grossberg et. al. *Cultural Studies* directly engaged with cultural history.[42] The history generated through from this scholarly raid has been lacking in scale, depth and subtlety. David Harris recognized this problem when he argued that within Cultural Studies,

> Sociology has been discussed in a highly selective manner. Lack of expertise means I can do little more than suggest similar significant selections and omissions in the debates with history or linguistics.[43]

Cultural Studies practitioners working with history should be commended for their desire to engage in interdisciplinary work. It is time-consuming, complicated and, as shown by the problems facing Richard Johnson and John Hartley, intellectually and politically treacherous. The problem with Cultural Studies' version of history is that the historical clock stopped, while sociological and semiological watches (and knowledges) continued to be wound, scrutinized and updated. This methodological freeze coincides, uneasily, with Johnson's engagement with *History Workshop*. Andrew Milner, by 1997, affirmed that "Cultural Studies suffers from an endemic lack of historical memory, a characteristic it shares with and perhaps derives from, the two disciplines most commonly recognized as its intellectual predecessors, sociology and semiology."[44] With the founding triumvirate of Raymond Williams, Richard Hoggart and E.P. Thompson increasingly being replaced by Williams/Hoggart/Hall, Cultural Studies is drained of history and historiography. As the attention to class has wavered, the nature of the political economy, social change and social justice has also been sidelined. The few named and acknowledged historians working in Cultural Studies is disturbing and has consequences on these few practitioners. Michael Pickering stated that his book, *History, Experience and Cultural Studies*, has grown out of a sense of frustration. There has now developed a wide division between history and Cultural Studies, and my frustration derives from the experience of social historians and practitioners of Cultural Studies talking past each other.[45]

A dialogue between social history and Cultural Studies not only theorizes popular culture with subtlety and care, but generates a diachronically delicate investigation of political change.

The way in which Cultural Studies writers have claimed the word 'history' is an intriguing trace upon the 'taken-for-granted' interchangeability between 'actually existing past', 'chronicle' and 'history', Windschuttle recognized that "when the proponents of Cultural Studies write about the past they now have few reservations about calling their practice 'history', However, they are usually careful to distinguish this from the discipline of traditional history, in which very few of them have trained".[46] Obviously, he has over-stated this case, but there is evidence for his judgement. I am one of many (trained) historians who moved in and through the Cultural Studies paradigm. But others like Meaghan Morris have justified Windschuttle's concern by stating that "wanting history, I read for the theory and skip the facts".[47] Such a maxim dismisses the subtle overlay and dialogue between discursive frameworks and the interpretation of evidence. There is no separation of source and interpretation, fact and theory and such a mantra serves to (over)stabilize the sanctity of both historical evidence and historiographical approaches. Her belief that "after all, history dates",[48] does not recognize that the discipline does the exact opposite. Historian's histories move through time and become primary sources for new inflections and interpretations. Similarly, Lawrence Grossberg too easily displaces the function of history in terms of political change and public profile.

> As history loses its sense, it can no longer be a source for the values by which one chooses and validates one's actions ... As history becomes mere change – discontinuous, directionless, and meaningless – it is replaced by a sense of fragmentation and rupture, of oppressive materiality, of powerlessness and relativism.[49]

This statement is worrying. Firstly, history is not – and has never been – 'about change', At its most reified, simplistic and undergraduate, it is an oscillation between change and continuity. At a time where the heritage industry is expanding rapidly, bleeding into tourism, education and environmental studies and when history has become the basis of popular film, television and literature, Grossberg's point is troubling. How he understands, defines and applies 'history' – as a noun, discipline and politicized node for action – is not clear.

Such an ambiguous Cultural Studies rendering of history can be tracked back to the Birmingham Centre for Contemporary Cultural Studies. Fresh insights into youth were hampered, not through intentionally obstructionist theories, but through an unsubstantiated conflation of 'history' and 'context', 'History' was used as an ideological tool in Birmingham to affirm difference: the Centre was *not* aligned with the overtly ahistorical *Screen* and was neither Weberian nor functionalist. Through the indeterminacy of the Centre's understanding of 'history', many gaps and absences haunted their investigations. The 'problem' of memory in the configuration of youth culture was not considered. The histories of spaces, margins and ambivalences that cannot be 'reclaimed' through empiricism were omitted from the Centre's research brief. To move beyond positivism required a recognition of the unknowability of the past. Source material cannot offer a politically correct and 'obvious' truth, but alludes to what may have been. Most communities – particularly the disempowered – leave few traces of their lives.

For a cultural future

History is made by those who say 'No.'[50]
Jon Savage

If any collective or community offers potential to be subjected to the vagaries of fact and fiction, truth and ideology, then it is Generation X. While the main axis of knowledge within the historical discipline relates to time, the Cultural Studies clock is locked in a loop: past, present and future are positioned within a confused and violently unstable temporal landscape. The crisis of legitimation after postmodernism forms a series of truths that play on the surfaces of 'credible' history. As Giroux suggests, "postmodernism conceives of the everyday and the popular as worthy of serious *and* playful consideration".[51] This valuable yet contradictory approach permits the development of plural subjectivities and conflictual meanings. Historians, trained in scholarly methods of rationality, authenticity and verification, reacted with vehemence and anger against the possibility of postmodern-inflected cultural history. Eric Hobsbawm argued that postmodern historians were claiming that there is no clear difference between fact and fiction. But there is, and for historians, even for the most militantly antipositivist ones among us, the ability to distinguish between the two is absolutely fundamental. We cannot invent our facts.[52]

Hobsbawm, the empowered historian of 19th century revolutions, has slammed those who 'invent their facts', Yet history is not a collection of facts, it is an amalgam of relevancies. Hobsbawm also frays his own thesis. While affirming that "what historians investigate is real",[53] he also admitted that "we cannot help comparing past and present".[54] Still, Eric Hobsbawm's historical method is based on verification: "Either Elvis Presley is dead or he isn't. The question can be answered unambiguously on the basis of evidence, in so far as reliable evidence is available."[55] While the mortality of Elvis Presley may be confirmed with certainty, a greater question is why his music and iconography continue to 'live' in our present. 'Why' questions are always more interesting than studies of 'the when',

Culture and history are sites of struggle. Like Cultural Studies, cultural history is an approach or a directive, rather than a discipline. It is a sphere of knowledge that overlaps with social history, women's history, men's studies, urban studies, cultural geography and historiography. Both inside and outside history, inside and outside Cultural Studies, this paradigm floats in and through both disciplines, interrogating the easy ranking and judging of sources. A cultural history textualizes history and contextualizes Cultural Studies. In researching popular culture, the goal is not an empirical journey to discover reality, but a watchful monitoring of sign systems and their movements. The resultant approach or method is tentative and interrogative, translating and transforming the past, not reclaiming it. History is a totalizing discourse, yet in that search for truth (transitory) legitimation is granted to those whose pasts are forgotten, whose visions are lost in shadows. Cultural Studies can effectively augment historical analysis by inflecting 'facts' through sites of social intervention. Meanings and pleasures are not found 'in' a text, but are generated through the act of seeing, listening and reading. A cultural history is also more conscious of readerships. History is not written for its own sake: it is always written for an audience. Different histories are owned and granted value by disparate communities. The sources of popular culture are dangerous to the form, content and ideology of traditional history: in compressing and perhaps collapsing the distance between history and reader, the historical past that survives in the present can be touched, accessible and owned.

In 'changing the rules' for the investigation of history, an historian transforms into the watcher of fans, the listener to gossip and the speaker of rumours, rather than a stoic figure conveying truth. This effacement of a knowable and containable past demands other skills, such as a pervasive and proactive sense of the present. As Hebdige suggested in the conclusion of *Hiding in the Light*,

> We're on the road to nowhere. All of us. There's nowhere else but here for us. No other time but now. This is all there is and it's enough to be getting on with. It's not so bad. In fact it can make us laugh.[56]

Cultural history confirms a recognition that there is 'no other time but now', This awareness changes the selection of topics and source material, renewing suspicion of written sources. This critique generates 'enough to be getting on with', although this process may appear lacking in radicalism or 'original thought', It may be on a road to nowhere, but the journey becomes significant.

A functioning paradigm of cultural history is necessary to investigate Generation X. Such an invented community can only be approached historically. Cultural history, as an interpretation of representations rather than the real, offers a method to trace the residue of memories, music and ideas. The youth of the 1980s and 1990s no longer exist. Their clubs have been closed or renovated. Their music has ceased to be played, returning only as nostalgia or film soundtracks. In recognizing the incomplete nature of evidence and the impossibility of capturing the past 'as it really existed', the historian is freed from the task of ventriloquy. Generation X are phantoms, who phase in and out of the present in an amalgam of half-remembered song lyrics and discarded fashion accessories. As Cassidy asked,

> Who listens to Duran Duran nowadays? Who can remember the name of that nice young man in Wham? No, not George Michael, the other one.[57]

These semi-remembered imaginings of the past grant a temporal frame to the study of youth culture. Should this past and the pop knowledge that remembers the names of the band members from Duran Duran (Simon, Nick, Roger, John and Andy) or the other half of Wham (Andrew Ridgeley) be reclaimed? Is such a past relevant to the construction of a history?

(Post) youth cultures are banal and non-spectacular. As Douglas Coupland, the sage of X, articulated, "history does not record my response".[58] There are reasons for this lack of acknowledgement. History imposes an ordered path through the past. In attempting to prove that a culture is always wrong about itself, historians deny the workings of memory. If history is relinquished from its responsibility to account for change, then 'causes' and 'explanations' do not need to be offered. Facts are loosened from their ordered positioning between origins and endings. With the past/future and form/content nexus loosened, the resultant 'history' will not resemble a narrative. Instead, spaces, margins and gaps are highlighted. Through revealing the absences, writers recognize not only who is left out of history, but who tells the tales and writes the fictions that are believed and trusted as history. In exploring popular memory, historians shift their focus from written to aural and visual literacies.

The relationship between Cultural Studies and historical paradigms remains conflictual, particularly over cultural value. As Graeme Turner suggested,

> despite the importance of the *category* of history to the developing protocols of Cultural Studies, the field's relation with academic professions – the discipline and institution – of history has never been without tension or ambiguity.[59]

Through this ambiguity, tension and contradiction, a popular cultural literacy can be created to track meaning from memory. There is a seductive potential in watching the absence as much as the presence, the gaps and silences as well as moments bubbling with activity, 'blank' margins rather than burgeoning text. Meaghan Morris, asking a question within the 1990 Cultural Studies Conference in Urbana, Illinois, detailed her 'quarrel' with history. In the end, she concluded that, "History is the name of the space where we define what matters."[60] Keith Jenkins concurs, arguing that "those who will be the best guides in history today are those who not only know all about the collapse of both upper and lower case versions [of History] into uncertainty, but who like it and can accept it".[61] In shifting the mental furniture of the past, a present can be created with political and theoretical honesty, if not credibility. Social change does not emerge from definitive historical judgements and narrative closure, but the free play of metaphor, metonymy, synecdoche and irony.

If history becomes a collection of Lipstick Traces, smears on disused coffee cups, champagne flutes and cigarettes, then the status and fixity granted to evidence is disrupted and lost. As the lipstick bleeds pervasively over the historical paradigm, a new meaning system is tinctured. These Lipstick Traces are not 'historical', but offer a history of/for the future. To utilize Andrew Ross's description of Greil Marcus's book,

> Because of its bad faith with history, Lipstick Traces has no alternative, then, but to present a history that can only be taken on faith.[62]

That infusion of emotion and politics into meaning systems may not be scholarly, but remains radically contextual and determinately pertinent. A history to be taken on faith, lacking an intellectual apparatus but doggedly pursuant of relevance, grants historians an aperture through which to explore the political potentials of the past in the present.

Notes

1   This story was related by Keith Windschuttle in "Journalism and the Western tradition", *Australian Journalism Review*, Vol. 21, No. 1, 1999, p. 60. I confirmed these events through a personal email to John Hartley, sent on December 26, 2000.

2   L. Hunt, "Introduction: History, Culture and Text", in L. Hunt (ed.), *The New Cultural History* (Berkeley: University of California Press, 1989), p. 22.

3   E.H. Carr, *What is History?* (London: Penguin, 1963).

4   K. Windschuttle, *The killing of history: how a discipline is being murdered by literary critics and social theorists* (Paddington: Macleay Press, 1994), p. 2.

5   L. Johnson, "The study of popular culture: the need for a clear agenda", *Australian Journal of Cultural Studies*, Vol. 4, No. 1, June 1986, p. 1.

6   L. Grossberg, *We gotta get out of this place* (New York: Routledge, 1992), p. 1.

7   I am unable to address in this book the very important relationship between Cultural Studies and Australian Studies. Both paradigms occupy an ambivalent relationship with Australian history. The *Journal of Australian Studies* captures many of these debates, but an outstanding entry point into this discussion is Richard Nile's "Australian Studies: Australian History, Australian Studies and the new economy", *Journal of Australian Studies*, June 2002, pp. 201-216.

8   M. Wark, *The Virtual Republic: Australia's Culture Wars in the 1990s* (Sydney: St. Leonards, 1997), p. 168.

9   G. Marcus, *The dustbin of history* (Cambridge: Harvard University Press, 1995), p. 5.

10 Importantly though, hierarchies of 'evidence' still exist, even in social history. Jay Hopler, when researching the literature of contractual murder, tells of her relationship with pulp fiction: "the stories themselves were shallow and formulaic; the characters were cardboard cut-outs that meandered from one almost-sexual encounter to another and, no matter what the plot was or where the story was set, someone inevitably ended up unconscious in an alley behind some strip bar or juke joint ... *The Mammoth Book of Pulp Fiction* confirmed what I had always suspected – pulp fiction was worthless", from "Watching the detectives", *Journal of*

Social History, Winter 2002, p. 460. She later realized that by moving away from text-based models of literary criticism and granting the audience of these books a context and' space through Cultural Studies methods, the genre gained meaning in a particular time and place. Hopler's article is an outstanding 'journey piece,' capturing how even the most liberal of social historians was able to discount 'evidence' because a history degree provides few skills in audience analysis.

11   Even when utilizing photographic and filmic sources, a notion of cultural value is deployed in a way that excludes other ways of reading visual culture. For example, please refer to Horst Bredekamp's "A neglected tradition?   Art History as Bildwissenschaft", *Critical Inquiry*, Vol. 29, Spring 2003. This research, while appearing to incorporate a wide range of visual culture, offers singular readings of 'art,' wherever it may be found.

12   G. Marcus, *Lipstick Traces* (London: Secker and Warburg, 1989), p. 6.

13   This work is seen in the Niall Ferguson edited collection, *Virtual history: alternatives and counterfactuals* (London: Macmillan, 1997).

14   As Georg Iggers has argued, "the distinction between truth and falsehood remains fundamental to the work of the historian. The concept of truth has become immeasurably more complex in the course of recent critical thought", from *Historiography in the twentieth century* (Hanover: Wesleyan University Press, 1997), p. 12.

15   To view the importance of these historical representations, rather than realities, please refer to Iain Chambers "Migrancy, culture, identity", in Keith Jenkins (ed.), *The postmodern history reader* (London: Routledge, 1997), pp. 77-81.

16   An extraordinary piece of research into how indigenous knowledge systems have been valued and judged is David Chambers and Richard Gillespie's "Locality in the history of science: colonial science, technoscience, and indigenous knowledge", *Osiris*, Vol. 15, 2001. Particularly, in terms of the relationship between evidence and indigenous history, the writers explore the "network of exchange and control", p. 231. Such a network demonstrates why some knowledge systems enter the "global information network", and other truths are discarded.

17   G. Marcus, *The dustbin of history* (Cambridge: Harvard University Press, 1995), pp. 17-18.

18   The consequences of this silence are seen in Gayatri Chakravorty Spivak's "Can the subaltern speak?" from L. Grossberg and C. Nelson (eds) *Marxism and the interpretation of culture* (Urbana: University of Illinois Press, 1988) and bell hooks' *Talking Back* (Boston: South End Press, 1989). hooks investigates the silence of the weak, less recognized discourses, suggesting that "madness, not just physical

abuse, was the punishment for too much talking if you were female. Yet even this fear of madness haunted me, hanging over my writing like some monstrous shadow. I could not stop the words making thought, writing speech", p. 7.

[19] For example, in the case of indigenous Australians, an interpretation and negotiation with film is particularly important. Such films as *Radiance*, written by Louis Nowra (Sydney: Currency Press, 2000), offer a distinct look, accent and inflection on indigenous women's lives in contemporary Australia.

[20] A. Bloom, *The closing of the American mind* (London: Penguin Books, 1987), p. 55.

[21] An outstanding exhibition of how Cultural Studies and historical approaches align through feminist theory – and offering a stark critique of Bloom's rendering of American 'progress' – is Anne McLeer's "Practical Perfection? The nanny negotiates gender, class, and family contradictions in 1960s popular culture", *NWSA Journal*, Vol. 14, No. 2, Summer 2002, pp. 80-101. She demonstrates that *Mary Poppins* and *The Sound of Music*, because of their 'foreign' settings, are able to "speak to the 'Hollywood imaginary,' addressing their oblique, allegorical manner, concerns and anxiety that surrounded the notion of the family and changing gender roles in the United States in the 1960s", p. 80.

[22] Stephen Muecke assessed the consequences of this demarcation. "The grammatical differences between the two discourses … serve to locate the subject in different positions in relation to the text. The reader of 'history,' for instance, is not directly addressed by the writer, and is temporally removed by the tense from the sphere of action. The overall effect is for the text to become authoritative and the reader unquestioning", from S. Muecke, "Discourse, history, fiction, language and Aboriginal history", *Australian Journal of Cultural Studies*, Vol. 1, May 1983, p. 73.

[23] F. Braudel, *The Mediterranean and the Mediterranean World of Philip II* (London: Fontana, 1986).

[24] T. Masuzawa, "Original lost: an image of myth and ritual in the age of mechanical reproduction", *Journal of Religion*, Vol. 69, 1989.

[25] Raymond Williams stated that "an adequate sociology of culture must … be an historical sociology", *Culture* (London: Fontana, 1981), p. 32.

[26] R. Johnson, "Thompson, Genovese, and Socialist-Humanist History", *History Workshop*, Issue 6, Autumn 1978, p. 77.

[27] *ibid.*, p. 85.

[28] *ibid.*, p. 98.

[29] T. Putnam, "'Structuralism' and 'humanism,'" Letters – *History Workshop*, Issue 7, Spring 1978, p. 222.

[30] R. Shenton, "Socialist-Humanism", Letters – *History Workshop*, Issue 7, Spring 1979, p. 224.

[31] R. Johnson, "Socialist History", Letters – *History Workshop*, Issue 8, Spring 1979, p. 196.

[32] G. Stedman Jones, "History and Theory", *History Workshop*, Issue 8, Spring 1979, p. 202.

[33] R. Johnson, "What is Cultural Studies, anyway?", *Departmental paper*, Department of Cultural Studies, University of Birmingham, September 1983, p. 6.

[34] I interviewed Richard Johnson on August 15, 1991 while in Birmingham. In his discussion with me, he exhibited great knowledge and concern for the nature of history. When I met him, I was 21 years old, straight out of a history honours degree. The only knowledge of Cultural Studies that I held was self taught and eclectic to the extreme. Yet his commitment and skill in explaining the nature of 'National memory' and 'National popular' has stayed with me since that meeting.

[35] B. Henkes and R. Johnson, "Silences across disciplines: folklore studies, cultural studies and history", *Journal of Folklore Research*, Vol. 39, No. 2/3, 2002.

[36] R. Johnson, D. Chambers, P. Raghuram and E. Tincknell, *The Practice of Cultural Studies* (London: SAGE, 2004).

[37] E.P. Thompson, "The politics of theory", in Raphael Samuel (ed.), *People's history and socialist theory* (London: Routledge and Kegan Paul, 1981), p. 399. For an outstanding discussion of E.P. Thompson and the *History Workshop* debate, please refer to Dennis Dworkin's *Cultural Marxism in postwar Britain: history, the New Left and the origins of Cultural Studies* (Durham: Duke University Press, 1997), particularly pages 243-245.

[38] R. Evans, *In defense of history* (New York: W.W. Norton, 1999), p. 7.

[39] I also want to acknowledge the increasing confluence between Cultural Studies and Pacific Studies, and the important disciplinary outreach that has been a characteristic of the latter paradigm. For example, Edvard Hviding stated that "a rapidly and unpredictably transforming world requires transformed research approaches, as reflected in calls for interdisciplinarity – a concept easily invoked but a research approach less easily implemented. Regionally-oriented research of wide thematic scope such as Pacific Islands studies – whose past we want in the present context to honor, and to whose future we would like to contribute – aspires towards understanding a wonderful diversity of human lifeworlds that can hardly be interpreted within a single-discipline framework", p. 43. His piece, "Between knowledges: Pacific Studies and academic disciplines", *The Contemporary Pacific*, Vol. 15, No. 1, Spring 2003, is an innovative account of the function of interdisciplinarity in the investigation of cultural difference.

40 S. Hall, "The emergence of Cultural Studies and the crisis of the humanities", *October*, No. 53, 1990, p. 16.

41 Cultural History Group, "Out of the people", *Working Papers in Cultural Studies*, No. 9, Spring 1976, p. 29.

42 C. Steedman, "Culture, Cultural Studies and the historians", in L. Grossberg, C. Nelson and P. Treichler (eds), *Cultural Studies* (New York and London: Routledge, 1992).

43 D. Harris, *From Class Struggle to the politics of pleasure* (London: Routledge, 1992), p. 15.

44 A. Milner, "Cultural Studies and cultural hegemony", *Arena Journal*, No. 9, 1997, p. 133.

45 M. Pickering, *History, experience and Cultural Studies* (Houndmills: Macmillan Press, 1997), p. 1.

46 Windschuttle, *The killing of history*, p. 15.

47 M. Morris, *Too soon too late: history in popular culture* (Bloomington: Indiana University Press, 1998), p. 5.

48 *ibid.*, p. 3.

49 L. Grossberg, *Dancing in spite of myself: essays on popular culture* (Durham: Duke University Press, 1997), p. 34.

50 J. Savage, *England's Dreaming: the Sex Pistols and punk rock* (London: Faber and Faber, 1990), p. 541.

51 H. Giroux, "Rethinking the boundaries of educational discourse", *College Literature*, Vol. 17, 1990, p. 21.

52 E. Hobsbawm, "Fact, fiction and historical revisionism", *Higher Education Supplement*, The Australian, December 8, 1993, p. 35.

53 E. Hobsbawm, *On history* (London: Weidenfeld and Nicholson, 1997), p. viii.

54 *ibid.*, p. 24.

55 Hobsbawm, "Fact, fiction and historical revisionism", *op. cit.*, p. 35.

56 D. Hebdige, *Hiding in the Light* (London: Routledge, 1988), p. 239.

57 F. Cassidy, "Young people, culture and pop music", *Youth Studies*, Vol. 10, No. 2, May 1991, p. 34.

58 D. Coupland, *Generation X* (London: Abacus, 1992), p. 36.

59 G. Turner, *British Cultural Studies* (Boston: Unwin Hyman, 1990), p. 181.

60 M. Morris, question time during C. Steedman, "Culture, Cultural Studies and the historians", in L. Grossberg et al. (eds), *Cultural Studies* (New York: Routledge, 1990), p. 622.

61 K. Jenkins, *On 'What is history?'* (London: Routledge, 1995), p. 10.

62 A. Ross, "The Rock 'n' Roll Ghost – Lipstick Traces", *October*, Number 50, 1989, p. 112.

Chapter four

Always on my mind:
building Popular Memory Studies

You can explain the past only by what is most powerful in the present.[1]

Friedrich Nietzsche

There is a dense tragedy in the life story of Frank Wren. My maternal grandfather who I never knew, he was functionally illiterate, only attending a rural Western Australian school for barely six months. During that time, he learnt about numbers and how to sign his name. Like many strong young men of the time, he was needed in his father's log hauling business and book learning was not a prerequisite for the job. There are few family stories that survive about this extraordinary man. Revelling in his bushman heritage, he had a temper. On one occasion, he locked himself out of the house. Frank became so frustrated that he attempted to open the door – with an axe. The axe had been a feature of his working life as well. In his early adulthood, he was log hauling in the south west of the State, single-handedly being responsible for increasing the greenhouse effect on Australia through his felling of large Jarrah and Karri trees. While working one day, an axe head fell from a branch above, slicing his face and damaging his skull. These scars would remain for the rest of his life. His first daughter Alice would not survive the damage to her skull, being killed before the age of two. Her tiny head was crushed in the mechanism of a kalamazoo. Frank was operating the machinery at the time. After the accident, he carried the bloodied body of Alice on his shoulder for several miles to find a doctor. It was a futile, desperate act.

Frank died relatively young – his body was worn out from cigarettes as well as hard work. I have no memory of him: but my brother supposedly bears his resemblance. For a man who lived a life of such gothic tragedy, there is no trace that he ever existed. His cremated ashes were placed around a rose bush of a house long sold. No diaries or letters capture his handwriting or feelings. He avoided photographs because of facial injuries. There is a battered silver pocket watch that stopped working before he did. Little remains of this man's life, but there is a residue of memory.

One splinter of information always relayed by my mother is that Frank had a secret love. He adored Ginger Rogers. While words and photographs have failed us, there is a trace of Frank's feelings, pleasures and hopes in film. When watching *Top Hat, 42nd Street* or *Roberta,* I feel closer to him, to a possibility of what he could have been like. We share nothing but this popular culture – separated through decades and death – but there is something of him in the moving images of a bubbly blonde with a weak voice and magnificent frocks.

Frank's story is the reason why I enrolled in a history degree at university. I wanted to find a way – as we only do in our youth – to 'reclaim' the lives of those who are lost to time because they were not part of the good and the great. Ordinary people with extraordinary stories seem so expendable. However history did not provide me with a method to raise the dead of those who left no record. I was then drawn to Cultural Studies as a way to 'read' texts like Ginger Rogers. I found some assistance but wanted more. It was through Popular Memory Studies that it seemed possible to transform popular culture into useable culture.

Popular memory is the intellectual nexus of Cultural Studies and history. While *From Revolution to Revelation* retheorizes and applies the popular memory paradigm, with attention to (post) youth culture and Generation X, the book also has a wider aim. As revealed through the last two chapters, I argue for the necessity of a renewed dialogue between Cultural Studies and cultural history. Popular Memory Studies is the evocative and compelling rivulet. This chapter gathers the debates from this first section, assembling a workable model of Popular Memory Studies, attending specifically to the potentials and problems of popular culture.

Popular memory should have been a far more visible and significant part of contemporary Cultural Studies. When Richard Johnson, Gregor McLennan, Bill Schwarz and David Sutton published *Making Histories* in 1982, they focused attention on how the fibres of the past are woven into the present. A dialogue between radical scholarship, political change and critical history was forged. The Popular Memory Group, which met between October 1979 and June 1980, drew attention to the limits of academic history. Their experiments with popular autobiography and community-based scholarship were a starting point of not only a site or object of study, but an organic, realizable politics. While the group sketched how public representations operated through private memory, they left popular culture an untouched and untethered part of their analysis. Oral history was of greater interest. Their focus on power, domination and social change was stark. They discussed the power and pervasiveness of historical representations, their connections with dominant institutions and the part they play in winning consent and building alliances in the process of formal politics.[2]

They stressed that there is always resistance to dominant memory and contestation is always possible. Their work displayed how empowered representations are cut up by oppositional ideologies, while also placing attention on how public discourses intervene in private lives. Most significantly, they reminded historians that through Popular Memory Studies, the past is neither pristine nor static, but a living skeleton on which the flesh of the present clings.

The Group's neglect of popular culture was odd. The post-war period has been punctuated by pop retro-glances. We cannot separate our knowledge of popular representations such as music and film from the experiences of life. Significant songs are the grammar and fodder for our troubles, pleasures, joy and pain. We fall in love, break up, become inspired and seek respite from pop. Particularly, it is important to watch the popular culture that, while connected to dominant institutions, also creates a space for difference and critique. Therefore, it is important to focus on – overtly and clearly – the relationship between popular culture and Popular Memory Studies.

Popular culture is a conduit for popular memory, moving words, ideas, ideologies and narratives through time. It is distinct from both collective memory and history. Popular memory, by its nature, is a fount of consensus and a building block of 'the mainstream.' Collective memory, such as that formed by and with working class communities, women or citizens of colour, can hold a radical or resistive agenda. Collective memory is often forged by unpopular culture and is the 'minority report' of an era. The greatest difficulty for disempowered groups is the survival of their stories, truths and differences. The dustbin of history is hungry for those voices and views that disagree with the justifications of the influential. Popular culture – like films, music, television, food and magazines – preserves something of a life lived, pleasures shared, joyous laughter or empathic tears. It is not accurate or verifiable, but it is affective. Life is extinguished through death. Popular culture – if preserved – cuts through the finality of mortality. Oral history can certainly offer a corrective to the gaps in dominant narratives, but it is impossible to interview the dead. Popular memory theorists are able to use a wider range of media to capture the scale, depth and feelings of the past.

Popular culture, as a memory conduit, has two functions: to translate and transform. Firstly, it is able to translate texts into a new context. So *24 Hour Party People* is able to take the Hacienda nightclub from 1987 and move it into

the 2000s, activating new audiences and literacies. Yet popular culture also holds another function: transforming a sign system into a site of political opportunity, pushing it forward into a new, creative and productive space. There are no political guarantees with popular culture – it can be both conservative and progressive. For writers working with popular memory, we can intervene in the popular culture that survives – reading with or against the grains of meaning – providing texture, taste and energy to the past and past lives. We can translate and transform old texts with new interpretations. Proactive preservation is important. Unless this material survives, there will be little for Popular Memory scholars to either translate or transform.

Popular Memory Studies is a new way of thinking about popular culture, beyond the high/low binary, beyond intrinsically resistive readings and beyond textual poaching. It requires skills to decode the tactics of the desperate and forgotten. Frequently, these sources express trivial concerns in flighty ways. For example, the now departed journal of style, The Face[3] offered a sassy space to express disenchantment with the massive post-compact disc reissuing from record companies in the 1990s. As David Toop, the legendary musical reviewer for The Face, stated, "All I seem to hear from other rooms, other radios, other TV sets is Fleetwood Mac's 'Albatross'".[4] It is not simply the recycling of the 1960s, as a mythic formation, that has blocked the memory and specificity of Generation X. Punk and the late 1970s provided another watershed. By the arrival of punk, the connection between youth, music and style was naturalized and taken for granted. Punk was still able to shock through an ability to cut up the fabric of normality and post-war youth subcultures and then fasten it back together with safety pins. Chambers defined this type of cultural pillaging as "ransack[ing] ... post-war subcultures for fashions and signs to re-cycle and re-live".[5] This shock iconography offered a strong critique of baby boomer culture. Punk arrived during the year that the first baby boomers were turning thirty. The semiotic realities of the 'fat hippies' that the punks decried were splintered through the mobilization of 'shocking objects' like swastikas, syringes and suspenders. The punks attacked the fodder of myth, credibility and authenticity through the apparatus of triviality, trash and humour.

The Sex Pistols released their single 'God Save the Queen' to coincide with the Queen's Silver Jubilee. It was a far cry from the 'safe' rock celebrations of Paul McCartney and Cliff Richard for Elizabeth's Golden Jubilee Concert in 2002. The anger of the Pistols' lyrics and the violence of their stage performances offered far more than a critique of the 'United' Kingdom. The success of their 'anthem',[6] which reached number two on the British charts in June 1977, typified the manner in which style, consumption and resistance were blended through a solid link between youth culture and popular music. Ironically, it was the Pistols and not the Queen, who could not be saved.

The politics of pop that resulted in 1980s journalists affirming the credibility of Simple Minds, the Smiths and REM while dismissing the triviality of ABC, Scritti Politti and Rick Astley continued post-war modalities of authenticity. Certainly the 1980s had its political pop figures: Bruce Springsteen, Billy Bragg, the Style Council, UB40 and the Communards. But the disruption of the relationship between production, class and consciousness meant many of the concerns of this political pop appeared hackneyed, rather than popular.

Finding a radical or resistive popular memory is difficult, perhaps impossible. It is a consensual and mainstream formation, knocking the sharp corners off hard-edged differences and forceful critiques. This is perhaps one reason why Richard Johnson and the Popular Memory Group overlooked film, television and popular music, focussing on oral history and photographs. Denying popular culture because it does not provide a 'clean' or definitive resistance is no longer an option in a time of war, political extremism and heightening inequalities. The Third Way has 'managed' – not negated – odd allegiances between neo-conservatives and neo-liberals. In such an environment, wars, weapons and willing coalitions spiral from view. Through these caveats and contradictions, Popular Memory Studies provides a database of ideas and icons for both Popular/Cultural Studies and cultural history. It provides interdisciplinary options during a period when research in universities is assessed and judged within strict subject areas.

The tracing of popular memory through the conduit of popular culture is a promiscuous intellectual business, refusing to obey disciplinary boundaries. The re-presentations of place, time and identity envelop theories of power, transgressing the limits of history, heritage studies, Cultural Studies and geography. As Liliane Weissberg has recognized,

> Memory's stock has not only had a low and a high. Memory's own history, our understanding of what it is and how it functions, has radically changed in recent years. The computer is not the sole challenge to our notion of a personalized, individually owned memory.[7]

The careful recycling of popular culture – particularly music – has frayed the textual fibres of remembering and forgetting. Popular memory does not signal the end of history, but a collectivizing and preservation of 'private' experiences that rarely survive beyond the death of the subject.

Popular memory was defined by the Birmingham Centre's Popular Memory Group as "first an object of study, but, second, as a dimension of political practice".[8] While the Group argued that all histories are histories of the present, their imperatives actually extended the nature of historical writing. Memory is a composite construction and finds a fertile incubator in popular culture. For example, during the Second World War, there were many individual experiences and memories, but certain moments arch beyond the self. The memory of particular songs, like Glenn Miller's 'In the Mood' and Noel Coward's 'London Pride', or the connection of particular films like *Casablanca* with events in the war, are fully textualized and become the foundation of community building. While these textual sites offer many ways of reading, there is a shared recognition of relevance and importance. Popular memory provides a way to assemble a sense of how the past is produced outside of historical disciplinary borders. History is a dominant memory and frequently based on written sources. Private or individual memories have a limited circulation and operate within photograph albums and everyday conversations. Collective and popular memories rebound in the liminal space between private reminiscence and national narratives.

Popular culture slops clumsily into the cup of memory. Oral history is far more methodical and precise in its collection, storage and application. Popular culture is different, being seldom marked as significant or important. The memory of shoulder pads and lip-gloss, Raybans, fingerless gloves and Wham, grasps an ordinariness and banality that is rarely useful for museum curators or historians. This is the role of Popular Memory Studies – to translate and transform past popular culture into relevant sources in the present. Such a process reveals roughened surfaces, ragged edges and contradictory interpretations. Thinking about popular memory demonstrates that there is a political imperative of the past beyond scholarly and professional responsibilities. Occasionally, we need to put down our notebook, silence the clatter of keys, pick up a camera and flood the shutter with meaning. While popular memory is an itinerant (and playful) amalgam of media, its survival, collection, research and (re)writing requires new methodologies. Popular memory is a practice, not an inheritance.

The passage of time is volatile, fragile and passionately heated, not objective, predictable and linear. Memory is not safe: it is messy, corrosive and/or empowering. As Janet Zandy has revealed,

> Memory has purpose. It is a bridge between subjective and intersubjective – the private and unprivileged circumstances of individual lives – and the objective – the collective history of class oppression.[9]

70

Songs, fashion and stories pass through families. The multigenerational layering that is a characteristic of popular memory leaves its mark in language and is seen more obviously through photographs, stories, scribbled notes and popular culture. The distress in remembering the lives of parents and friends is a pain of living life differently, the possibility of taking an alternative path. The great difficulty for researchers is speaking with – rather than shouting over – the disempowered and disembodied voices whispering through popular memory. Popular culture seems too superficial and compliant to offer the trigger of a socialist revolution. To track revelation – the building of consciousness – is more complex and ultimately more important. This work probes borders, margins, ambiguities, hybridities and transgressions. Little is left of the ageing or the dead, particularly those who were poor, 'ordinary' or weak. The loss of whole lives through a lack of historical evidence is not good enough for those of us who believe in change and justice. Even if popular culture is inadequate, it provides a delicate, tissued trace of lives lived and lost. What are our options? Unless we gather, preserve and interpret songs, films, photographs, dancing, fashions and styles, generations of disempowered communities will continue to have their lives, words, movements and memories scattered to the winds. As Chris Healy affirmed, "ruins are never simply gone or in the past; ruins are enduring traces; spaces of romantic fancies and forgetfulness where social memories imagine the persistence of time in records of destruction".[10] Popular/Cultural Studies is in a position to enter metaphoric textual ruins. For the groups who do not leave a ruin but only the residue of laughter, pain and pleasure captured through and by popular culture, the analysis is more difficult. The hardened faces of the past stare down the alternative stories and images that are lost to us. By methodically piecing together the slithers of sounds and visions, Popular Memory Studies can commence the difficult process of translating and transforming popular culture. The present is not a smooth, clear pane of glass, but a shattered, roughened surface that conceals and warps as much as it reveals. This obscure, fractured and oblique memory requires interpretation and intervention to discover the potential for social change and marking cultural difference.

The past is mediated and moulded. The hierarchization of events allows a determination of what is to be valued as (capital H) History. Raphael Samuel realized that "it fetishizes archive-based research", with "argument ... embedded in dense thickets of footnotage".[11] Through this method, the past is narrativized, edited and controlled. While History is organized, popular memory is chaotic. Peter Carroll realized that "Clio is a jealous muse and research is her weapon."[12] The difficulty is discovering how to return the passion, enthusiasm, pain and despair of life to the page. By utilizing the non-standard ontology of music, dancing, television, film, food and fashion, the contradictory and convoluted pop past can be restored to the cultural debate. Popular culture is important because, as Lipsitz has suggested, it is "a repository of collective memory that places immediate experience in the context of change over time".[13] Popular culture is not intrinsically valuable because it is resistive. It may be conservative. Popular culture is not intrinsically valuable because it offers alternatives. It may reinforce the status quo. Popular culture is important because it provides a database and safe house for the lives of those who leave few other sources. Without this intellectual intervention, too many groups are swept into the dustbin of history.

Remembering requires a conscious selection of events and people, with a desire to hide some uncomfortable or embarrassing moments and ideas. There is a layering of the past that transforms popular memory theorists into cognitive archaeologists, carefully removing skin layers from the present. The aim is to create a map of emotion, a link with specific subjectivities, that develops a consciousness of community.

Pop goes history

An excess of history seems to be an enemy to the life of a time.[14]

Friedrich Nietzsche

Trashy popular culture is the undiscovered country of history. While classic film has been accepted as 'reasonable' source material, other texts have been dismissed as trivial or irrelevant. As Robert Rosenstone has affirmed, "history is an agreed-upon game that creates its own rules, including rules for assessing what it is to contribute to the game".[15] To follow Rosenstone's metaphor, history is a site of contest and conflict. The 1980s, as an era of leg warmers, big earrings, chalk stiff hair, patterned stockings and big trousers, has suffered from an intense credibility crisis in the battle over truth, meaning and politics. The memory of the 1980s remains almost captivatingly masculine. Leia has been overwritten by Luke. Molly Ringwald lost out to Judd Nelson. Bruce Springsteen outlasted Chrissie Hynde. Even Annie Lennox effaced her own past through a tragic erasing of her swish 1980s iconography. She now appears as boring as Dave Stewart. This is hard to do.

There were extraordinary women who changed and challenged the imaginary of the acceptable feminine. This truth was not only performed by pre-yoga Madonna. Ponder Cyndi Lauper's video for 'Money changes everything.' It features a live vocal and show. Her just-from-the-op-shop wardrobe is attended by mis-matched shoes and the strangest hair in pop. What I am most interested in though is her make-up. After endlessly running around the stage, her foundation is tracked with sweat, the eye liner has streaked her entire face, contour powder has moved from cheek to chin and traces of lipstick have vacated her mouth. Part witch, part banshee, part hooker, she is simply captivating, exciting, riveting.

Streaked make-up, lycra, bike pants and mullets are not the foundations of history, but are the fodder of memory. Imagination is a unique force, a creative energy that extends beyond intelligence, relevance and truth. Through its insights, new knowledges are invented, preserved or questioned. If scholars and particularly historians, do not use this type of trivial 'pop', then they will limit their relevance and future. Dominic Strinati has recognized the consequences of forgetting or undermining the popular:

> The symbolic power of intellectuals over the standards of taste which are applied to the consumption of cultural goods becomes more difficult to protect and sustain when people have made available to them a mass culture which does not depend on intellectuals for its appreciation and its definitions of pleasures.[16]

Judgements of taste are often hidden through scholarly discussions of methodology. With so much at stake in the study of popular culture, it is not clear how it should be researched. There is something extraordinary about the popular: it is part of daily life, but also passionate, excessive and textually complex. Being both accessible and polysemic means that texts hail and connect with different viewers/listeners/readers through time. Popular culture, at its flashy best, has the capacity to transform a way of knowing, being, feeling and sensing. Cultural life in industrial societies must be meshed with politics: too often it is framed by discussions of aesthetics and cultural value. With the making of a present requiring the making of a past, a history of ephemera can be noted, recognized and interpreted. Popular Memory Studies frames a method of meaning making where a self and community is connected. The archival survival of popular culture is required to commence this process.

The function of Popular Memory Studies is to move beyond commodification, heritage and celebration, to prise open the space between historical events and representations. At the margins of established disciplines, alternative narratives are revealed. The Manchester Institute for Popular Culture at the Manchester Metropolitan University worked between disciplines and paradigms, to assist the development of Popular/Cultural Studies.[17] While much rhetoric emerges about interdisciplinarity in university mission statements and lists of generic competencies, it is a productive initiative to unsettle the rigours, citations and standards of academic research. Popular Memory Studies continues the goal of oral history in broadening out the range of accessible source material, while using the insight of curatorial preservation strategies and librarianship. Men's and women's studies, education, history, sociology, literature, film, internet and television studies and Cultural Studies are all required to actualize the two stages of Popular Memory Studies: to translate the popular culture of the past with the aim of transforming the present.

Much popular culture relies on the literacies and experiences of the viewer and there is power in carrying forward these competencies. Legislation and educational curricula perpetuate the values, ideas and memories of history's winners. Douglas Rushkoff realized the need to democratize this empowerment:

> Media literacy is dangerous – not to the individuals who gain it, but to the people and institutions that depend on our not having it. Once we master the tools of media literacy, we cannot apply them selectively.[18]

Popular memory remains politically crucial because it unmasks the limits of reality and the arbitrary relationship between sound and vision, time and space, fact and fiction. Ideas suddenly have a context and origin, rather than a bland tethering to 'traditional' values. The final part of this chapter shows how literate citizens may use popular memory to change the present.

Meaning in the movement

> We do need history, but quite differently from the jaded idlers in the garden of knowledge, however grandly they may look down on our rude and unpicturesque requirements.[19]

> Friedrich Nietzsche

Cicero, in *De oratore*, described history as "vita memoriae", or "the life of memory".[20] Similarly, Herodotus wrote to maintain a memory – to stoke the fire of a life so that embers of meaning survive. As Burke has realized, "memory reflects what actually happened and history reflects memory".[21] This demarcation of history and memory is simple and clear, but actually they embrace, slap and scratch in a troubled, firey fight. Both are sites of interpretation, bias, selection and politics. Maurice Halbwachs, a French sociologist and anthropologist, was a serious scholar of memory in the 1920s. He argued that an individual may remember an event, an idea or moment, but a community or social group actually determines what is memorable and the form in which it will be remembered. So the collective memory on which national history is based is heavily socially constructed.[22] While Marc Bloch criticized Halbwachs's approach, he did mobilize the phrase *memoire collective*, to display how traditions are circulated and moved between eras.[23] Therefore historians and Cultural Studies theorists must think more about popular memory. It is not only an historical source like oral testimony, or a method like oral history. Memories are moulded by dominant ideologies. To understand contemporary politics requires a tracing of how ideas are lost – or remain – in the bedrock of consciousness. Social amnesia has profound consequences on the disempowered and the dispossessed.

The best Popular Memory Studies seeks out the discordance in the past and the contradictions between public time and lived or subjective time. The struggles over popular music, for example, are clear and traceable. Music traverses many eras and ears. While a song may be in the charts for weeks, it is located in a back catalogue for years and popular memory for decades. Particular songs are summoned to hook onto specific cultural events or moments. While Jon Savage argued that "the basis of pop music is that it provides a refuge from chronology",[24] actually it does the reverse. It ties the notes, syncopation and screeching vocals to many clocks and many times. While it is easy for Savage to read this time-music-memory nexus as "a generational war, expressed in time and perception",[25] popular music no longer – did it ever? – offers a grenade for a youthful revolt. Instead, different revolutions, revelations and memories are summoned through each selection on the jukebox. Sourcing the past through music creates many possibilities, but few definitive answers. Forgetting and remembering builds the database from which histories are constituted.

We live the narratives and tales that have been written for us. While historians occupy a subject position, they rarely weave mourning through prose. Memory is charged with trauma and popular memory is punctuated by pathos. To ruthlessly divide memory from history may be academically rigorous but ignores the potential of writing a cultural history through popular culture, pounded by rhythms, seared by cinematography, infused by scents and traumatized by captivating photographs.

Popular culture burns in and through the present. While high culture pickles the past, popular culture denies it. The popular memory theorist must be far more proactive in protecting, reclaiming and re-creating texts from earlier eras. We must be pop curators as much as pop critics. It is a great time for this project. At the very point that students are turning away from the study of history, interest in the past has exploded. That is why Harvey Kaye is so staunch in his recommendation that "it is time for us to establish, or re-establish, the connections between 'history' and 'the people.'"[26] Popular culture researched through Popular Memory Studies is a method to accomplish Kaye's project.

For the past to be political, it must be useful and useable. There is no reason to study the past for its own sake. It must be immersed in present concerns and relevancies. The difficult intellectual task becomes connecting popular culture in a justifiable and convincing way to the present. Historical source material does not show reality, but what people thought happened. It is memory by proxy. So when an historian writes a history, it is a record *of a record* of what people thought happened. To prioritize Popular Memory Studies is an honest acknowledgement of how and why past truths move and change. Theorists then rewrite the Foucaultian-inspired archaeology of the discipline.

> History, in its traditional form, undertook to 'memorize' the monuments of the past, transform them into documents, and lend speech to those traces ... . In our time, history is that which transforms documents into monuments.[27]

Popular memory does not build a monument to the past. Instead, it walks through the ruins to rebuild a relevant past. It translates and transforms phantom whispers and rubbled buildings into the stories and structures that build the now. In moving beyond the grand narrative, a series of disciplinary dialogues around history can be promoted, triggered by the epistemological discovery of the other, the discord, the dissonant in our midst.

There are many experts in history. Expertise in *why* we study history is harder to find. While the New Right has fetishized history, the left has been unable to construct a critical, analytical and politicized popular memory. In such a context, history is a contagion that risks infecting and decaying other paths through the past. My grandfather, Frank Wren, is lost. When my parents die, all who knew him are gone. While prime ministers, presidents, sportsmen and writers live through legislation, world records and library catalogues, we are losing too many lives to the mortician's table. The task of Popular Memory Studies is to unsettle the assumptions that value a few and discount the many. In the spaces, margins and silences, there is good intellectual work to be done. The remaining four chapters in this book explore the popular memory of dance, popular music and film, applying the ideas assembled in this first section. We carry forward and apply the theories of Generation X, Cultural Studies, history and popular memory. With nothing predetermined or inevitable – except in retrospect – we muddy up the calm waters of the present, agitating the truths, tales and lies weighted by the sediments of sanitized stability. In slicing up the past in a new way, maybe Frank's axe, at least metaphorically, can cut through time and death.

Notes

1 F. Nietzsche, *The use and abuse of history* (Indianapolis: Bobbs-Merrill Company, 1957: 1949), p. 40.

2 Popular memory group, "Popular memory: theory, politics, method", from R. Johnson et al. (eds), *Making histories: studies in history writing and politics* (Minneapolis: University of Minnesota Press, 1982), p. 207.

3 "Face magazine, the epitome of 1980s cool, publishes final issue", *Lifestyle.co.uk*, April 8, 2004, http://news.lifestyle.co.uk/lifestyle/629-lifestyle.htm, accessed on July 1, 2004.

4 D. Toop, "Static in the groove", *The Face*, No. 82, February 1987, p. 69.

5 I. Chambers, *Popular culture: the metropolitan experience* (London: Methuen, 1986), p. 170.

6 'God save the Queen', written by Jones/Matlock/Cook/Rotten, from *Never mind the bollocks here's the Sex Pistols* (Virgin Records, 1977).

7 L. Weissberg, "Introduction", in D. Been-Amos and L. Weissberg (ed.), *Cultural memory and the construction of identity* (Detroit: Wayne State University Press, 1999), p. 13.

8 Popular memory group, "Popular memory: theory, politics, method", p. 205.

9 J. Zandy, "Introduction", from J. Zandy (ed.), *Liberating memory: our work and our working-class consciousness* (New Brunswick: Rutgers University Press, 1995).

10 C. Healy, *From the ruins of colonialism: history as social memory* (Cambridge: Cambridge University Press, 1997), p. 1.

11 R. Samuel, *Theatres of Memory* (London: Verso, 1994), p. 3.

12 P. Carroll, *Keeping time: memory, nostalgia, and the art of history* (Athens: The University of Georgia Press, 1990), p. 87.

13 G. Lipsitz, *Time passages: collective memory and American popular culture* (Minneapolis: University of Minnesota Press, 1990), p. 5.

14 F. Nietzsche, *op. cit.*, p. 28.

15 R. Rosenstone, "Introduction", from R. Rosenstone (ed.), *Revisioning history: time and the construction of a new past* (Princeton: Princeton University Press, 1995), p. 5.

16 D. Strinati, *An introduction to theories of popular culture* (London: Routledge, 1995), p. 45.

17 To view the rationale and motifs of the early MIPC, please refer to Steve Redhead's *Unpopular Cultures* (Manchester: Manchester University Press, 1995).

18 D. Rushkoff, *Coercion: why we listen to what 'they' say* (New York: Riverhead Books, 1999), p. 24.

19 Nietzsche, *op. cit.*, p. 3.

20 Cicero, *De oratore*, ii, cited in Peter Burke, *Varieties of cultural history* (Ithaca: Cornell University Press, 1997), p. 36.

21 Burke, *ibid.*, pp. 44-45.

22 Please refer to Maurice Halbwachs, *Les cadres sociaux de la memoire* (Paris: Albin Michel, 1994: 1925) and Maurice Halbwachs, *La topographie legendaire des evangiles en terre sainte: etude de memoir collective* (Paris: Alcan, 1941).

23 M. Bloch, "Memoire collective, tradition et coutume", *Revue de Synthese Historique*, Vol. 40, 1925, pp. 73-83.

24 J. Savage, *Time Travel* (London: Vintage, 1997), p. 8.

25 *ibid.*, p. 6.

26 H. Kaye, *The powers of the past* (New York: Harvester Wheatsheaf, 1991), p. 162.

27 M. Foucault, *The archaeology of knowledge* (New York: Routledge, 1989: 1972), p. 7.

Section Two
Sound and Vision

Chapter five

Reading on your feet and dancing through the revolution

Interviewer:	Oh, so when will you be playing your instruments then? ...
Robbie Williams:	Look, some of us can play instruments – not me, I might add. But that's not the point – we're not U2, we're entertainers. You wouldn't ask U2 when they're going to learn to dance properly would you?[1]

The notion of Bono and The Edge strutting to Donna Summer's 'Hot Stuff' is a ludicrous and luscious image. The craggy faces of authentic Celtic rock are above such triviality. For rock journalists, playing a twelve bar blues is more credible and difficult than executing intricate choreography, or elevating the body through the air with style and boldness. The dancing body denies fixity and flits through social, economic and political contradictions. That is why Take That was an easy target for a rock reporter. Attacking boy bands and (ex) Spice Girls is our most popular spectator sport.[2] It is too easy to ridicule five good-looking men who skilfully move their bodies and audiences while singing complex harmonies. When attacked, Robbie Williams reminded the interviewer that dancers need to be acknowledged for their integral place in popular culture. Too often, dancing is attacked by those who cannot do it. Dance is under-researched, demeaned and ridiculed. Through the twist and stomp, the joy, community and humour of the past can survive.

Striking a pose and other euphoric posturings is a strategy for bad times. Such moments are not escapist: they are transcendent. Popular culture always affects the body, resulting in screams, laughter, tears, desire and dancing. Emotion is frequently the first layer seared from history, as it erupts from transitory significations rather than more stable structures like nation, class, race or gender. Dancing offers a memory trace of past movements and sensibilities. It is a life lived by proxy, having sex without removing clothing, seemingly rich while maintaining nothing but credit card debt, working the body hard because there is nothing else at which to work and grasping the ecstatic moments on a dance floor because the rational world is too painful. The dance floor is not adjacent to real life. It enacts a life by corporeal metaphor. Past rhythms pound present politics.

This chapter investigates dancing as a readership strategy, reading beat through the feet. To enact this project, my words mimic a dance floor mix. The research (re)plays well-trammelled intellectual samples. The first part, the bedrock beat, exposes the weathered surfaces of popular music writing. The second section clears the floor, cranking up a head-banging critique of masculine rock narratives. The next task is to scratch race into the mix, adding loops, anger and dynamism. The final stages of the night sample some disco, move the beat around the world and end with popular memories of the night before.

So, let the music lift you up. Everybody in the house say 'way-oh'. Reach for the lasers. Feel the rush. But even with arms extended and head lowered, feel the rhythm and think about the movement(s) in the mix.

Writing the beat, forgetting the feet

> Listening to music is the most universal mass communication behaviour, requires neither literacy nor advanced electronic media. [3]
>
> Steven Chaffee

Popular music is a misunderstood part of cultural life. Twenty years ago, Steven Chaffee's statement undermined the aural, visual and corporeal literacies triggered through the 'simple' practice of listening. Instead of this banal interpretation, a craving for rhythm feeds a desire for difference. Music provides a history of magic, excess, power and desire, offering "an inextricable chronicle of feelings".[4] To write about music transforms the affectivity of a text into the realm of mediated abstraction. There is no correct position from which to write about music. There is a desperate need to place in prose what is felt through the feet. Cultural Studies offers potential through its ability to move between scholarly and journalistic writing modalities. To value one mode of prose over another returns to the tired debate about who has the right to mediate and translate meaning. Grossberg's theoretical corrective is important: "my research questions about rock have always been about its political possibilities rather than about any judgement of its aesthetic quality or cultural authenticity."[5] Grossberg is highlighting far more than New Labour dalliances with Britpop[6] or Bill Clinton's use of Fleetwood Mac. Writing about popular music is difficult. It always feels like we are draining the life from the beat, image, fabric or feeling. Because so much of music is non-linguistic, there is a necessity to access the meaning systems of fashion, rhythm, space and bodies. This writing of the popular does not capture the real, but widens the terrain of the imaginary, the probable and the possible. Music is a discourse of maybes. In a time of rigid definitions of us and them, right and wrong, a Coalition of the Willing and an Axis of Evil, ambivalence has an important function.

Theorists of popular music are intellectual trolls. Watching shadowy bodies through smoke and mirrors, we write of shapes and scents of meaning. The irony of dance writing is that the recent 'histories' of rave and electronic dance music are invariably banal in their structure and methodology. While Simon Reynolds attempted to create the definitive history of modern electronic music in *Energy Flash*, he used a highly conservative chronological structure to shape his story. The utilization of an historical narrative has displaced the volatile temporal and spatial movements of the dancing body. He presents a(nother) tale of great men: DJs, mixers, producers and club owners. He readily admits that his "take on dance music was fundamentally rockist".[7] This explains why the focus remains on 'the artist', rather than audiences, reception practices or consumption. In many ways, *Energy Flash* is an inferior, dance culture equivalent of Hebdige's *Subculture*: it invents and freezes the very events and people that it appears to be chronicling.[8]

The oddity is that so much writing about dance is boring and lacking energy. There is also a damaging obsession with personal experience, rather than collective and popular memories. As Simon Reynolds has stated,

> Participation is essential ... or at least, you have to have gone through a phase of being intensely into clubbing and dancing at some point to really understand the appeal.[9]

Part of me, the dancing part, wants to raise my hands and touch the lasers with Reynolds. Moving on the bouncing floor, jumping with the shining faces, feeling beat reverberate from the heels to the head, is an unforgettable experience. The buzzing lights illuminate an audience of dancers into a morphing shimmer. With electronic music synchronized through the lasers, it is like living in a computer game, dancing through the rhythm of the night. The problem with this type of experiential dogma is that it stops the clock, denying present movements and interpretations in favour of a mystical, personal nirvana. It also does not permit the presentation of diverse theories, sources and inflections. It is important to note that *mobile* bodies dance through the prose, thereby developing a critical history – not a static narrative – of dance music.

The higher purpose of Reynolds' analysis is not only an affirmation of experience. He is also denying the right of academics to comment on, critique and create culture. Too often in his career, Reynolds has excluded Cultural Studies theorists from the right to enter the metaphoric dance floor. He observed that

> Just as punk and rap became grist for the cult studs mill, rave music may be next on the academy's menu. Once upon a time, rave was just a case of London proles escaping workaday drudgery by losing it on the dance floor every weekend. But where once there was mere madness soon a thousand dissertations will bloom.[10]

In this way, experiential ideology becomes a way to protect terrain from academics and secure cultural territory for journalists. The great revelation of dance music is that it does not allow anyone to sit comfortably in such distinctions. The beat pushes us – either physically or metaphorically – out of a seat and into the grip of sinewy, spiralling keyboards.

Academics must remember – and remind Reynolds and others – what makes Cultural Studies important and intellectually revelatory. The paradigm takes (on) the popular forms that most people spend their time enjoying, thinking about and living through. In all honesty, census figures, shipping information, dates and immigration data are easier to interpret than popular music, film, radio, hypertexted documents and television. To deny these popular cultural sources because they are ambiguous, contradictory and ephemeral is to cut the heart out of the past and the people who populate it. While affirming radicalism, Reynolds actually argues a complementary position of a conservative historian like Keith Windschuttle, valuing a narrow range of sources.

> Burning with an inferiority complex towards the 'high' culture in whose discourse they are fluent, their [Cultural Studies scholars'] overweening concern is to validate pop culture. This they have done by bringing to bear on it all the gamut of 'high' cultural tools and terms.[11]

The lads obviously have a secret knowledge that the scholar could never understand. In this way, academics are denied an identity. They – we – become one-dimensional shadows of a self. The knowledge and language we possess become dangerous, difficult and irrelevant. No one would deny a medical doctor the need for a specialist language, or a lawyer the necessity for torts to be precisely framed. Cultural Studies has a specialist vocabulary because it enables us to understand the texture of culture with all its light, intricacy and passion.

Disempowered groups – young people, women, gay and lesbian communities, working class, indigenous populations and citizens of colour – leave few traces in historical sources. I am not prepared to allow generation after generation of the disempowered to be written out of history because journalists have mortgaged cultural credibility. A graft between history and Cultural Studies provides the tools for pop to be interpreted and made available for future researchers to ignore, incorporate or critique. Scholars with this revisionist urge are easy targets for journalists who desperately need to cling to the cutting edge of culture.

> Over 50 up-for-it academics attended a two-day conference on clubbing at Leeds University ... But the weekend wasn't just for dry analysis. A 'field trip' had been planned – in the end, five or six dons made it to a drum 'n' bass night at Leeds's Met Bar, where an eyewitness saw the academics dance badly to drum 'n' bass, only to sit down again ten minutes later.[12]

A great revenge narrative is triggered through such arrogance. These journalists will inevitably be bladed by their own discourse.[13] The 'it' boys and girls of the year inevitably end up looking like Mick Jagger in a bad jumpsuit, repeating bizarre dance steps which looked a bit silly in the 1960s, but now appear like a broken down rooster. Few of the academics attacked by this journalist would abuse him for an inability to construct a coherent sentence. Relying on an eyewitness serves the polemical purpose of this piece, but is not verifiable. In my experience – that is, a real eyewitness account – DJs cannot dance either. That is how they actually landed behind the decks. Understandably Hillegonda Rietveld – a fine scholar of house – rose to the journalistic bait:

> Whether its editors like it or not, *Mixmag* is part of an ongoing reflection on dance culture. However unlike cynical journalists, cultural commentators (like the ones you point your little finger at) have a respect for the topics they write about. In order to grow and change, it is important to discuss dance culture in an intelligent and inspiring manner, instead of drowning it in a bandwagon jumping muddiness so well demonstrated by your ignorant tabloid style.[14]

It is unwise to blame tabloids for being tabloids, or journalists for mobilizing journalese. To sample Jane Austen, it is a truth universally acknowledged that most music journalists have the stylistic flair of a ceiling fan on slow rotation. Although Rietveld was right to jab, cross and hook the hypocrisy of *Mixmag*, she also perpetuated the binarized division of academic and journalistic thinking and writing.

Dance culture falls *between* academic and journalistic spheres of influence. The aim must be to write through both these discourses, to evaluate dance music at its textured best. Kodwo Eshun offered a more effective inflection on dance journalism:

> Allegedly at odds with the rock press, dance-press writing also turns its total inability to describe any kind of rhythm into a virtue, invoking a white Brit routine of pubs and clubs, of business as usual, the bovine sense of good blokes together.[15]

Eshun recognizes that journalists do not have the vocabulary to write the rhythm. To mask this shortcoming, experiential ideologues flood the semiotic field. This explains much of the odd, derogatory treatment of IDM (intelligent dance music), or to cite Reynolds, "acid-jazzy, Rhodes-fetishizing tossers".[16] There is the nostalgic desire to return to the "Really Big, Really New Idea",[17] which invariably is the cultural moment in which the journalist was most confident and literate. Journalists have credibility: academics possess the credentials. One baits the other with a different type of 'cred'. Each mobilizes a different investment in the music and the meaning.

The trajectory of the young rock journalist who grows old is always uncertain. In moving outside the music/youth nexus, these writers become 'above the title' columnists or historians of the street. Neil Tennant, one-time writer for *Smash Hits*, became a pop star through the Pet Shop Boys. Tony Parsons turned into a tree-hugging men's movement loser and his ex-wife Julie Burchill transformed into a cool – if conservative – celebrity. Writing about dance music remains the archetypal war of position: it is a debate about who owns the mobile, twirling body and the pulsating context in which this form spins. As the mythical moments of Acid House, Techno and Jungle spiral back into the bedrock of the mix, there will continue to be debates about who has the right to write about the dance music archive.

A crucial recognition is that writing about music *must* enact critical distance and detachment. Once grasping this premise, the contested and textured nature of popular music can be discussed. While much is made of what is lost through prose, writing about dance provides a way to chart its social and political potential. The long-term consequences of the 1980s and 1990s in terms of capitalism, identity and meaning are only now being recognized. The division between journalists and scholars increased. The upshot of this partition was, as Frith and Savage suggested, "to increase the importance of journalists as cultural ideologues while undermining the cultural authority of educators".[18] The boom in the magazine market meant that there was an explosion of transitory and frequently ill-researched ideas that became the reverential truths of a music culture. Journalists accomplish far more than a reflection of their own era. They do more than repeat narratives, myths and stereotypes. Writing about dance music is difficult to situate in disciplinary terms. Resonating between the intellectual and the popular, its quilted theories must be stitched with both cultural practices and contemporary politics to make it suitable for publication. To focus overtly on the drug element of house, techno or jungle is to simplify the pleasures and the politics. Similarly, to affirm the protolinguistic bliss moment of dance is too convenient. If it is impossible to theorize and discuss the feelings of dance because it is outside language, then we must ask why all culture is not dismissed in this way. The euphoria of fandom – for paintings, opera, film or fashion – is also difficult to track and represent. Thinking and writing are anti-euphoric. To connect the inscription of the page and the dancing inscription of space summons a movement from the confirmation of knowledge into a sampling of discourses. Dance music is a site of knowledge, a way to learn about sex, identity, memory and bodies. If rock is presented as the only mode of popular music, then the diverse, playful politics of the last twenty years is undermined and perhaps lost.[19]

Reynolds referred to modern dance culture as a "collective autism".[20] He did not follow through on his own metaphor. Dance promotes non-standard thinking, distance from assumed modes of living and unexpected snatches of creativity and brilliance. It is ironic that this great music triggers such poor writing about it. With multiple narratives and myriad trajectories, dance music has lessons to teach theorists who write (about) popular memory and history. The notion that rock music is meant to have *a message* conveyed through a predictable structure of verse-chorus-verse-chorus-bridge, is decimated by dance. The repetitive, cyclical structure is built over a dominating bass and beat.

In silencing the mind and effacing the word from the grind of bass and the swirl of keyboards, the dream is always the same. The intense urge is to capture a moment of passion, happiness and deep, pulsing rhythm. As our fingertips reach for the lasers, there is a desire to reach for a referent – a myth – to affix the smeared charcoal of a dancer's movements. The point of dance writing is to understand the space between the lasers and our fingertips, or between rhythm and the body. Histories of dance music will never capture this swirling sonic complexity. The easiest way to grasp the rhythms of the past is via a nostalgic narrative, rather than a critical history. It is difficult to opt out of the chronology, while also undermining the singular locations of 'Manchester', 'Chicago', 'Sheffield', 'London', or 'Detroit'. The quest for origins uses a location to limit the meanings of the temporal, the popular memory. National memories of dance culture are not appropriate: such an approach has rotted the corpse of rock and punk. The key is to float dance music through multiple styles, locations, rhythms and movements. We may invest in a different beat.

We are Spinal Tap

All men have a bit of Mick Jagger in them, a lip licking, sleazy attitude matched by a complete inability to dance with rhythm and grace. In some ways, rock writers continue Jagger's jagged avoidance of regular beats, suave moves and the needs of others. This tradition of rock and roll facilitates the survival of white, male (post)rock music, recycling struggles between authentic, credible musicians and corporate profiteers. The fear of 'selling out' dominates the rock journalism archive, alongside a desire to reward pseudo-deviance and resistance. While popular music has a long history both before and after the Beatles, during the 1960s and 1970s rock was the soundtrack for social change. As Arnold Shaw stated in 1969

> The traditional tension between generations has grown to a point where the gap is almost that between classes in a revolutionary era. Condemning the supermaterialism, duplicity and hypocrisy of the older generation, they are raising the banners of a new ideology embodying communal sharing.[21]

Such generationalism always appears humorous and overdrawn in retrospect. A Baby Boomer community who condemned supermaterialism has gone on to be the market for banal and pointless consumer items.[22] We have to blame someone for the popularity of Ikea. Lapsed radicalism becomes a shared knowledge and memory, triggering conformity and mediocrity. The 1960s revolution itself is now a marketable formation. As rock became a commodity, rock's greatest sons such as Jagger, Richards, McCartney and Lennon entered knighthood, sainthood or rehab. Rock performers are museum artefacts, visited by curious semiotic tourists. Rock has become the can(n)on, firing at differences, with both punk and grunge following the path of disavowing the status quo and then perpetuating it. Ironically both these rock movements emerged during an era of innovative dance: disco and acid house. To stress the impact of Johnny Rotten and Kurt Cobain is to perpetuate and validate rock[23] and exclude and trivialize dance. Actually, dance and rock, as genres and categories, elegantly slide over each other. However, there is a core of rock writers that need a clean divide between the authentic, credible and masculine and the flighty, foolish and feminine. Ponder Marcus Breen's description of Nirvana's 1991 album *Nevermind*:

> It marked a new engagement with physicality which opened up the constraints of rock's prevailing orthodoxy to an optimistic re-reading. This was rock that mattered.[24]

Actually, it is the writing about rock that frames it as significant music. Authority and credibility is established by both journalists and scholars. Robert White is wrong to suggest that the study of rock music "enrich[es] our understanding of young people's attempts to create their own cultural history".[25] Elvis's significance is as much a product of Greil Marcus's words as the teenagers swooning to 'Love me tender'. Journalists have constructed, filtered and sold an authentic history of rock resistance. Rock's credibility did not emerge, intrinsically and organically, from the shrill screams of bobby soxers. This political overloading of rock has decentred the long and potent power of dance. It is too convenient in the current political and critical environment to dismiss dancing as ephemeral, fragmented and blissful. By verifying such a claim, dance theorists are sucked into a crisp separation of trivial dance music and authentic, serious (post)rock. The revolution had already happened: through the 1990s, technics outsold guitars. By 1994, Lawrence Grossberg suggested that "rock's operating logic might no longer be either effective or possible".[26] Let us take him at his word and dance through this alternative history that has already happened.

To endlessly retell the narratives of Anglo-American, male-dominated music is to – implicitly – reinforce their importance. As Katha Pollitt has recognized, "As long as we're talking about white men competing with each other, we tacitly acknowledge that we live in a realistic world ... Add women and blacks into the picture, though and suddenly the scene shifts."[27] If we acknowledge gays, lesbians, young people and citizens with disabilities, body memories and histories are more ambivalent, contradictory and volatile. Therefore this singular, truthful, combative masculine trajectory – I refuse. Like the best of dancing, the best of dance writing offers an affirmative refusal. In walking away from empowered histories, new narrative threads and rhythms are claimed. Analysis and thinking replaces an easy restatement of the rock 'n' roll chronicle. So, let us revel in the bridge for a time.

The Anglo-American dominance of music is caused through emphasizing particular literacies, notes, time signatures and rhythms over other structures of meaning. It is also supported by journalistic methods and languages, which reinforce and empower these sonic codes. At its most basic, the application of this power determines the boundary between music and noise. Dance music never reveals a clear centre – either spatially or temporally. While particular clubs may be mentioned, the historical palette is invariably washed clean as a new venue, DJ and rhythm assumes popularity. The Paradise Garage closed in 1983, with Chicago's Warehouse following in 1987. The Hacienda was built, but then demolished. These closures allowed the emergence of new clubs – Shoom, Spectrum, The Trip and The Globe. Dance cannibalizes its past, leaving Oldskoolsamples as scratches in the mix. While it is easy to focus on the big clubs, DJs and tracks, there is no centre for dance music: peripheries, edges and boundaries abound. It is therefore difficult to create a definitive dance history. The archive is carried to every new night out. The big nightclubs – the shrines to the rhythm – close. There is no easy origin and no definitive ending. The focus on clubs is understandable: it allows an anchoring of the beat and a micro-geographical negotiation of governmental policies, social injustices and private memory. It is a site for the living renegotiation of institutions and organizations. Also, it allows prior memories of dance to re-emerge in new places in new ways.[28] Such dynamic imaginings must disempower the critic. Dance music cannot be contained, pigeonholed or described. Earlier beats, lyrics, voices and rhythms are carried forward through the music of the present.

Rock and roll brought new instruments to popular music: amplified guitars, electric basses and a prominent drummer. These innovations in sound forged sonic differences with the big band and string era. The decline of violins and reed instruments opened the way for new music structures – of a 32-bar chorus followed by a bridge. The standardized rock discourse feeds into the ideologies of globalization, communicating the post-war imperatives of societal, economic and technological *development*. Those left outside of globalization – and rock – are dancing on the margins.

Nik Cohn, along with Greil Marcus, has produced extraordinary writing on American rock music. He offered the hypothesis that in tough times, the entertainment industries become 'sloppy', light and uplifting.[29] The 1960s, as a time of relatively high employment and affluence, could broach darker topics and ideas. The 1980s, the era of youth unemployment and HIV/AIDS, was also the time of Spandau Ballet, Haircut 100 and Jason Donovan. His thesis appears to be functioning well. Well, maybe not. The 1980s and 1990s was also the era of New Order, who has provided a soundtrack for the poignant, dense, difficult and tremulous moments.

> I feel quite extraordinary
> Something's got a hold on me
> I get the feeling I'm in motion
> A certain sense of liberty.[30]

Like the best of dance music, 'True Faith' was marinated in the context of its original release, but has continued to absorb new meanings through time. An anthem to the hyper-present dance floor has become a carrier of time and a conduit for memory.

Via the passionate commitments of 'True Faith', it is clear that New Order has released an even more significant song. 'Blue Monday' is probably the most famous post-disco extended remix.[31] This track accomplished nothing less than re-educating a generation of dancers about rhythm, bodies and movement. Its success is remarkable, considering that it was written to test out the band's new drum machine.[32] It is a powerful site of popular memory because of its groundbreaking role in creating new sonoric and corporeal literacies. It defamiliarizes the relationship between bodies and beat. Andrew Goodwin realized the significance of the drum patterning.

> The famous drum break that interrupts New Order's 'Blue Monday' is a good example of a fill that few drummers would have considered trying to play, not only because it would be technically quite demanding, but because it is just very slightly removed from what one's hands and feet would normally do with a rock drum set.[33]

In opening out the reading capacity of the feet, it remains a bouncing buoy of dance history. When this song pulsates out of a dance floor, it triggers excitement, energy and movement. Paul Morley 'explained' the innovations of New Order's music and the (ir)rationale for the committed focus of fans.

> The very best of irrational pop music, a question of identity, confession cut with dry wit, a deflecting adventure in thought and space, a question of style, a parting of ways, the end and the beginning, a celebration of alienated consciousness, a sincere sell out, a voyage into the present, a full stop, a semi-colon, a question.[34]

New Order punctuate ambiguous, tortured phrases with a hostile beat. The ambivalent lyrics are appropriately framed by the rigid rhythm. They dissipate the white heat of rock, twist commonsense and open a new paintbox of sounds. Importantly, they create an alternative vocabulary to American rock genres. They broke the rule of four young men with guitars and a drum kit. The presence of Gillian Gilbert behind a keyboard and a stack of samplers created a new space for women in popular music.[35]   New Order's pre-history as Joy Division adds even more complexity to the understanding of their music. They survived the death of a lead singer, Ian Curtis. Emerging from the sanctified ashes of Joy Division, love did not tear New Order apart, but fashioned a dance of mourning – a dance with an agenda.

For dancers, Ian Curtis' death is far more significant than the suicide of Kurt Cobain. Significantly, his dancing determined the rhythm of the band. As Bernard Sumner remembered,

> To me, a drummer is the clock of the band, but Steve wouldn't be the clock, because he's passive: he would follow the rhythm of the band, which gave us our own edge. Live, we were driven by watching Ian dance; we were playing to him visually.[36]

This inverse relationship, of a dancer leading the rhythm, defamiliarizes acceptable time signatures and beats. Paul Morley has always known this. His obsession with New Order and Joy Division has accompanied him throughout his writing career. He described 'Love will tear us apart' as the greatest song ever written.[37] He is correct in his hyper-confident value judgement: the trajectory of dance in the last twenty years was foreshadowed by the shift between the eight and the ninth bar of 'Love will tear us apart'. In this space, *something* happens. The music transfers from a minor to a major key. On a dance floor, the repercussions of that shift is a feeling of euphoria, that anything is possible, we can dance all night and be young forever. There is also a shift from the guitar-based past of rock music towards the synthesized future of dance music. The shift is significant, self-evident and pronounced. It is no surprise that the Pied Piper trajectory of this ninth bar was followed by so many. New Order dance with black armbands – like most of us. New Order dance with popular memory.

After disco's demise, rock was a soundtrack for growing old. Dance music is the endlessly inventive genre. The brazen hedonism of disco was the basis of 1980s pop: ten years earlier Kylie Minogue and Madonna would have been termed disco divas. Dance music during the 1980s and 1990s was an aural Esperanto. Sampling translated and transformed aural and tactile memories into a bricolage of possibilities. Digitized divas warbled with a re-energized beat and imported rhythms from Spain, Italy, France and Germany. Techno, offering a break with Motown's past, fused with the intensely European sounds of Kraftwerk,[38] Giorgio Moroder and Tangerine Dream. While Kraftwerk is frequently praised by critics (who have never heard their music), what makes this German powerhouse so important is that they prised open the gaps between the notes. They knew the value of silence and noise. Their embrace of technology created new theories of meter, melody and mixing. These fusions were continued through the 1980s by Cabaret Voltaire, Depeche Mode, Heaven 17 and Human League. Techno brought this link of the corporeal and computer into clearer profile.

Like the digital and analogue platforms on which they are based, these sampled origins of dance are unstable, unlike the authentic histories of the Beatles, Sex Pistols and Nirvana. Steve Redhead described this process as "a fracturing of the conventions which have commonly structured the body and dance in pop history".[39] Through denying rock narratives, spaces emerge for movement, change and difference. Race, gender, sexuality and age reconnect and dissociate in novel ways. Only after the beat stops, the sweat dries and the DJ packs away his gear do uncomfortable questions emerge of cultural appropriation and 'stealing' of disempowered rhythms.

Bass in the place

Whitey could dance, with a pill in him.[40]

Mani

It would take the white bass player from the Stone Roses to assemble a truth of the age. With some chemical stimulation, even a white boy can dance. Race-based questions etch an ambivalent, difficult and distinctive path through dance music. Notions of hybridity, discomfort and transgression are evocative metaphors to summon the conflictual politics of indigenous and black cultures. Dance provides an underwritten refrain to these larger histories of appropriation and reinscription.

Dance music semiotically strips popular music. Undressed of lyrics and the biography of an artist, it is marinated in cosmopolitanism, transculturality and the diaspora. Dance genres are promiscuous. Theorists must therefore be watchful of any claims for purity or essentialism, particularly with regard to race. For example, Simon Reynolds suggested that, "jungle contains a non-verbal response to troubled times, a kind of warrior-stance. The resistance is in the rhythms".[41] There is a meta-racist stance here. While much attention in the 1980s was focused on the two 'bad' musics – rap and heavy metal – both were marketable to young men, the Beavis and Butthead market. The success of white rappers, from the Beastie Boys to Vanilla Ice and Eminem, created a culture of crossovers, raising questions of cultural property and appropriation. From this serious political debate about authenticity and credibility, dance music summons an alternative energy to the binarized thinking of black and white, gay and straight, bitches and bootie. As Homi Bhabha suggested, "the body is always simultaneously inscribed in both the economy of pleasure and desire and the economy of discourse, domination and power".[42] From this perspective, both colonization and resistance continue through dance music. The trade route has been replaced by a rhythm route. It is a mode of musical tourism. Dance music fetishizes the new, opening the ears and body to new styles of music. This spice for the ears is pepper for the body, developing innovative sounds and choreography.

After the Seattle – and flannel – explosion of 1991, the primary audience for popular music was no longer American. While grunge allowed a rewriting of the power chord, The Who's legacy had been in a death rattle decline for decades. The disco pulse was still beating and about to increase its beats per minute. Dance music's transfusion through black-framed genres created new relationships, beatlines and samples of rhythm. Yet Michael Freedberg mourned the lack of American electronica:

> One of the greatest challenges for a U.S.A.-based writer is that we live in a kind of 'no-dance music zone'. We have to travel, usually overseas, to hear the best 'dance music'.[43]

Actually, disco, house and techno were born in the United States. But they were conceived in black, Hispanic and gay clubs, an alternative America that can easily be forgotten, marginalized or e-raced. Dance music revels in this non-Anglo/American musical space. Cut with colonial interrogations, dancing has almost too much race history. Being popular memory in motion, it is difficult to wash the mobile body of prior cultural readings. Colonized beats pulse through (frequently) white clubs. This marking and marketing of blackness continues to be a soundtrack for thinking about postcolonialism and race-based social justice.

Blackness operates within popular music as a transnational movement of signs, summoning questions of cultural property. Of concern is that the effects of racism are masked or negated through affirmations of cultural hybridity in the mix. Dancing to jungle decentres more intense discussions about inequality, slavery, genocide and semiotic theft. With authenticity determined through representation, the politics of sounds and their distribution are ambiguous. With the Caribbean influence on jungle, the melodic bass formations duel with aggressive drum programming. This migration of a bass line also allows the potential for new meaning systems that offer the opportunity for resistance and change. But ownership and responsibility are important.

Britpop bleached the history of Empire and denied the blackness living on the edges of colonial history. Ska, with its sped-up rendering of reggae, was attended by bass riders and post-hippies. Pseudo crusties got down to Goa Trance.[44] All these movements offer precise examples of what Stuart Hall described as "the extraordinary diversity of subject positions, social experiences and cultural identities which compose the category of 'black'".[45] To actually pinpoint a black experience or musical style is increasingly difficult, as it has been burnt so tightly into the grooves of the mix. David Toop – rhetorically – asked if "drum 'n' bass [is] reducible to the repressed black youth theme, then?"[46] Identities and ideologies of black youth are not vacuum-sealed sociological formations. Instead, the sounds move around the dance floor mix, perhaps opening out dominant histories to moments of contestation and questioning.

If Britpop has one lasting legacy, it is that it "cleaned house",[47] exfoliating the roughened surface of rock, pop and dance. It toughened music, permitting the construction of a more critical history, rather than a liquid papering of British colonization. More significantly, the Cool Britannia project (finally) rendered ridiculous any restating of a London-centred approach to music, fashion and style.[48] It was built on the changes to Britain and music through (post) house music. Dance culture created new communities of movement – between the north and the south, colonizer and colonized and Britain and Empire. It is no surprise that Oasis was the only rock band to ever feature an album review in the home of dance journalism, *Mixmag*.[49] This supposed national revival of the British music industry only increased the proliferation of alternative sounds and sensibilities. Britpop was an affirmation not of British singularity, but of a panicked desire for a stable, coherent English identity. It was an attempt to create an alternative to America's rock dominance. Britpop's greatest success – Oasis' 'Wonderwall' – was crushed by Underworld's 'Born Slippy'. This song, which most famously featured on the *Trainspotting* soundtrack, demonstrated that there were potent and strange cultural forces pounding the clubs, more than could be conveyed in a three-minute pop song. The Chemical Brothers, Prodigy and Underworld showed that new spaces were being formed that did not rely on either London or Los Angeles as a reference point. While America is a large domestic market, the declining significance of the lyric has meant that the linguistic domination of English is no longer a block to chart success. Bhangra house, which entered popular culture in the late 1980s, was a smooth presentation of sonic hybridity through Anglo-Asia collaborations and dialogues. Similarly, house and jungle attacked nationalized histories, but in distinct ways.

House is not – and has never been – an underground formation. It is simply a dominant culture in very specific spaces and times. There is global house geography that links Manchester, Chicago, Singapore, Perth, Auckland and thousands of clubs into capillaries of a bodily, rhythmic history. While house and techno claim significant origins in the United States, dance music has remained bigger than America. There remains a tissue of connectiveness in these trans-local histories. Jungle's intervention though was of a distinct order.

Jungle was fast, a frantically accelerated beat that bladed dance mixes. Put bluntly, it is a hip hop rhythm at 160 beats per minute. By creating two beats and tones, a complex sonic layering is created. When I first heard Goldie's 'Angel', I immediately thought that it was impossible to dance to – the rhythm was too demanding. The bass made my clavicle crackle and a jackhammer found residence in my middle ear. Once more, the bodily movements and dance choreography changed in response to the manic metronome. The dancing body always makes sense of the rhythm. The beat is pedagogic. Similarly, drum 'n' bass claims many origins, emerging from the hardcore techno pulses of 1991-2. By 1997, it was carving a specific groove in post-house musics. Its characteristics are marked: the distorted bass line is accompanied by an amphetamine-rush rhythm and hip hop inflections. It is a stripped down jungle and lacks the layering of beats and tones. Finally, when Coldcut released *Seventy Minutes of Madness*[50] the mix enfolded hip hop into soul and funk, techno with drum and bass. This strategy worked against the genre-based style of the DJ and denied the easy labelling of ambient or trance, house or jungle. The separation and promotion of race-based resistances, black music or national histories became even more difficult to define. Goldie won out over Gallagher. If we could cut away the keyboards and slow the jackhammer for a moment, we inevitably reveal Donna and disco.

Donna's revenge

Disco is therefore audibly where the 21st C begins.[51]

Kodwo Eshun

Dancing is a listening with more than the ears. It is a hearing through sinew, muscles, blood and bone, tissues and nerves. Popular memory twirls around the pleasuring body to frame a disco(urse) of dancing. Disco was a special moment of big wigs, polyester shirts, body glitter and bright disco ball-inspired exhilaration. Determining its politics is more difficult. Richard Dyer worried in *Only Entertainment* that, "It's not just that people whose politics I share don't like disco, they manage to imply that it is politically beyond the pale to like it".[52] It remains a maligned music genre, with roots in African-American, Latino and gay clubs. The air was filled with smoke and mirrors, cutting through Philadelphia strings, funk bass lines and tacky handclaps. A popular memory of dance exists, not in the form of a linear narrative, but splaying out from disco as a central moment and motif. While race has been seismic in its role in dance culture, sex and gender are (at least) as important.

Disco, as a chart and map for popular music, was a chronologically short-lived moment. The Disco Sucks campaign was triggered by Steve Dahl, a Detroit DJ, in 1978. The tenor of this attack was racist, misogynist and homophobic. The burning of the records offered tantalizing and disturbing reminders of Nazi book burnings. Like books, disco survived, going underground and then bursting with the power of recognition, memory and magnificent female vocals. David Toop, who like Paul Morley is exuberant in his passion for great pop music, affirmed that "Disco, as we all agree, is the best music of all time. Disco is on the way back (right on!)."[53] The gap between Toop's excited affirmation and Hebdige's dismissal of "vacuous disco-bounce"[54] requires an interpretation of a genre thirty years after its emergence. Disco was renamed and reconfigured through HiNRG, techno, handbag and house. It lives on through emulation and sampling. Donna Summer and the Village People survive because they offer a quirky and pleasurable path through the potentials of the body. The edgy, pounding beat overwhelms subtle melodic manifestations.

In the mid 1970s, with clubs proliferating in New York, DJs wished to maintain a continual rhythm so that dancers would not exit the floor at the conclusion of a song. The three-minute single was simply too short a duration to allow an extended affective experience. To keep the dance floor alive and active, the twelve-inch mix was formulated to permit the seamless connection of songs. Beat was and is the blood of a club, providing the textual information for a dancer to commence movement. As music made for the dance floor rather than the home stereo, disco promoted a specific sensibility. This world, populated by gay clones and disco divas, boomed with a 4/4 pulse under a disco ball on full rotation. The decadence of nightclubs provided a model for an alternative society based on fleeting moments of euphoria and expectation that filled the body and then drained. Disco triggered a pleasure-seeking mentalitae that was captured in so many anthems to disco, such as Sister Sledge's 'Everybody dance'.[55]

Politics, pain and challenge drain from the edges of this dance floor. It was left to Richard Dyer to present a concise review of the political choices available within this disco(urse) dancing.

> Disco can't change the world, make revolution. No art can do that, and it is pointless expecting it to. But partly by opening up experience, partly by changing definitions, art, disco, can be used. To which one might risk adding the refrain – If it feels good, use it.[56]

Dyer offers important advice for theorists of dance music. In moving beyond the making of revolution to consider the fashioning of revelation, dance music leaves few textual residues of bodily shapes and sensibilities.[57] Feelings and passion flicker through popular memory

What makes dance music so important is that it carries its beat history on a textual journey. To poach the great Blackbox track, dancing allows the body to ride on time,[58] to translate and transform old sounds into new mixes. While writing and music are scriptic and sonic, both are marinated in loss and nostalgia. Memorials to dance are difficult to erect, because the great parties and big nights continue in our minds. Dominant historical and critical protocols interrupt the metaphoric lasers in the memory. This dance music continues to beat in the present. The metronome may increase in speed, but keeps pulsing. This principle is embodied by both Robbie Williams' 'Supreme',[59] with the sample from Gloria Gaynor's 'I will survive', through to the *Casablanca* of dance records, 'Bass in the place, London'.[60] The latter song, like the cult film, embodies Umberto Eco's notion that "the clichés were talking among themselves".[61] It recycles all the slogans of the era: calling out to the house to 'make some noise' and locating bass in a place – in this case, London. Most potently, the rhythm track is lifted from New Order's 'Confusion'. This is far more than a sample: the entire track is built on this foundation.

Such 'commemorations' of rhythmic history are not rare. Dance music is proud of its past. The opening track of madisonavenue's album, *Polyester*

Embassy, offers a rapped history and aural pilgrimage to the vinyl histories of the beat.

> Such said vinyl being the vehicle by which, what we call 'music' has been recorded on for decades. What some might consider an antiquated storage system has become the trademark of a new generation. The 12". The logo of the culture of the 'club'. … Take the sounds of a bygone era, combine it with the sound of 'here' and 'now'. Clarity, Beauty, Aggression. Create a face an identity and a voice and a sound that spans 3 generations, 4 decades, 2 genders, 10 years in the making, and a partridge in a pear tree.[62]

Such a popular history, which discursively frames the dance experience on the album, has been a characteristic of the best post-disco. Enigma, in their hymn to the chill out room and/or the burning of aromatherapy oils, presented a similar introduction, wishing listeners and dancers a "good evening" while commanding them to "turn off the light, take a deep breath and relax".[63] Such lyrical instructions provide information about the music and instructions about bodily movement and behaviour. They also grasp significant beacons in dance history.

By 1987, the cry of 'Aceeeed' was matched with Smiley t-shirts and endlessly screeching whistles. Numerous DJs and promoters allege to have invented the genre, with Frankie Knuckles' claim probably being the most likely.[64] Mobilizing sparse, but powerful diva vocals alongside a fast disco beat, the rhythm was created through the 808 drum machine. Men did not respond well to this mix. As John Lee recognized, "as soon as those divaesque vocals appear you will see damn near every straight guy run for cover away from the dance floor".[65] House continues many of disco's legacies, including a repetitive hypnotic structure through dub and drop outs, energetic keyboard riffs and high levels of sampling. Through house, popular music became dance music. More worrying though, the changes to the dance genre became a way to discredit its disco origins. As Reynolds stated, "house music, in its … hands-in-the-air, handbag form, has reverted to mere disco".[66] The 'mere' is significant here. House's long-term survival and success has surprised even experts in the field. Phil Cheeseman, from *DJ magazine*, remembered that

> it's seven years since it was being said house couldn't last, that it was just hi-NRG, a fast blast that would wither as quickly as it had started. But then the music reinvented itself, and then again and again until it gradually dawned on people that house wasn't just another phase of club culture, it was club culture, the continuing future of dance music. The reason? It's simple. People like to dance to house.[67]

What people liked was the stutter technique, originally found in the dub remixes, overlaid big strings and a pounding piano. This combination is most clearly associated with Marshall Jefferson, whose 'Move your body' was the start of the house explosion in the United Kingdom and Australia. Lyrics were bled from the music, with Jim Silk's 'Jack your body' only working through three words – the title. Jack and jacking are obviously resonant – describing the jerky dance moves to house. By 1988, Acid House diversified and popularized, mixing industrial origins with disco rhythms.[68]   Through the summer of 1989 a movement into the rave setting allowed Acid House to live within a new all-night venue. The Euro-inflection of this sound created the first house number one since 'Jack your body'. The legendary 'Ride on Time' featured the biggest piano, biggest voice and more repetitive stuttering syllables than any other track. It is the Mona Lisa of the genre and is a potent anthem of the time, a pedagogic song for the dancing body. The transition from acid house to techno that occurred in 1990 was marked by the presence of a heavier, more atmospheric beat. As the rhythm became more frantic, techno developed into a beat blitzkrieg, vanquishing other styles. The famous DJs, Derrick May and Kevin Sanderson among others, increased the 120bpm to the 130-150 range, incorporating (even) more break beats and sampled drum patterns into the mix.[69]

The study of dance is not only part of aesthetics, but histories of beat, affectivity, style, sampling and sexuality. A body cannot escape rhythm. Through dance, we read music – through our feet. The rigid step choreography that survives in ballroom dancing lessons to this day has given way to variable choreographic vocabularies. Without teachable steps, much of the post-twist dancing formations do not survive beyond their moment. While the Pride of Erin or the birdy dance can be summoned at weddings, other steps are washed away with the transitory tracks that triggered them.

Dancing to popular music gains its potency and power from this ephemerality, from the response to shallow bodily displacements and eclectic shifts between past and present, beat and meaning. Dance offers the most evocative apparatus through which to convey the sensuality of bodily surfaces. If we look carefully enough, the future can be glimpsed through the flickering lights and sweltering bodies stretching and crunching on the dance floor. The 1980s and 1990s have been framed as eras of recession and profound inequalities, granting dance moments significant political and social meanings. Nightclubs offer a site to forget history and efface the past. In assuming many possible identities, or none, they offer a place for the performance of a flirtatious self. Operating late at night, when families, children and married couples have vacated the streets, nightclubs offer the promise of eroticism without the certainty of gratification. As the most evocative apparatus through which to convey the sensuality of bodily surfaces, dancing transforms polished floors, disco balls and laser lighting into a dance floor.

To reveal the discourses of dance involves more than a narrative history from jitterbug to jungle. When beat hits the body, meaning is generated. Narratives are written through flesh. There is a body memory that we as cultural critics must start to theorize. Dance is a vital feature of leisure culture, entertainment, sexuality and numerous cinematic narratives. The dance floor is a space that frames the body, engulfing the moving form into a disciplining cycle of motion and stillness. Where there is movement, there is meaning.

Dancing feet totter at the edges of time. They also foreshadow knowledges of intimacy, sex and desire. The rhythm teaches us to stretch our skin and test the limits of our identities. Dance music is much more than a smoke alarm set to a drum beat. While there is a desire to control and constrain the dancing body, it always breaks free of such a suffocating embrace. The aim of a good DJ is to match a record's beat with the affectivity of the club. Writing about dance music is rarely this smooth. It often lurches between time and space, men and women, bodies and desires. Such stylistic jacking is a significant metaphor to block the easy, celebratory tales of great clubs, greater DJs and the greatest night of them all.

Dancing in Berlin

There is a deep, bright honesty to the dance. If a dancer – as a mobile semiotician – does not like the DJ's mix, then they leave the floor. The textures of the beat, samples, keyboards, warbling vocal, lights and smoke grants the music an ironic authenticity and gritty texture. Watching a dancer in a moment of intense connection to the rhythm is a revelation: of eyes closed, arms extended towards the ceiling, legs anchoring a deep energy of commitment, passion and control.

The spaces of the dance floor are flooded with desire, nostalgia and an effervescent ever-present. It is also a site of drug use and has been through much of its history. Picture drinking prohibition gin while dancing to trad jazz, or rock 'n' roll halls with the hip flask stashed in the inner pocket of a jacket, or the speedy highs of the mods, or the ganja-inflection of reggae and progressive rock. Every generation discovers the drug it needs to make sense of its time and place. These other histories of dance and drugs are lost through the overwhelming criminalization of MDMA, or ecstasy.[70] The context and consequences of the drug have been decentred through the 'shock horror' quotient of the stories. To understand the spaces of the post-Acid House dance floor, we need to grasp how ecstasy puffed out dance rhythms into an experience, feeling and politics. There was a chemical rejection of institutional realities that has left a mark on such films as *The Basketball Diaries*, *Kids* and *Trainspotting*. The earlier ideology – so resonant in *Easy Rider* – is a desire to use drugs to check out from life. As with all drug stories, it is easy to overrate ecstasy's pervasive presence, but it certainly triggered experimentation in the form of dance mixes and the bodily movements overlaying the back beat.

Just as too much discussion of music videos has focused on the sex and violence, so have too many words about electronic dance music been wasted through discussion of drugs. The aim of MDMA (Ecstasy) is to isolate a part of the brain that produces serotonin. But Ecstasy has a 'natural' law of diminishing returns that prevents addiction. After regular weekend use, it starts to have little effect. The greater problem of its usage is social, rather than physical or medical. Ecstasy creates a euphoric sense of community and sensory belonging. The working week can never match the explosion of sound and meaning of 'the big weekend'. Therefore, there is a nostalgic desire for a return to that moment on the dance floor when life made sense. The loss of the big community becomes the addictive trigger. After the chemical saturation of dance culture, the comedown was always going to be pendulous and dark. Lowenthal affirmed the potent, but destructive potential of this sanitized past.

> People flock to historic sites to share recall of the familiar, communal recollection enhancing personal reminiscence. What pleases the nostalgist is not just the relic but his own recognition of it … less the memory of what actually was than of what was actually once thought possible.[71]

Obviously, the collective dreaming of the ultimate dance floor moment embodies Lowenthal's principle. The innovative, critical and creative music force *Shut Up and Dance* is best known for the track 'Raving I'm Raving'. It was not – as it may appear – a celebratory anthem to the techno moment. Instead, by lifting the entire melody from Marc Cohn's 'Walking in Memphis', a deep doubt was expressed about the euphoric dance experience.

> Bought myself a first-class ticket
> Everybody was happy
> Ecstasy shining down on me.
> I'm raving I'm raving
> But do I really feel the way I feel?[72]

Such a denial of lived experience is profoundly destructive to the formation of popular memory. In every drug culture, there is a moment of Darth Vader-inspired darkness. The ecstasy buzz evaporates through heavy past use. The decaying depression is triggered through emptying the brain of serotonin.

There is a troubling irony and accuracy, to Shaun Ryder's statement that "we're Thatcher's children".[73] Obviously, as the bastard progeny of capitalism, operating on the wrong side of the law but the right side of rhythm, dance music has cannibalized its own popular memory. Jarvis Cocker related in the anthem to the outdoor raves of 1989, 'Sorted for Es & Whiz',

Oh is this the way the future's meant to feel?
Or just 20,000 people standing in a field. [74]

Ecstasy was – at its most politicized – a medication for an atomized self. The drug re-collectivized disparate selves for a journey through rhythm. It is no coincidence that ecstasy emerged at the end of the self-absorbed 'me' decade. From Thatcher to Reagan, from Hawke to Muldoon, individual rights replaced collective goals. Ecstasy built bonds between bodies and music, self and syncopation. The drug has two parts: dopamine and serotonin. The former is the speedy component of the experience. The latter initiates the textured, 'loved up' response to music, fabric, skin and other dancers. The psychological effects of the drug are embedded in two descriptions: entactogenesis (the sensation of a calm, peaceful relationship with the world) and empathogenesis (creating emotional closeness with strangers). The displacement of sexualized energy into sensualized movements was always going to be transitory. Jungle, as a genre, no longer required the ecstasy buzz, replacing organic herbalism with chemical stimulation.

Dancing and dance music occupies space. The multi-sensory cacophony on the dance floor uses technology – even more than drugs – to amplify its intentions. It is not a pointless, progressivist technology, but embedded in the social sphere, enlarging the revelation in surfaces and sensuality. Angela McRobbie was wrong – seriously wrong – in her description of rave as "a culture of avoidance".[75] She has expressed a desire to restate the simpler and more obvious politics of the punk years. She has little sense of how dancers read their environment. The past is incorporated, but subordinated into the present. Ironically, that is also a definition of effective politics.

Prior rhythms are quarried, exploited or laughed at. We need to recognize that contemporary musical listeners and dancers have more to remember and recognize than previous generations. There is more popular memory to play with in the present than during the punk years. As Collin recognized, the notion that electronic dance music has no politics overstates the significance of slogans and manifestos from political parties.[76] All cultural formations are determined by the context of their emergence. Bodies create particular literacies and ways of ordering space and flesh. Dance culture has built an alternative map of movement,[77] from Europe to Africa, Asia and the Pacific. It is a global exchange of sounds.[78] The success of Fatboy Slim and The Chemical Brothers conveyed an alternative mode of dancing, thinking and reading. Concurrently Daft Punk and Air in particular show how nu-disco offers a movement beyond England's colonial boundaries. The house that smiley built has created a mansion of promise.

Dissonant sounds clash and reverberate, ripping through the sonic tissues of time. The dance floor is frequently a dark space, which is occasionally lit with possibilities. The beat makes us move: that is its power and its politics. What makes a great dance record? Too many woo-yeah-babies or calls to the house do not capture the luminescence of the genre. Dance music is a cultural ismis: a discursive river between the land masses of politics and pleasure.

Dancing through the revolution

The revolution wasn't plotted, not even expected or defined.[79]

Dave Haslam

In remembering his time at Manchester's mythical Hacienda from 1988-90, Haslam recognized that the revolution rarely arrives when expected. The affirmation of the weekend as the centre of joy, power and revelation can be over-stated. Once the night is over, how is that energy, community and passion sustained to create a bigger, brighter and stronger future? There is a need to textualize the structural nodes of inequality and regulation. The grammatology of gratification results in an unrepresentable space: endlessly different, unknowable and decentred. This manner of morphology offers space for multiple selves, experimentation and disarray, not perspective and empiricism. By focussing on the unstable and contestable, Reynolds reminded us that "even bliss can get boring".[80] The aim is to honour the feeling, while negotiating a path to a better future.

Popular music tells stories of place and identity. Dance music is marked by great clubs. The club at the centre of house myths is the Hacienda, named after the famous Situationists' slogan.

And you, forgotten, your memories ravaged by all the consternations of two hemispheres, stranded in the Red Cellars of Pali-Kao, without music and without geography, no longer setting out for the hacienda ... Now that's finished. You'll never see the hacienda. It doesn't exist. The hacienda must be built.[81]

As can happen in the dance discourse, the Hacienda was built, founded and funded by Factory Records and New Order. The problem and strength is that these hyper-significant sites that seemed the centre of the dancing world inevitably close. They survive through popular memory and are carried forward by popular culture, as seen through the film *24 Hour Party People*.

Dance music, throughout much of its history, has been a resource for the creation of a youth culture. A song can puff out an emerging consciousness. The command to stand up and dance is, at times, breathtaking in its compulsive simplicity. While there has been some discussion of how baby boomer musical tastes have been commodified, little has been written about how Xer cultural frameworks, which were frequently under the radar, become capitalist fodder and the modality of memory. Remarkably, some theorists are surprised that dance music was not a trend, or a fashion. Gavin Hills found this situation

Curiouser and curiouser. Another year on and the dancing isn't over. A few summers ago most of us thought the explosion of drugs and dance music which formed that four-letter word rave would wither and die like so many youth cults before. Usually such things shoot up like a rocket from a milk bottle, sprinkle in the sky with starlight glory, then quickly fall to earth in a burnout shell of their former selves. But something funny has happened with house music and the drug culture it spawned. Instead of burning out it has spread out, sprinkling its pixie dust across our country.[82]

That pixie dust has spread through the academy as well. Rave research has become a successful intellectual industry. The jacking scholars are trolling through history and sampling rhythmic popular memories.

It is easy to dismiss or demean dance culture, particularly in retrospect. Elvis Costello, for example, stated that "there is nothing to speak of from the 80s, the decade that music forgot".[83] Dance music was not the perdition of a generation, but constructed a startling life out of the ordinary. If any political lessons are derived from the 1980s and 1990s, it is a need to believe in the present tense and not celebrate a seamless investment in 'tradition' or 'the fifties'. Clubbers are such a demanding audience because they desire innovation, while instigating a reflexive, ironic interpretation of the past. The abandonment of a linear narrative allows the multiplicity of identity filaments to be aligned and stretched in creative ways. Writing about dance music may not always appear to be of political interest to the left, or a part of revolutionary change. Yet we need to ponder Andrew Ross's thesis that "the dance floor has always offered a safe haven for the socially marginalized".[84] I demand more of *that moment* than shared ghettoization and consciousness building. Sarah Champion did not have such hopes: "For one brief naïve moment in the late eighties, in a field off the M25 at an acid house party or at an urban warehouse party, we all believed that things might change. Like our parents did in the sixties. And maybe for a time things were different."[85] It helped at the time to verbalize that movement, the feelings of space and rhythm. Yet the gloss of translucent faces has created a potent afterglow that we must use, remember and historicize.

Dancing is pedagogic. It teaches us about movement, change and community. The aim in creating critical, popular memories of dance is to not only make them historically and culturally relevant, but to connect knowledge and experience. At the conclusion of Shakespeare's comedies, a wedding dance signified the end of the action. Eliza Doolittle sashayed through her new identity and accent, believing she could dance all night. The ignorance or avoidance of dance culture by 'serious' scholars is a way to drain passion from history. As Sarah Thornton has stated, "dancers have been regarded as narcotized, conformist and easily manipulated".[86] Perhaps they are carving out new spaces, movements and communities.

There is no split between mind and body. Dancing and thinking about dance are synergetic and healing. Much of feminism, particularly the work of Adrienne Rich and Jane Gallop, has argued that this Decartean split is the foundation of patriarchal culture. For women therefore, dancing is the site for commencing a revelation, a way to thrust bodies into popular memory. As Leslie Gotfrit reminded us,

> Dancing precipitates an incredible longing. To recover the pleasure – in the imagining and remembering, the connecting again with my limbs, my breath, my body – is to ignite desire. These are rare moments of realizing my body and mind are not distinct, and of feeling the power of creativity when embodied. This is my history, and investment in dance, always in the shadow of the writing.[87]

The dancing feet lead the writing hand. Dancing is transcendent, not escapist. It is impossible to remove the self, the consciousness and identity from the pounding of rhythm and the movements of feet. The task for writers of dance music is to stress the connection between body/politics, beat/meaning and self/sensibility. We must grant dancing a big, bright and textured history, capturing something of the energy and feeling, so that the collectivity and consciousness may survive through time. In an era of individualized failures and achievements, it is even more important to widen and lengthen those times of commitment and belief in something more than stock market movements and interest rate hikes. Histories and theories of dance are thoughts without shape, but can be woven with community through a recognition of what we shared, what we believed in and how we can continue that passion in our present. Dance conflates many histories – of sex, economic dislocation, race-based prejudice, affirmative feminism or generational memory. Tick a box and see where it takes us.

All of us share something of the dance. Our task now is to remember – with an agenda. No textual trace has represented this goal more than the film *Human Traffic*.[88] It exists in an odd semiotic space, resonating between documentary and fiction, off-screen memories and on-screen dialogues. It captures a cultural landscape of spatial disorientation and disassociation, jarring between displacements of story and space, audience and text. Without a strong, propulsive narrative, it jaggedly affixes micro memories of the post-Acid house experience. The time codes on the screen are a chronology of Friday night, Saturday morning or the weekend. There is no year in which to situate the text. This is remarkable, particularly considering that we live in an era where music and movements are charted and carolled into years, genres or summers. As Jon Savage affirmed, "history is being rewritten fast these days".[89] With the characters directly addressing the camera, it is a dancing *Spinal Tap*, maintaining the humour of the earlier mockumentary. With Carl Cox playing a cameo in the film and Pete Tong responsible for the soundtrack, the film lightly grazes the simulacrum, allowing us to caress the discarded sounds and sensations of the past. The film's success is obvious when compared with *Groove*, which is so gutless in its rendering of 'the rave scene' that it does not mention ecstasy. Oprahfied techno is no replacement for a tough, critical gaze at the past – and the present – inscriptions of dance culture.

Critics were split in their interpretation of the film. Xan Brooks described it as "a frustrating hodge-podge ... with so many ham-fisted gimmicks".[90] Alix Sharkey framed it as "a fantastical pseudo-documentary".[91] Mark Morris saw – it appears – a different film from these other critics, describing it as "an honest depiction".[92] From a bag of gimmicked clichés, to a mockumentary and a photographic representation, *Human Traffic* is a popular memory text, connecting past feelings with present visuality. Riding the clashing clichés, the film offers a tribute to the affectivity of club culture.

The scene of *Human Traffic* which always stops the show is situated on the 'nostalgia couch' in the club on the Friday night. While the lounge is located in the same temporal frame as the rest of the film, actually the clubbers, who appropriately are not dancing because they are too busy complaining about not dancing, are located (in time) much earlier in the decade.

Clubber 1:   I don't care what anyone says. It's not like it used to be.
Clubber 2:   It's gone too widespread. It used to attract open minded people who were looking for something new.
Clubber 1:   Yeah. Yeah. People were a lot more friendly.
Clubber 2:   Now it's almost a cliché to talk to a stranger in a club, for some reason ...
Clubber 1:   We have lost the fundamental reason we use Es in the first place.
Clubber 2:   Which was to leave your ego at the door and feel comfortable enough to communicate with strangers ... Do you remember when this was Tom Toms?[93]

Like these *Human Traffic* popular historians – ignoring the current vibe to remember an earlier buzz – every past club and past clubber lives and complains in the spaces of the four-four bass line. While dance music may seem a cold, digital, technologically determinist part of popular music, the mix is analogue, warm and cyclical.

So while the record spins, dance writers circulate, sampling and scratching notions of revolt, revolution and revelation into the mix. This process does not grant significance to banality, but passion to memory. Dance theorists must remain focused on what Hebdige brilliantly describes as the "knowledge that comes up through the feet".[94] Dancing is an active archaeology, denying history was maintaining the popular memory of the past in the present. By deploying a semiotics of movement, we may not only reach for the lasers, but see political alternatives. This magpie music fosters a magpie memory. Dance is made in the dark, but is written in the white light of morning.

Notes

[1]   Anonymous interviewer and Robbie Williams, from A. Kadis, *Take That in private* (London: Virgin, 1994), p. 41.
[2]   It is important to recognize the role and place of boy bands in fostering popular cultural manifestations of dance music. Norman Cook is not only known better as Fatboy Slim, but was also the bass player for the 1980s indie band, The Housemartins.

3   S. Chaffee, "Popular music and communication research: an editorial epilogue", *Communication Research*, Vol. 12, No. 3, July 1985, p. 416.

4   M. Breen, "Woof, Woof: the real bite in *Reservoir Dogs*", *The UTS Review*, Vol. 2, No. 2, November 1996, p. 5.

5   L. Grossberg, "Re-placing popular culture", in S. Redhead (ed.), *The clubcultures reader: readings in Popular/Cultural Studies* (Oxford: Blackwell Publishers, 1997), p. 230.

6   For a discussion of the relationship between New Labour and popular music, please refer to Martin Cloonan and John Street's "Politics and popular music: from policing to packaging", *Parliamentary Affairs*, Vol. 50, No. 2, April 1997, pp. 223-235.

7   S. Reynolds, *Energy Flash* (London: Macmillan, 1998), p. xi.

8   It was Mark Miller who realized the irony of music journalists writing history. In *Boxed in* (Evaston: Northwestern University Press, 1988), he stated that "A pop journalist whose reviews could be forgotten along with the music ... has become a historian in spite of himself. Like rock, his work was meant for consumption, not preservation and yet he must now look back on the development of this evanescent subject and establish its official record", p. 176.

9   S. Reynolds, "Writing about dancing: disco critics survey", http://ww.rockcritics.com/Disco-Crits_Intro1.html, accessed on March 30, 2001.

10   S. Reynolds, "A philosophical dance stance", *The Australian Higher Education Supplement*, December 11, 1996, p. 35.

11   S. Reynolds, *Blissed out* (London: Serpent's Tail, 1990), p. 10.

12   "Rave scientists exposed!" *Mixmag*, August 1998, p. 25.

13   As the dance journalists age, they become trapped by their own experiential discourse. For example, Simon Reynolds stated in 2000 that it "seems like each year an ever larger percentage of my opinions are simply unsellable on the 'ideas market' (sick joke) that is music journalism – being either too ultra-specialist/insidery, or too vehement/vituperative, or too pretentious/theoretical", from "Simon Reynolds' FAVES of 2000", http://members.aol.com/blissout.fave2000.htm, accessed on March 30, 2001.

14   H. Rietveld, "Letters", *Mixmag*, September 1998, p. 5. What Rietveld does not acknowledge is that readers of the magazine have actually consented to *Mixmag* maintaining a position of leadership. As Lawrence Grossberg has stated, "By making certain things or practices matter, the fan 'authorizes' them to speak for him or her, not only as a spokesperson but also as surrogate voice", from "Is there a fan in the house", in L. Lewis (ed.), *The adoring audience* (London: Routledge, 1992), p. 59.

15   K. Eshun, *More brilliant than the sun: adventures in sonic fiction* (London: Quartet, 1998), p. 7.

16   Reynolds, "Simon Reynolds' FAVES of 2000", *op. cit.*

17   S. Reynolds, " Glitches with attitude", *The Village Voice*, http://www.villagevoice.com/issues/0034/reynolds.shtml, accessed on March 30, 2001.

18 S. Frith and J. Savage, "Pearls and swine: intellectuals and the mass media", in S. Redhead (ed.), *The Clubcultures reader: readings in Popular/Cultural Studies* (Oxford: Blackwell Publishers, 1997), p. 10.

19 For example, the ambivalent capitalism of dance music encases myriad histories reinforced by new technologies such as the MP3, I-Pod, digitized sampling and hypertext.

20 Reynolds, *Energy Flash*, p. 414.

21 A. Shaw, *The Rock Revolution* (New York: Crowell, 1969), p. 5.

22 Terry Bloomfield has recognized the irony of this movement. As he stated, "there has been a pattern that music which at first expresses opposition to the social order is then inexorably commodified by the capitalist structures of production", from "It's sooner than you think, or where are we in the history of Rock Music?" *New Left Review*, No. 190, 1991, p. 80.

23 The verification of this principle is found on the cover of Clint Heylin (ed.) *The Penguin Book of Rock and Roll Writing* (Harmondsworth: Penguin 1992). This cover features Elvis Presley, Janis Joplin, Johnny Rotten, Bono, Keith Richards, Jim Morrison, Michael Stipe, Joe Strummer, Mick Jones, Jimi Hendrix, Bob Dylan, John Lennon, Mark Bolan, Patti Smith, Led Zeppelin and Bruce Springsteen. There are many exclusions from his cover. The oddest – but perhaps most telling – is that the performers are mostly white, there are only two women and only two post-punk acts are mentioned.

24 M. Breen, "Woof, Woof: The real bite in *Reservoir Dogs*", *The UTS Review*, Vol. 2, No. 2, November 1996, p. 1.

25 R. White, "Perspectives: bring music back in", *Communication Research Trends*, Vol. 5, No. 1, 1984, p. 6.

26 L. Grossberg, "Is anybody listening? Does anybody care? On 'the state of rock'" in A. Rose and T. Rose (ed.), *Microphone Fiends: Youth Music and Youth Culture* (New York: Routledge, 1994), p. 56.

27 K. Pollitt, *Reasonable creatures* (London: Vintage, 1995), p. 83.

28 For example Sarah Champion explored how her memory of acid house and techno re-emerged during a trip through the Midwest of America. She stated that "I have a weird sense of deja-vu. It transports me back to Shelly's Laserdome in Stoke-on-Trent in the north of England in the early 1990s, when the UK's race scene was in its emergent stages", from S. Redhead (ed.), *The clubcultures reader: readings in Popular/Cultural Studies* (Oxford: Blackwell Publishers, 1997), p. 114.

29 N. Cohn, *AwopBopaLooBopALopBamBoom* (London: Weidenfeld and Nicholson, 1969), p. 11.

30 New Order, "True Faith", *Retro* (London: London Records, 2002), disc one, track three.

31 Simon Reynolds referred to this song as "hi-NRG and '80s, gay disco genre whose distinctive butt-bumping rhythm is most easily identified by the

words 'Blue Monday'," from "Energy Flash", *The Village Voice*, http://www.sonicnet.com/news/archive/story.jhtml?id=1122936, accessed on March 30, 2001.

32 Please refer to 'Blue Monday', http://home.wxs.nl/~frankbri/facstory.html, accessed on January 12, 2003.

33 A. Goodwin, "Drumming and memory; scholarship, technology and music-making", from T. Swiss, J. Sloop and A. Herman (eds), *Mapping the Beat* (Oxford: Blackwell, 1998), p. 125.

34 P. Morley, "What did you say the name of the compilation was?" sleeve notes (*the best of) New Order* (London Records, 1994).

35 Obviously I am not suggesting that women have not had a potent and powerful history in popular music before Gillian Gilbert. However the focus on women as either a singer and/or guitarist means that female instrumentalists are frequently minimized in their role and influence.

36 B. Sumner cited in J. Savage, *Time Travel* (London: Chatto and Windus, 1996), p. 364.

37 Similarly, the *New Musical Express* listed Joy Division's 'Love will tear us apart', as the greatest single of all time in their November 12, 2002 listing. Please refer to http://www.worldinmotion.net/newsroom.htm, accessed on January 12, 2003.

38 It is important to recognize the significant foreshadowing of 1990s dance music through Kraftwerk's 'Techno Pop'. Written by Florian Schneider and Ralf Hutter, they critiqued the separation between music and everyday sonic experience. The lyric also moulded this ideology. For a magnificent discussion of their work, please refer to Tim Barr's *Kraftwerk: from Dusseldorf to the Future (with Love)* (London: Ebury Press, 1988).

39 S. Redhead, *The end of the century party* (Manchester: Manchester University Press, 1990), p. 6.

40 Mani, cited in Simon Reynolds, *Energy Flash*, p. 70.

41 Reynolds, *Energy Flash*, p. 239.

42 H. Bhabha, "The other question", in R. Fergus, M. Gever, T. Minh-ha (eds), *Out There* (New York: MIT Press, 1990).

43 M. Freedberg, "Writing about dancing: disco critics survey", http://www.rockcritics.com/Disco-Crits_Intro1.html, accessed on March 30, 2001.

44 It is important to recognize that Goa Trance, like the Balearic Beat, was actually a genre created in retrospect. The genre refers to the music played at beach parties in Goa, India. This then became the marketing label for a mode of music, rather than a type of soundtrack played in a particular location. For a further discussion of Goa, please refer to Morgan Lang, "Futuresound: techno music and mediation", http://music.hyperreal.org/library/fewerchur.txt, accessed on March 30, 2001. To investigate how this dance genre has been commodified through the tourism industry, please refer to A. Saldanha, "Music tourism and factions of bodies in Goa", *Tourism Studies*, Vol. 1, No. 1, 2002.

[45] S. Hall, "New ethnicities", in H. Baker, M. Diawara and R. Lindeborg (eds), *Black British Cultural Studies* (Chicago: University of Chicago Press, 1996), p. 166.

[46] D. Toop, "Metal Guru", *The Face*, July 1995, p. 92.

[47] This evocative phrase is derived from Erich Boehm's article, "Pop will beat itself up", *Variety*, Vol. 373, No. 5, December 14, 1998, p. 89.

[48] Joyce McMillan remained disappointed at the conservativism of this post-Britpop renaissance, describing it as "hopelessly superficial and London-centred, the 'Cool Britannia' project has done no justice at all to the radical potential for new kinds of community within the rich network of nations and cultures in these islands", from "Remind me who I am again ..." *New Statesman*, July 5, 1999, p. 30.

[49] "Pub rock", *Mixmag*, September 1997. The reviewer stated that "It's important to remember why Oasis are so big in the first place – and also why they're the only rock band that ever get reviewed in *Mixmag*. It's because they took the attitude of house music – the joy, the comedowns, the 'tonight, I'm a rock'n' roll star' – and put them into rock. It's because they celebrated having a laugh. It's because they went to the Hac and necked E's and understood", p. 133.

[50] Coldcut, *Seventy minutes of madness* (Music Unites Ltd., 1995). Coldcut are Jonathan More and Matt Black.

[51] Eshun, *op. cit.*, p. 6.

[52] R. Dyer, *Only Entertainment* (London: Routledge, 1992), 149.

[53] D. Toop, "Music", *The Face*, No. 88, August 1987, p. 99.

[54] D. Hebdige, *Subculture* (London: Methuen, 1979), p. 60.

[55] Sister Sledge, 'Everybody dance', from *70s party* (Milano: New Music, 1993), track 12.

[56] Dyer, *op. cit.*, p. 158.

[57] One of the brilliant exceptions to my rule is "How to dance properly", http://home.earthlink.net/~zefrank/invite/swfs/navigation.html, accessed on March 30, 2001.

[58] Blackbox, 'Ride on Time', *Dreamland* (Deconstruction, 1990), track six.

[59] Robbie Williams, 'Supreme', *Sing when you're winning* (Chrysalis, 2000), track one.

[60] Public Domain, "Operation Blade (Bass in the place, London...)" (Xtravaganza Recordings, 2000), track one.

[61] I am reminded of Greil Marcus's assessment of how clichés may be used politically. He stated, "I am a cliché, I don't even exist, there's nothing you can do to hurt me, I am a zero, I can start from nothing, you made me up out of your fantasies and now reality is up to me", *In the fascist bathroom* (London: Penguin, 1993), p. 404.

[62] 'This is your introduction', from madisonavenue, *Polyester embassy* (Vicious Grooves, 2000), track 1. As a significant side note, madisonavenue not only thank their record company and parents on the sleeve notes, but the designers and fashion labels that supplied their clothing.

[63] Enigma, 'The Voice of Enigma', from *MCMXC a.D.* (Virgin, 1991), track one.

[64] Garage music also has a similar club based origin, being founded at New York's Paradise Garage, through the DJing of Larry Levan. Therefore, both types of music – house and garage – are derived from the crucible clubs of their origin. The description of 'Garage' was used to demarcate between the sounds from Chicago and New York/New Jersey.

[65] J. Lee, from Miles Pearce, "Rave History", http://www.hyperreal.org/raves/spirit/culture/Rave_History.html, accessed on March 30, 2001.

[66] S. Reynolds, "Rave culture: living dream or living death?" in S. Redhead (ed.), *The Clubcultures reader* (Oxford: Blackwell Publishers, 1997), p. 103.

[67] P. Chesseman, "The history of house", http://music.hyperreal.org/library/history_of_house.html, accessed on March 30, 2001.

[68] Sterling Void's 'It's Alright' is the anthem of this area. The Pet Shop Boys later recorded this track as a single – one of the few cover songs released through their career. Please refer to The Pet Shop Boys, *Discography* (EMI Records, 1991), track 12.

[69] Also, significant subgenres emerged that were to signify the future of post-acid house music. The early divide between techno pop and hardcore techno became more marked, inevitably splitting into handbag and jungle.

[70] For an investigation of the relationship between legal theory, deviance and Cultural Studies, please refer to Steve Redhead's *Unpopular cultures* (Manchester: Manchester University Press, 1995).

[71] D. Lowenthal, *The past is a foreign country* (Cambridge: Cambridge University Press, 1985), p. 8.

[72] Shut up and dance, 'Raving I'm Raving' (Shut up and dance records, 1992). For further information about Shut up and dance, please refer to http://www.shutupanddance.co.uk.

[73] S. Ryder, from Reynolds, *Energy Flash*, p. 73.

[74] Pulp, "Sorted for Es and Wizz", from *A different class* (Island, 1995), track eight.

[75] A. McRobbie, "Shut up and dance: youth culture and changing modes of femininity", *Cultural Studies*, Vol. 7, No. 3, 1993, p. 423.

[76] M. Collin, *Altered state: the story of ecstasy culture and acid house* (London: Serpent's Tail, 1997), p. 5.

[77] Simon Frith recognized the alternative mode of music and space. He stated that "there are reasons to suspect that 'Europe' is becoming a new mythical space, with rhythms of memory and identity, war and migration, colonialism and return, which are decidedly un-American", from "Anglo-American and its discontents", *Cultural Studies*, Vol. 5, 1991, p. 269.

[78] Obviously there have been slippages in this cleanly configured narrative history between rock and dance. Oasis attained a review in *Mixmag*, the core magazine of dance culture. Please refer to *Mixmag*, September 1997, p. 133.

[79] D. Haslam, "DJ Culture", in S. Redhead (ed.), *The Clubcultures reader: readings in Popular/Cultural Studies* (Oxford: Blackwell Publishers, 1997), p. 175.

[80] Reynolds, "Rave Culture", *op. cit.*, p. 106.

[81] Ivan Chtcheglov, "Formulary for a new urbanism", in K. Knabb (ed.), *Situationist International Anthology* (Berkeley: Bureau of Public Secrets, 1981), p. 1.

[82] G. Hills, "Wonderland UK: why people take drugs and go to clubs", in R. Benson (ed.), *Night Fever: club writing in The Face 1980-1997* (London: Boxtree, 1997), p. 12.

[83] E. Costello, 'Costello's 500', *Vanity Fair*, November 2000, p. 62.

[84] A. Ross, "Introduction", from A. Ross and T. Roce (ed.), New York: Routledge, 1994), p. 10.

[85] S. Champion, "Introduction", in S. Champion (ed.), *Disco Biscuits* (London: Sceptre, 1997), p. xv.

[86] S. Thornton, *Club cultures: music, media and subcultural capital* (Cambridge: Polity, 1995), p. 1.

[87] L. Gotfrit, "Women dancing back: disruption and the politics of pleasure", from Henry Giroux (ed.), *Postmodernism, feminism and cultural politics* (Albany: State University of New York, 1991), p. 176.

[88] *Human Traffic*, written and directed by Justin Kerrigan (Fruit Salad Films, 1999).

[89] J. Savage, *Time Travel* (London: Chatto and Windus, 1996), p. 233.

[90] X. Brooks, "Human Traffic", *Sight and Sound*, Vol. 19, No. 6, June 1999, p. 37.

[91] A. Sharkey, "From chill out to sell out", *The Guardian Weekend Magazine*, May 22, 1999, p. 33.

[92] M. Morris, "Something for the weekend", *The Guardian Unlimited Archive*, May 16, 1999, p. 1.

[93] *Human Traffic*, op. cit.

[94] D. Hebdige, "Hiding in the Light", *Art and Text*, 1987, p. 68.

Chapter six

Dancing with the chairman of the board

Men play on the sensitive role. Most men I know have one thing on their minds and if they can get it, they'll take it. I don't mean to sound callous, but there's a Robbie Williams in all of us.[1]

Neil, 29, Lawyer

Very little is known about Neil. As an interview subject for *Cosmopolitan* magazine, the missal for pseudo-It girls, he is granted the privilege of a *Playboy* centrefold by only possessing a first name. Yet unlike the bunnies of old who express fondness for cats and candle-lit dinners, Neil confirms both an age and occupation. Indeed, it is endearing to know that a lawyer can concurrently sound callous and play on sensitivity. Most startling though is his testament that Robbie Williams, the deity of levity, is the combustible core of contemporary masculinity.

To paraphrase Austin Powers, Williams returned the ger to singer. He single-handedly inserted the word sodomy into an aerobic class soundtrack.[2] Williams also triumphed in a captivatingly original way. He is one of the few members of a boy band who created a successful solo career without regurgitating the middle of the road mantras of boys, girls, love, loss and whining about it. Williams' journey through post-war popular music, encompassing influences from both Sinatra and Sonique, forms a functional collage, rather than patchwork, of masculinity. He has been prepared to not only age in public, but to discuss the crevices and cracks in the facade. Robbie Williams is a Dorian Gray for Generation X, without the decaying portrait in the attic. Surfing the simulacrum, he is prepared to reveal paranoia, weakness and confusion. He strips, smokes, plays football, wears interesting underwear and drinks too much. This chapter trails behind a combustible masculinity, problematizing the gap between text and readership, beat and ear, music and men. Using Popular Memory Studies, Robbie Williams arches beyond the brief of boy bands to create a reflexive space for commentary on contemporary celebrity, constructing a moment of masculinity through movement.

Let me entertain you

Boy bands have a history only slightly shorter than rock and roll. The Beatles were the first group to mark each individual member with attributes, specificity and personality. In this way, a diverse audience of women (and men) was drawn to one (or all) of the shy/pretty/funny/smart Beatles. Few groups of the 1960s, 1970s and 1980s managed this together-alone relationship as effectively as the fab four. The Supremes were Diana Ross. The Osmonds were Donny and later Marie. The Jacksons were Michael – and then the rest. By the 1980s, this trend was continued by Wham, Bros and Spandau Ballet. Duran Duran, for a time, managed to maintain support for all band members and therefore had a wider audience and longer pop life than Andrew Ridgeley's fan base. If the 1990s had a marked generic form, then it was the presence of male and female singing groups. The personalities were managed, marketed and performed. The intensification of this principle was obviously the Spice Girls, where the name of the group infiltrated the personality of the singers: Ginger Spice, Posh Spice, Baby Spice, Scary Spice and Sporty Spice.[3] These names were secondary to their tightly toned role. Their trajectory had an earlier resonance in British music, a model that was followed to fame.

Take That was the archetypal postmodern doo-wop group. They were marked by custard bowl haircuts, baggy trousers that could conceal the contents of a minibar and an over-scrubbed complexion derived from a severe Clearasil addiction. Like the Spice Girls, they were English and there were five of them. Each band member was granted a role in the pop drama and a personality small enough to be swallowed with a spoon full of sugar. Gary Barlow, the self-deprecating songwriter,[4] was mates with Jason Orange, the kind, animal lover. Mark Owen, the heart throb, was friends with Robbie Williams, the "cheeky, cheery chappy".[5] Howard Donald was the silent, ugly one, with odd facial growths and bad hair. Most thirteen-year-old girls and a few thirty-year-old men – *Arena* readers all – found them irresistible. Their only hit in the United States, occurring months before their break-up, was the single 'Back for Good'. For audiences in the United Kingdom, Europe, Australia, New Zealand and Singapore, they created new models of masculinity and triggered a combustible female fandom.

The narrative trajectory of boy bands is now a standard morphology. An ambitious manager/producer holds an audition. He finds the best looking twenty boys, discerns who can dance and sing and then makes the cut for the final five. At this point, choreographers, managers, singing coaches and record producers groom, move and train the vocal chords and muscles for synchronicity. Invariably, cover songs are selected. The publicity machine is cranked and a fan base summoned. Williams remembers that

> We were told what to say, how to behave, how to dress, where we could and couldn't go. All the thinking was done for us. It was a prison, I lived in that prison for six years![6]

Here we scrutinize the careful grooming of cropped masculinity. Take That provided a basis for Williams' celebrity, but also a framework for disciplining men.

This startling fame had to be built, rather than assumed. Take That's first single, "Do What U Like" only reached 82 in the British charts. Their second and third singles, "Promises" and "Once You've Tasted Love" skimmed around the extremities of the top 40. As their *Greatest Hits* collection, released at the time of the group's demise, reported

> Gaining acceptance was no easy task in the early days. There had been no British group quite like Take That and so they were establishing a new form of pop as well as a career. Having laid the way, today the Take That template is used time and again for other groups with varying degrees of success.[7]

The TTT (Take That Template) has been followed by Boyzone[8] and Westlife most obviously, but can also be monitored in the marketing of New Kids on the Block,[9] the Backstreet Boys, Five and N'Sync. The time was right for this model of pop. The sustained combustion of dance music discussed in the last chapter – initiated through acid house, trance, techno and jungle – pulsated through the lasers and cut up the chart. Yet dance culture did not abide by the rules of pop. The invisibility of producers, conducting an orchestra of samples, beats and basslines, did not fit into *Top of the Pops* or the *Pepsi Chart*. Therefore, boy and girl bands were necessary. The facelessness of dance music was masked by the many faces of good looking men and women in vocal groups. They emphasized lyrics, had an identifiable verse, chorus and bridge structure and danced utilizing safe and recognizable choreography in their videos. They were highly visual, compared to the hidden, quasi-legal, ecstasy-inflected, volatile and cold cut technology of post-acid house music. The vocal groups were television and video friendly and highly appropriate to the context of girl's bedrooms, just as dance music was appropriate to warehouses, clubs and outdoor venues.[10] Concurrently, the rock genres also filled the visual void of the dance vacuum, by the promotion of the Britpop antics of Oasis, Blur, Suede and Pulp.

Take That's chart dominance is difficult to grasp in retrospect. The 'five lads from Manchester' blended dance rhythms and ballads, while single-handedly transforming anoraks into a fashionable item. Combining good looks, smooth choreography, well-chosen cover singles and talented songwriting, they sold eleven million albums worldwide.[11] The fan allegiance and commitment from this base was neither solid nor dependable. As Pride realized,

> While the teen market can be very profitable when the right act hits the right note, loyalties can suddenly vanish as the fans grow and wish to distance themselves from their embarrassing pasts.[12]

Take That split in early 1996. The fan allegiance evaporated very quickly. While a Take That Appreciation Page survives on the web,[13] the bulletin board shows highly intermittent messages. There are very few regular members, so few that an event scheduled to commemorate the group's dissolution became embarrassing in its unpopularity.

> It is with much sadness that we have to announce that the 2001 Thatters Reunion has been cancelled due to lack of response. We are very surprised that so few Thatters wanted to get together to remember the guys on the 5th anniversary of their split, but we guess a lot of fans have moved on. We have received a total of 25 payments so far but unfortunately because we have to pay the hotel by the end of February, we cannot wait any longer to see if more fans will be coming.[14]

Melancholy punctuates this message. There is a tragedy in establishing a relic of youth that no one visits. It is a virtual ghost town. This unpopular culture is odd not only when considering the place of Take That in recent memory, but also the current fame of Robbie Williams. His present fans practise textual amnesia about his boy band past. "Thatmania"[15] has disappeared even faster than the Duranmania, Rollermania and Beatlemania. The popcult clock is increasing in speed. To make this dismissal of the fan's past even more bizarre, those who leave messages on the discussion forum now deny their own commitment of five years earlier. As Deborah suggests,

> I remember I was so down after they'd split up and I never thought I'd be able to cheer up again. I wouldn't say that I'm a TT-fan now. I don't think I ever was actually. I was just a teenybopper having a huuuuuge crush on Mark Owen.[16]

This statement was made at the same time that the Beatles, thirty years after their break-up, were holding a number one chart position for a retrospective album of their singles. Some memories are more acceptable than others. The obsessions and desires of the girls (we were) are exfoliated off the skin of memory. We lose, deny and forget much of our selves through this process. Popular music is a demanding musical form and young women are a demanding audience. Willie Dixon realized that "the men don't know, but the little girls understand".[17] Sadly, women grow to deny what, as a little girl, they comprehended and shared.

The power held by these screaming girls is difficult to pinpoint. Yet the grazing female gaze and the intensity of its desiring power, is a troubling concern for Men's Studies. The siren song of feminism is calling out men's uncoiled fear of the feminine. As Kevin Goddard feared,

> Medusa's gaze is deadly because it is self-defensive, the snakes obvious phallic symbols – the female assuming male power, turning the male into stone.[18]

Once more, the female gaze is a threat to masculine expectations and executions of power. When reviewing the footage of Take That at their height, there is no doubt that the spearing attention of the young women is combustible and shrill. In their feminine collectivity, there is safety in moving outside of normative sexual behaviour. These fans express desires that, because of their ephemerality, cannot be contained within heteronormative discourses of sexuality. Although loud, the voices of these girls are vaporized from historical sources. Sheryl Garratt has reclaimed some of this past.

> One of my clearest memories from nine years ago is of a bus ride from my housing estate in Birmingham into the city centre. An atmosphere like a cup final coach, but with all of us on the same side and with one even more radical difference – there were no boys. At every stop more and more girls got on, laughing, shouting, singing the songs we all knew off by heart. We compared the outfits and banners we had spent hours making, swapped jokes and stories, and talked happily to complete strangers because we all had an interest in common: we were about to see the Bay City Rollers ... Most of us scream ourselves silly at a concert at least once, although many refuse to admit it later, because like a lot of female experience, our teen infatuations have been trivialized, dismissed and so silenced.[19]

Garratt has added much to the historical record because of her disclosure. While most post-boy band singers insist that they have serious (male) fans, this affirmation invariably decentres the millions of female screamers who granted them an original audience. Not surprisingly as these girls become young women, they decry these memories within themselves, dismissing them as a stage, phase or crazy summer. When these desires and collective hopes are lost, so are significant micro-moments of power and autonomous sexuality. Significantly, because the 'serious music press' is written for men and by men, the source material survives through time. This tendency only increases through the digitization of documents. While *Billboard* and *Rolling Stone* are enfolded into the Expanded Academic and ProQuest databases, *Smash Hits* and *No. 1* remain outside the parameters of their interest and, one would assume, a university market.[20]

After the demise of Take That, their record company signed Barlow and Owen, but not Williams. Certainly his early post-TT career was not stellar. In the late 1990s, being an (ex) member of Take That must have seemed a life threatening illness. Indeed, Williams' situation was described as "starting his career buried alive in the boy-group Take That".[21] The situation could be worse. After all, Britney Spears was in the Mickey Mouse Club. But women's pop pasts are handled differently. When pondering the case of Madonna for example, her consistent and diverse career over nearly twenty years should have guaranteed her the status of legend, enabling her to retire comfortably to critical acclaim, yoga and a macrobiotic diet. Steven Daly recognized the contradictions of her continually capricious career.

> Had Madonna been a male performer blessed with the same assets, she would surely have critical respect to burn at this stage of her career. Look, for instance, at George Michael … most of Madonna's best work has been dance music, a frivolous form with roots in gay, Latino, and black culture.[22]

For (ex) members of Boy Bands, George Michael offers hope: if he could survive 'Wake Me Up Before You Go Go,' then popular endurance is possible for anyone. His 'credibility' and 'talent' became a lighthouse of survival from the shrill screams and naff trousers. Gary Barlow, from the moment of the group's demise, assumed Michael as his career model.[23] Robbie Williams took George Michael's lessons far too literally and actually recorded 'Freedom' as an anthem for his new career and wardrobe. At this stage, Williams still had to prove he was a better man than permitted by the Take That anorak.[24] He became the group's renegade, leaving (or being pushed out of) the band because of drug and alcohol excesses.[25] Ironically, he was able to mobilize this decadent past to create a distance from it. As he had been famous in Europe since the age of sixteen, Williams realized that his audience had seen my trials and tribulations, seen me rise and take loads of drugs and fall down and look stupid, then get back up. They know my sense of humour, and they've come to know what to expect.[26]

His explosive chart placings in 1999 and 2000 seemed unexpected, considering that his first solo album only sold 33,000 copies, compared to the multiple platinum power of Take That.[27] Yet his career was saved, quite appropriately, by a ballad titled 'Angels'. After this breakthrough, the 1998 album *I've been expecting you* entered the chart at number one and after one week became platinum. Similarly, the single 'Millennium' topped the charts. From 1999, Robbie Williams became a dominating solo performer, pushing other Thatters into the Ridgeley zone.

Dance when you're winning

While American listeners require the overt parody of a Weird Al Yankovic to signify audio humour, Robbie Williams is Spike Milligan in Armani. *Sing when you're winning*, his third release, presents enough aural explosions to satisfy the most violent of Goon Shows. 'Kids'[28] is the masterpiece of the album, a comedy song that made it on the pop charts, which gave terms like knowingness, reflexivity and consciousness new depths of interpretation. A duet between Kylie Minogue and Robbie Williams, it is an Xer (soap) opera. Within two verses, there are references to three decades of culture, via AC/DC, Frank Sinatra and James Bond.[29] The rhyming rap weaves Billy Connolly with Sean Connery, serial monogamy, ornithology and sodomy. The video adds *Grease* references to the text,[30] with a black-clad Minogue and Williams reprising a 'You're the one that I want' style, by trading lyrical lines and dance steps.

Through such references, Williams has targeted an audience poorly represented by rock journalism. An ignorance of consumer behaviour of the twenty/thirty somethings is revealed in the confusion surfacing over *Sing when you're winning*. Tom Sinclair was baffled at the explosion of cultural references.

'I don't mind doin' it for the kids', sings U.K. upstart Robbie Williams on 'Kids', an infectiously percolating number from his second U.S. album, *Sing when you're winning*. He's presumably talking about making music, but you wonder if he's targeting the right demographic ... lyrical allusions to Gloria Gaynor and John Coltrane in 'Supreme' will probably escape them entirely.[31]

Robbie Williams does not mind 'doin it for the kids', because they are merely one of his markets. Mobilizing Kylie Minogue to verify his point, both the Xer singers claimed a teen market in their youth, but then aged with their audience. The video and audio references play on credibility, predicability and authenticity. In this context, style no longer signifies symbolic resistance. The Williams bricolage is complex and unstable and, like *The Goon Show*, risks being misread or ignored as noise or nonsense. At its worst, the 'clever clever' pop cultural tourism can be reduced to allowing "a self-absorbed and self-important generation to rationalize its own existence, ascribing significance to meaninglessness".[32] Such statements demonstrate the necessity to monitor how popular culture translates and transforms through time and which texts and ideas remain to circulate in popular memory.

The Robbie Williams discourse took years to attract an audience who held a literacy of this cultural range. Much of the rock press expresses an inability to grasp his codes. There is a fervent assumption that rock and resistance will forever be entwined in a guitar-drums embrace. This notion, as Terry Bloomfield suggests, "reflects the dominance of white adult male definitions of popular music ... too many commentators are of an age that they remember sixties music as a sentimental accompaniment to excursions into adulthood".[33] Bloomfield made this realization in 1991, the year of pummelling hardcore techno on the dancefloors. The evidence for Bloomfield's interpretation is shown not only through rock journalism in *Rolling Stone* and *Q*, but through the Cultural Studies musical analysis of the time. In the same year as Bloomfield's article appeared in the *New Left Review*, Simon Frith reported that

> The average teenager listens to pop music for 4 hours a day, 3 times more, it's claimed, than teens spent listening to pop in the 1970s ... The poll also reveals that pop is 'very low' on the list of 'the most important things in life.' ... The young listen to more and more and it means less and less.[34]

Frith may regret this application of sociological methods. The decade following his words renders his interpretation narrow and misguided. After all, breathing was probably not on the list of the most important things in life for these teens. Through the 1990s, popular music became the cultural equivalent of oxygen. It permeated everyday spaces and because of that significance, was taken for granted. While love, sex, death, family life, relationships and world peace may be more important, music is the language that provides the entry points to these other cultural formations.[35] Popular music is a soundtrack for living, providing an imaginative path through identity building formations.

Like Frith, Lawrence Grossberg could not stabilize or understand the cultural markings of post-Techno popular music.

> The various post-baby boomer generations seem barely able to use the music to mark any generational difference, and totally unable to mark intragenerational differences. While the music matters, it matters in not quite the same way ... Rather than dancing to the music you like, you like the music you can dance to.[36]

Grossberg has based a career on his expertize in the rock formation. He represented the growing body of critical writing that spoke on the behalf of, rather than to, Generation X. Certainly, there is much textual material that verifies Grossberg's analysis. Consider the performances and audience for Bruce Springsteen, Dire Straits or Jackson Brown. Indeed, the latter's performance of 'Running on empty' dates experiences with a mechanical precision.[37] Post-acid house popular music does not freeze time in this way. Through sampling and scratching, audio cut and pastes allow the past and present to dialogue in the mix.[38] Therefore, dancing, listening, boredom and fascination, affectivity and banality cannot be separated. As argued in the previous chapter, dancing is reading of beat on the feet and reading through the feet. Dance-inflected popular music replaced the rock drummer with a drum machine, brought back the brass section and strings and added sonic depth and texture to the strumming patterns.

Through the inflection of the complex rhythmic patterns of trance, house, jungle and ambient, the structure and grain of music changed. Obviously, there is a desire to locate progressivist politics and leftist struggle in popular culture during times of conservatism. However the post-1960s music and post-baby boomer youth cultures were always going to be disappointing to critics raised on Bob Dylan. The path from Lenin to Lennon was not the road to revolution. Of course, journalists are still looking for the next punk to promise anarchy and another anthem to youth.

> I think young people have got really bland. There's no gangs anymore. When I was about twelve you had to be a mod or a punk or whatever ... you don't see deep housers being chased down the road by drum & bass kids.[39]

The problem is not within the present. It never is. An imagined past, where generations of young people wore garbage bag dresses with colostomy bag belts, or buzz cuts and big boots, or colour-coordinated jackets and Vespas, never happened. The sociological renderings of radical subcultures have created a Cultural Studies dreaming of angry, visible resistance to the conservative order. Obviously, this was political wish fulfilment.

If a generation is to be summoned, hailed or claimed, then it must have shared literacy and popular memory. Pop is no longer only a tale of fast cars and faster women travelling on an unending Thunder Road. It is a fragmented, commodified, specialist and rapidly changing socio-technical configuration. Obsolescence was and is a marketing strategy to ensure a constant consumer of new musical product. Once commercially redundant, these texts assume a new function.

Popular memory is the fodder of Robbie Williams' lyrics, becoming an autobiography in motion

> My breath smells of a thousand fags
> And when I'm drunk I dance like me dad
> I've started to dress a bit like him.
> Early morning when I wake up
> I look like Kiss but without the make-up
> And that's a good line to take it to the bridge.[40]

The easy generationalism of rock writers is not found in this verse. Instead, a critical literacy of popular culture, from drinking to dancing, from Kiss to their make-up, is used to summon nostalgia for the present, but also the consciousness of a community who recognizes a good line and a bridge, when we hear it.

Rock journalists misread the popular sphere in 1996 and 1997. The post-Take That reviews of the lads assumed that Gary Barlow would have a stellar, middle of the road (tautology or contradiction?) career.[41] Robbie Williams, because of his humour, unpredictability and ambivalent sexuality, was a more dodgy option. The journalists and rock critics were wrong, underestimating the changes to music, men and women in the closing five years of the twentieth century. More precisely, their incapacity to track the selling power of Williams' humour and irony is an ignorance of Generation Xer music fans who were not ready to jump from Take That to the Elton John audio graveyard. While Barlow went for the syrupy ballads and limp lyrics, Williams wrote eulogies to youth, exposed fears of dressing like your dad and demonstrated a complete inability to manage a private life. The icons of the post-war period – like James Bond, Jackie Stewart, Kiss, John Travolta and Barry White – were woven through his videos, alongside wiry raps to sodomy and the lash. Such diversity is explained by Judith Halberstam, who recognized that "we find that excessive masculinity turns into a parody or exposure of the norm".[42] The difficulty for the other members of his old band was that they did not extend beyond the safe parameters of safe teenage masculinity. Such unexpected innovations were continued at the end of 2001, when Robbie Williams released a compact disc filled with standards: from 'Mack the Knife' to 'Mr. Bojangles' and 'One for my baby'. Quaffed to the max and photographed in the 1940s crooner's uniform of stylish suit – slightly dishevelled – he broadened out the spectrum and history of 'popular' music.[43] By 2002's *Escapology*, death, depression and loss were his motifs.[44] This compact disc spills over with disappointments, fears and paranoia. It offers an extraordinary testament to a year of political brinkmanship, war and xenophobia. That it was unsuccessful in comparison to his earlier releases is no surprise and provides a significant marker of the edge that separates popular and un/popular culture. The celebrity self was saturated: there was nothing left to know about Robbie Williams' public (and private) life.

After the – comparative – failure of *Escapology*, it was no surprise that the following year Williams recorded and released a live album, becoming a 'best of' hit collection. Recorded at Knebworth between August 1 and 3, 2003, it was released soon after its mixing. Confirming his incredible stage performance and the capacity to lead an audience in a terrace chant of his songs, there was a fascinating, if desperate, spoken introduction to 'Angels'.

> This is the best tour I've ever been on. The best tour by far. And I know I said it before but I'm going to get old and I'm getting older. I want you to come with me. You've watched me grow up so far. I want to get old with you lot. Please please don't leave me.[45]

As a testament to – and denial of – popular cultural ephemerality and redundancy, this is a poignant moment in the live performance and his career. As one of the very few boy band singers to survive beyond the bubblegum, he now has a more difficult task to accomplish: pop survival through his forties and fifties. Disconnecting popular music from youth culture and allowing the music to age with his audience, was commenced through the release *Swing when you're winning*. However finding strategies to continue this process, where much of his success has been based on his youthful appearance and tabloid antics, will become more difficult. The Pet Shop Boys confronted this moment in the release of *Behaviour* in 1990, their best album but one that attracted a more adult audience. From the point of this release, they had to discover how to age through popular culture. In the subsequent fifteen years, they have produced three-minute chart pop on the album *Very*, dance and rock crossovers through *Release* and stage musicals. Their audience has reduced in numbers, but their legacy has survived. *Pop Art* – the two-disc testament to their career – captures the scale of their influence in popular music. The title was revealing, affirming their journey from the 1980s to the 2000s, from Pop to Art. Williams has some challenges ahead of him.

Ironically, it is his former group leader, Gary Barlow, who most clearly explained Robbie Williams' ambivalent success. He stated, with remarkable clarity, that "you can't pick your audience, it picks you".[46] Generation X gave Robbie Williams an audience. Gary Barlow was not (as) significant because Baby Boomers did not need another white boy crooner. While rock journalists remain confident in charting the credibility of U2, they have actualized a misreading of a generation who danced to Take That, but wanted to dance – and think – to Robbie Williams. Significantly, nihilistic Xer politics in the United States exploded with anger through hip hop and death metal, but in Australia, New Zealand and the United Kingdom, a backbeat and soaring vocals triggered – not rage – but dancing and laughing.

While most of Williams' music has a pulsating, regular beat which can be remixed up by dance producers or down for acoustic presentation, the lyrics are important. Like Frank Sinatra and Dean Martin, he has impeccable diction and a clear, strong voice. He encourages live audiences to sing the words so that, at times, his concerts resemble a football match. Also, the presentation of lyrics and videos in his compact discs encourages a focus on the words as much as the melody and rhythm.[47] If the Williams' lyric have an overarching ideology though, it is of mourning and loss, a fear of time passing. His lyrics are effective aural medication for the passing of time. The only way to gain perspective on life is to live long enough to transform regrets into laughter. Williams is so important because, while living a life in the present tense, he understands that without a knowledge of history, we remain prisoners of the past.

Come follow me

Robbie Williams is a man for our age. Between dating supermodels and Geri 'Lost Spice' Halliwell,[48] he has time to "love … his mum and a pint",[49] but also subvert the Oasis cocaine cock(rock)tail by frocking up for a television appearance. Williams is important to theories of masculine representation. As a masculinity to think with, he creates popular culture with a history. In an era where Madonna practises yoga and wears cowboy boots, it is no surprise that by June 2000, Robbie Williams was voted the world's sexiest man.[50] A few months later, in the October edition of *Vogue*, he posed in a British flag bikini.

It is reassuring in an era where a 12-year-old boy states that "You aren't a man until you shoot at something",[51] that positive male role models exist who are prepared to both wear a frock and strip on national television.

Reading Robbie Williams is like dipping into the most convincing but draining of intellectual texts. He is masculinity in motion, conveying foreignness, transgression and corruption, bartering in the polymorphous economies of sex, colonialism, race, gender and nation. His career has spanned boy bands, try-hard rock, video star, crooner and hybrid pop performer. There are obvious resonances between the changes to Williams and shifts in masculinity. In 1988, Suzanne Moore described (the artist still known as) Prince as "the pimp of postmodernism".[52] Over a decade later, the simulacrum has a new tour guide. Williams revels in the potency of representation. He rarely sings about love or romance, as was his sonic fodder in Take That. Instead, he is fixated on becoming a better man, glancing an analytical eye over other modes of masculinity.

Notions of masculine crisis dominate contemporary media. Men's studies is a boom area within Cultural Studies, dislodging the assumed investments in popular culture.[53] William Pollack's *Real Boys* has created a culture of changing expectations for men.[54] The greater question arising from his concerns is why these problems, traumas and difficulties are emerging now. Pollack's argument is that boys and young men invest energy and time "disguising their deepest and most vulnerable feelings".[55] This masking is difficult to discern within dance and popular music. Through lyrics and dancing, videos and choreography, masculinity is presented as convoluted, complex, fragmented and emotionally complex. While rock music is legitimized by dominant ideologies, marginalized groups frequently use disempowered genres – like country, dance and hip hop – to present oppositional messages. These competing representations expose multiple versions of competent masculinity.[56]

Particular skills are necessary to rip the metaphoric pacifier out of the masculine mouth of popular culture. Patriarchal pop is punctated by the paradoxes within lived experience. Frequently these are nostalgic visions, which Kimmel described as a "retreat to a bygone era".[57] It is the recognition of a shared, simpler past that reinforces heteronormativity. Williams, as a gaffer tape masculinity, pulls apart the gaps and crevices in representation. Theorists must open the interpretative space encircling such popular culture, disrupting normalizing criteria.

There are many ways to judge masculinity. From sport to business, drinking to sex, masculinity is transformed into a wired site of judgement and evaluation. Popular music conveys a rite of passage, swimming in the spectacle of maleness. From David Lee Roth's skied splits to Eminem's beanie, young men are interpellated as subjects in patriarchy. Robbie Williams is a history lesson in post-war masculinity. While this nostalgia is conservative in nature, the ironic pastiche of past narratives of motor racing, heavy metal and James Bond are fragmented in their execution, thereby blasting the pylons of power and domination.

'Rock DJ' is Williams' most elaborate video. Set in a rollerdrome with female skaters encircling a central podium, the object of fascination and fetish is a male stripper. This strip is different: it disrupts the power held by men in phallocentralism. After being confronted by Williams' naked body, the observing women are both bored and disappointed at the lack-lustre deployment of masculine genitalia. After this display, Williams appears embarrassed, confused and humiliated. As Buchbinder realized,

> No actual penis could ever really measure up to the imagined sexual potency and social or magical power of the phallus. We might think of the relationship as, in the sense, intertextual.[58]

To render this banal experience of male nudity ridiculous, Williams then proceeds to remove skin and muscles. He finally becomes an object of attraction for the female DJ only in skeletal form. By 'going all the way', the strip reveals the predictability of masculinity and the ordinariness of the male body. For literate listeners, a higher level of connotation is revealed. The song itself is based on Barry White's melody for 'It's ecstasy (when you lay down next to me).' Such intertextuality accesses the meta-racist excesses of a licentious black male sexuality. A white boy dancer must deliver an impotent, but ironic, rendering of White's (love unlimited) orchestration of potent sexuality. Williams' iconography and soundtrack is refreshing, emerging from an era of "men who cling ... tightly to their illusions".[59] When the ideological drapery is cut away, the male body is a major disappointment. Fascinatingly, this deconstructive video has been demeaned through its labelling as pornography.[60] Oddly, a man who is prepared to – literally – shave the skin of masculinity is rendered offensive.

Men's studies, like feminism, has been defrocking masculinity for some time. Robinson, for example, expressed little sympathy for "whiny men jumping on the victimization bandwagon or playing Cowboys and Indians at warrior weekends and beating drums in sweat lodges".[61] By shredding men's identity back to the body, the link between surface and depth – or identity and self – is forged. 'Rock DJ' attacks the new subjectivities of the male body, by not only generating self-surveillance but humour through the removal of clothes, skin and muscle. He continues this play with the symbols of masculine performance throughout the album *Sing when you're winning*. Featuring photographs of soccer players, coaches and fans, closer inspection of the images reveal that Robbie Williams is actually every character, in every role.

His live shows also capture diverse performances. Singing a version of 'My Way', with cigarette in tow, he remixes Frank Sinatra into a replaying and recutting of masculine fabric. He follows one dominating masculinity with another: the Bond-inspired 'Millennium'. Robbie Williams is comfortably located in a long history of post-Sinatra popular music. He mocks the rock ethos by combining guitars and drums with a gleaming brass section, hailing the lounge act of Dean Martin, while also using rap and dance samples.

Although carrying fifty years of crooner baggage, the spicy scent of homosexuality has also danced around Robbie Williams' career. Much of this ideology can be traced back to the Take That years. As Gary Barlow and Jason Orange commented at the time,

Jason:	So the rumour is we're all gay now are we?
Gary:	Am I gay? I am? Why? Oh good. Just as long as we know.
Howard:	Does anyone think I'm gay?
Jason:	No, you're the only one people think is straight.
Howard:	Why aren't I gay? What's wrong with me?
Jason:	It's because you're such a fine figure of macho manhood.[62]

For those not literate in the Take That discourse, it should come as no surprise that Howard was the TT equivalent of The Beatles' Ringo or Duran Duran's Andy Taylor. Every boy band requires the ugly, shy member to make the others appear taller and more attractive. The inference of this dialogue is that the other members of the group are simply too handsome to be heterosexual. This ambiguous sexuality has followed Williams into his solo career, becoming fodder for those lads too unappealing to be homosexual: Oasis.

Born to be mild

Robbie Williams accesses a bigger, brighter and bolder future than Britpop. While the Gallagher brothers emulate and worship the icons of 1960s British music – from the Beatles' haircuts to the Stones' psychedelia – Williams' songs, videos and persona are chattering in a broader cultural field. From

Noel Cowardesque allusions to the ordinariness of pub culture, Williams is much more than a pretty-boy singer. He has become an icon of English masculinity, enclosing all the complexity that these two terms convey.

Williams' solo career from 1999 occurred at the time of much parochial concern that British acts were not performing well in the American charts. It is bemusing to read *Billboard* over this period. The obvious quality of Britney Spears is seen to dwarf the mediocrity of British performers. The calibre of Fatboy Slim, carrying a smiley backpack stuffed with reflexive dance culture, is neither admitted nor discussed. It is becoming increasingly strange to monitor the excessive fame of Williams in Britain, Europe, Asia and the Pacific when compared to his patchy career in the United States. Even some American magazines are trying to grasp the disparity.

> The swaggering king of Britpop sold a relatively measly 600,000 copies of his U.S. debut album, *The ego has landed* ... Maybe Americans didn't appreciate his songs about being famous.[63]

In the first few years of the 2000s, there was no unified Anglo-American musical formation, a coalition of willing listeners. Divergent discursive frameworks emerged through a British evasion. There was no agreed centre to the musical map.

Throughout 1990s Britain, blackness jutted out of dance floor mixes, from reggae to dub, jazz and jungle. Plied with the coldness of techno's precision was an almost too hot hip hop. Yet both were alternate trajectories to Cool Britannia. London once more became swinging, or as *Vanity Fair* declared, "the nerve centre of pop's most cohesive scene since the Pacific Northwest grunge explosion of 1991".[64] Through Britpop, the clock turned back to the 1960s, a simpler time before race became 'a problem' for the nation. An affiliation was made between a New Britain formed by the 1997 British election and the rebirth of a Swinging London.[65] This style-driven empire supposedly – again – made Britain the centre of the world.

Britpop was itself a misnaming. It was a strong sense of Englishness that permeated the lyrics, iconography and accent. Englishness requires a Britishness to invoke a sense of bigness and greatness. Slicing through the arrogance and anger of the Gallaghers was a yearning for colonial simplicity, when the pink portions of the map were the stable subjects of geography lessons, rather than the volatile embodiment of post-colonial theory. Simon Gikandi argues that "the central moments of English cultural identity were driven by doubts and disputes about the perimeters of the values that defined Englishness".[66] Britpop could not 'make it big' in the United States because it was recycling an exhausted colonial dreaming. Two old Englands were duelling for ascendancy: the Oasis-inflected Manchester working class fought Blur-inspired London art school flair. This insular understanding of difference had serious social and cultural consequences. The only possible representation of white, British youth was a tabloidization of Oasis's behaviour through swearing, drug excess and violence. Simon Reynolds realized that by

> returning to the three minute pop tune that the milkman can whistle, reinvoking parochial England with no black people, Britpop has turned its back defiantly on the future.[67]

Fortunately, the future had already emerged. The beats per minute were pulsing with an urgent affirmation of change, hybridity and difference. Hip hop and techno grafted an alternative cartography of race. While rock was colonialization by other means, hip hop enacted a decolonial imperative. While the Anglo-American military alliance was matched and shadowed by post-war popular culture, Britpop signalled an end to the NATO-like movements of music. From this point, English pop and American rock would not sail as smoothly over the Atlantic. While 1995 was the year of 'Wonderwall', by 1996 the Britpop bubble burst and corroded the faces of the Gallagher brothers. Oasis was unable to complete an American tour. Yet other cultural forces were already active, with 1996 the year of *Trainspotting*. This cultural force no longer required America as a reference point.[68]

Robbie Williams was able to integrate the histories of Britpop and dance culture, instigating a complex dialogue between the two. Still, concern peppered music and entertainment magazines that British performers were not accessing 'America'. As Sharon Swart stated

> Britpop acts, on the other hand, are finding it less easy to crack the U.S. market. The Spice Girls may have made some early headway, but fellow purveyors of pop, such as Robbie Williams, can't seem to get satisfaction from American fans.[69]

British performers had numerous cultural forces working against them. Flat global sales, the strength of the sterling and the slow response to the new technological opportunities of DVD, all caused problems. Because of the complex dialogues between the rock discourse and dance culture, time and space were unable to align into a unified market. American critics simply could not grasp Robbie Williams' history, motives or iconography.

It's Robbie's world, we just buy tickets for it. Unless, of course you're American and you don't know jack about soccer. That's the first mistake Williams makes – if indeed one of his goals is to break big in the U.S. (and I can't believe someone so ambitious would settle for less.) ... Americans, it seems, are most fascinated by British pop when it presents a mirror image of American pop.[70]

There is little sense that a different musical economy now circulates, where making it big in the United States is not the singular marker of credibility. Williams demonstrates commitment to the international market, focussing on MTV Asia, MTV online, New Zealand and Australian audiences.[71]

With Oasis still attempting to stand on the shoulders of English giants, the pop boom that began with Take That and East 17 and continued with the Spice Girls, became more unpredictable through the solo careers of Geri Halliwell, Ronan Keating and Robbie Williams. The ballad and dance mix of *Sing when you're winning* integrated the distinct histories of pop and rock, samplers and guitars, into a tight package. Retrospectively, this was his popular cultural high water mark. Williams' confident embodiment of liminality offered a model for different modes of masculinity and music. The Gallagher brothers spent much of the 1990s trying to be John Lennon. While Noel, at times, knocked at the door of rock legends through 'Wonderwall', he snubbed Williams' penchant for pop glory, describing him as a "fat dancer".[72] Dancing should not be decried so summarily. It conveys subtle nodes of bodily knowledge about men, women, sex and desire. While men are validated for bodily movement through sport, women's dancing is a performance of voyeuristic attention. Such a divide is highly repressive of men who dance, with gayness infiltrating the metaphoric masculine dance floor.[73]

Too often the binary of male and female is enmeshed into the divide of rock and dance. Actually, these categories slide elegantly over each other. The male pop singers are located in a significant semiotic space. Robbie Williams carries these contradictions and controversy.

NO! Robbie didn't go on NME's cover in a 'desperate' attempt to seduce nine-year old knickerwetters ... YES! He used to be teenybopper fodder. SO WHAT?! So did the Beatles the Stones, the Who, the Kinks, etc blah blah pseudohistoricalrockbollocks. NO! Making music that gurlz like is NOT a crime![74]

There remains an uncertainty in his performance of masculinity and at times, a deliberate ambivalence. He grafts subversiveness into a specific lineage of English pop music. The aim for critics of popular music is to find a way to create a rhythm of resistance, rather than melody of credible meanings. In summoning a pop archive, we can write new sonic histories. Robbie Williams enables the writing of a critical history of post-Anglo-American music.[75] Popular music captures such stories of place and identity, while also opening out spaces of knowing. There is an investment in rhythm that transgresses national histories of music. While Williams has produced albums, singles, video and endless newspaper copy, his most important revelations are volatile and ephemeral in their impact. He increases the popular cultural vocabulary of masculinity.

Suzanne Moore asked why men should "be interested in a sexual politics based on the frightfully old-fashioned ideas of truth, identity and history?"[76] The reason is now obvious. Femininity is no longer alone in the simulacrum. It is impossible to separate real men from the representations of masculinity that dress the corporeal form. Popular music is pivotal, not for collapsing the representation into the real, but for making the space between these states liveable and pleasurable. Williams demonstrates that the polemical is political.

Notes

1   Neil, "Inside the male mind", *Cosmopolitan*, Issue 334, April 2001, p. 100.

2   Both "Kids" and "Rock DJ" were featured in the first Body Attack tape, produced by Les Mills New Zealand, for the global market.

3   As the group have aged and gone on to 'solo projects', the labels have followed them. Spice World has become Spite World, Posh Spice (Victoria Beckham) transformed into Skeletal Spice and, with great cruelty, Sporty Spice's weight gain remade her into Sumo Spice.

4   Quite importantly, Barlow has maintained this humour in the post-Take That years. He stated in the superb 1998 APT documentary on Boy Bands, *Love me for a reason*, that "four of the guys did a lot of the dance routines. I was quite a few pounds heavier when I was in the group and in those competitions where they voted for the favourite member, I always used to end up with that shameful 2% on the results. My job was the music and vocals and getting the direction correct. I sort of left the sex appeal to everyone else."

5   A. Kadis, *Take That: In Private* (London: Virgin Books, 1994), p. 63. Importantly, although Take That are framed as 'five lads from Manchester', Robbie Williams was actually from Stoke-on-Trent.

6   R. Williams, *Let me entertain you* (London: Virgin Books, 1998), p. 8.

7   Liner notes (no author listed but probably Alex Kadis), *Take That Greatest Hits* (BMG, 1996), npn.

8   What remains surprising is that these boy bands, from the Beatles to Boyzone, are not from London. There is a need for a difference, an erotic separation between the empowered core

and the home of 'our lads'. The boys become (only) slightly exotic, but still known and safe. Boyzone, who accurately shadowed the narrative of Take That, were derived from Dublin. While rock success from Ireland is relatively common, from Thin Lizzy through to U2, the Cranberries, Pogues and Waterboys, pop achievement has been far more elusive. Clearly westlife, b*witched and the Corrs were the corrective to this principle.

9   An argument could be made that the success of New Kids on the Block actually prevented Take That from gaining more chart placings in the United States.

10 By the late 1990s, the facelessness of dance music had been solved by transforming the producer/DJ into music star. This is observed not only in the success of Dan Rampling and Goldie (who actually appeared as a Bond villain in *The World is Not Enough*), but also in the explosive hits of Fatboy Slim.

11 This figure is derived from Dominic Pride's, "Teen acts in the '90s present many faces", *Billboard*, November 2, 1996, p. 89.

12 *ibid.*, p. 89.

13 "Take That: the appreciation pages", http://www.geocities.com/Broadway/3005/takethat.html, accessed on March 30, 2001.

14 "3 February 2001: Thatters Reunion Cancelled", http://www.geocities.com/Broadway/3005/ttnews.html, accessed on March 3, 2001.

15 Alex Kadis, *Take That: In private* (London: Virgin Books, 1994), p. 10.

16 Deborah, http://pub17.bravenet.com/forum/fetch.php?id=9566345&usernum=1436661303, accessed on March 30, 2001.

17 W. Dixon, cited in Daly, *op. cit.*

18 K. Goddard, "'Look maketh the man': the female gaze and the construction of masculinity", *The Journal of Men's Studies*, Vol. 9, No. 1, Fall 2000, p. 28.

19 S. Garratt, "All of us love all of you", from Sue Steward and Sheryl Garratt, *Signed, sealed and delivered: true life stories of women in pop* (London: Pluto, 1984), p. 140.

20 A survey of *Ulrich's Periodicals Directory*, http://www.ulrichsweb.com (accessed on June 1, 2004) reveals that while *Melody Maker*, *Q*, *Rolling Stone* (Australia), *Rolling Stone* (US), *Vanity Fair* (UK) and *Vanity Fair* (US) are all distributed in alternative media such as online fulltext and CDRom, *Smash Hits* (Australia), *Smash Hits* (UK) and *No. 1* are only available in print form. There are no commercial publishers or distributors who make these popular cultural texts accessible to scholars.

21 D. Ansen, J. Giles, Jack Kroll, David Gates, N'Gai Croal and Karen Schoemer, "What's a handsome lad to do?" *Newsweek*, Vol. 133, Issue 19, May 10, 1999, p. 85.

22 S. Daly, "Like an artist", *Vanity Fair*, November 2000, p. 54.

23 Gary Barlow's respect for and modelling on, George Michael is revealed in Dominic Pride and Paul Sexton's "Take That's Barlow takes 'road' to Arista", *Billboard*, June 14, 1997, p. 7.

24 R. Williams, "Better Man" (Chrysalis Records, 2001).

25 Williams stated in an interview that "I was young and very stupid", cited in "Williams' 'Ego' to land in U.S." *Billboard*, Vol. 111, No. 14, p. 12.

26 R. Williams, cited in "The UK's reformed bad boy Williams enjoys slow climb to Stateside stardom", *Billboard*, March 4, 2000, p. 5. After the release of "Angels", the album sold 300,000 copies and became double platinum within two weeks.

27 These figures are cited in *ibid.*, p. 5.

28 "Kids", sung by Kylie Minogue and Robbie Williams, from *Sing when you're winning* (Chrysalis Records, 2000), track five.

29 While Robbie Williams enacted a parody of the Bond discourse in "Millennium", on numerous occasions he has been suggested as a replacement for Pierce Brosnan's Bond. Please refer to "Double agent of the week", *Entertainment Weekly*, Issue 570, November 24, 2000, p. 83.

30 The restyling of *Grease* was discussed by I-Lien Tsay in "Slick's back: grease is the word for a smooth new video duet", *In Style*, Vol. 6, No. 2, p. 162.

31 T. Sinclair, "Robbie Williams lets go his ego on the smart, since winning", *Entertainment Weekly*, No. 564, October 20, 2000, p. 77.

32 J. Cohen and M. Krugman, *Generation Ecch: the backlash starts here* (New York: Fireside, 1993), p. 11.

33 T. Bloomfield, "It's sooner than you think, or where are we in the history of rock music?" *New Left Review*, No. 190, 1991, p. 80.

34 S. Frith, "He's the one", *Village Voice*, October 29, 1991, p. 18.

35 For example, music is a soundtrack for shopping, driving, studying, dancing and sport.

36 L. Grossberg, "Is anybody listening? Does anybody care? On 'the state of rock'," in A. Rose and T. Rose (ed.), *Microphone fiends: youth music and youth culture* (New York: Routledge, 1994), p. 56.

37 Most famously, the lyric for "Running on Empty", proclaims "In '65 I was 17" and "In '69 I was 21." The precision of this dating has resulted in the song being used in two films to connote the passing of time. It was deployed in both *Forrest Gump* and *Mr Holland's Opus*. This song appears on Jackson Browne, *Running on Empty*, produced by Jackson Browne (Elektra/Asylum Records, 1977).

38 Samplers have a long history. The earliest synthesizers – Moog and Mellotron – were used in the 1970s. Their primary function was to replicate existing sounds, but also to pre-record musical movements. By the end of the 1970s, the Fairlight Computer enabled the manipulation of sounds. Through the 1980s, samplers became smaller, through the Akai SL 1200, the Casio series and Ensoniq Mirage. The late 1990s were marked by MP3 and the potentials of audio compression format.

39 Justin Robertson, *DJ Magazine*, Vol. 2, No. 10, March 14-27, 1998, p. 48.

40 "Strong", sung by Robbie Williams, from *The ego has landed*, track 2.

41 For example, Dominic Pride and Paul Sexton, "Take That's Barlow takes 'road' to Arista", *Billboard*, June 14, 1997, p. 7. In this article, Barlow was termed "the music linchpin." Mark Owen and Robbie Williams were dismissed as minor players in British music.

[42] J. Halberstam, *Female Masculinity* (Durham: Duke University Press, 1998), p. 4.

[43] Robbie Williams, *Swing when you're winning* (Chrysalis Records, 2001).

[44] Robbie Williams, "Feel", *Escapology* (Chrysalis Records, 2002), track two.

[45] R. Williams, Introduction to "Angels", *Robbie Williams Live Summer 2003* (EMI, 2003).

[46] G. Barlow, cited in Pride and Sexton, *op. cit.*, p. 7.

[47] Robbie Williams has made a habit of including his music video on CD singles, supplying Quicktime 4 on the disc.

[48] The fame of both Williams and Halliwell was at such a level that it was reported in the generally conservative pages of *Marketing*. The piece was titled "Will Geri's fling lose its fizz?" *Marketing*, August 2000, p. 17.

[49] Ansen et al., *op. cit.*, p. 85.

[50] For poll results, please refer to "Winners and Losers", *Time International*, Vol. 155, Issue 23, June 12, 2000, p. 9.

[51] Isaac, cited in Adrienne Mendell, *How men think* (New York: Fawcett, 1996), p. 19.

[52] S. Moore, "Getting a bit of the other – the pimps of postmodernism", in R. Chapman and Jonathan Rutherford (ed.), *Male Order* (London: Lawrence and Wishart, 1988), pp. 165-166.

[53] For a discussion of this growth in academic discourse on masculinity, please refer to Paul Smith's "Introduction", in P. Smith (ed.), *Boys: Masculinity in contemporary culture* (Colorado: Westview Press, 1996).

[54] W. Pollack, *Real boys* (Melbourne: Scribe Publications, 1999), p. 14.

[55] *ibid.*, p. 15.

[56] For example, Jillian Sandell argued that "what is needed … is for analyses of masculinity in popular culture to be more specific – socially, historically and politically – about how particular representations of masculinity present a challenge or a critique to questions of gender, male privilege and social power", from "Reinventing masculinity: the spectacle of male intimacy in the films of John Woo", *Film Quarterly*, Vol. 49, No. 4, Summer 1996, p. 23.

[57] M. Kimmel, *Manhood in America* (New York: The Free Press, 1996), p. 87.

[58] D. Buchbinder, *Performance Anxieties* (Sydney: Allen and Unwin, 1998), p. 49.

[59] S. Faludi, *Stiffed* (London: Chatto and Windus, 1999), p. 14.

[60] Steve Futterman described "Rock DJ" as the "least alluring porn video on MTV", in "The best and worst: honour roll", *Entertainment Weekly*, Issue 574-575, December 22-December 29, 2000, p. 146.

[61] D. Robinson, *No less a man* (Bowling Green: Bowling Green State University, 1994), p. 6.

[62] Jason Orange, Gary Barlow and Howard Donald, cited by Alex Kadis, *Take That: In private* (London: Virgin Books, 1994), p. 17.

[63] "Ask Dr. Hip", *U.S. News and World Report*, Vol. 129, No. 16, October 23, 2000, p. 72.

[64] D. Kamp, "London Swings! Again!", *Vanity Fair*, March 1997, p. 102.

[65] Michael Bracewell stated that "pop provides an unofficial cartography of its host culture, charting the national mood, marking the crossroads between the major social trends and

the tunnels of the zeitgeist", in "Britpop's coming home, it's coming home", *New Statesman*, February 21, 1997, p. 36.

66 S. Gikandi, *Maps of Englishness* (New York: Columbia University Press, 1996), p. x.

67 S. Reynolds, http://www.members.aol.com/blissout/britpop.html, accessed on April 15, 2001.

68 It is important to make my point clear. I am discussing a popular cultural 'America' which is a distinct formation to the territory, institution or defence initiatives of the United States. Simon Frith also made this distinction clear when he stated that "the question becomes whether 'America' can continue to be the mythical locale of popular culture as it has been through most of this century ... there are reasons now to suppose that 'America' itself, as a pop cultural myth, no longer bears much resemblance to the USA as a real place even in the myth." This statement was made in "Anglo-America and its discontents", *Cultural Studies*, Vol. 5, 1991, p. 268.

69 S. Swart, "U.K. Showbiz", *Variety*, December 11-17, 2000, p. 35. Also, please refer to Paul Sexton and Gordon Masson, "Tips for Brits who want U.S. success", *Billboard*, September 9, 2000, p. 1.

70 S. Woods, "Robbie Williams Sing when you're winning", *The Village Voice*, Vol. 45, No. 52, January 2, 2001, p. 98.

71 To observe the scale of attention paid to the Asian and Pacific markets, please refer to http://robbiewilliams.com/july13scroll.html, http://robbiewilliams.com/july19scroll.html and http://robbiewilliams.com/july24scroll.html, accessed on March 3, 2001.

72 N. Gallagher, cited in Michele Orecklin's "People", *Time*, Vol. 155, No. 10, March 13, 2000, p. 101.

73 At its most naïve, J. Michael Bailey and Michael Oberschneider asked "Why are gay men so motivated to dance? One hypothesis is that gay men dance in order to be feminine. In other words, gay men dance because women do. An alternative hypothesis is that gay men and women share a common factor in their emotional make-up that makes dancing especially enjoyable", from "Sexual orientation in professional dance", *Archives of Sexual Behaviour*, Vol. 26, No. 4, August 1997. Such an interpretation is particularly ludicrous when considering the pre-rock and roll masculine performance of dancing rituals such as the jive, Charleston and jitterbug. The role of dance in heterosexual narratives of love, sex and romance are downplayed through such an investigation. Once more, the history of rock music is obscuring the history of dance both before the mid 1950s and after acid house.

74 Steven Wells, "Angst", *NME*, November 21, 1998, p. 62.

75 Women, gay men and black communities through much of the twentieth century have used these popular spaces. For example, Lynne Segal, in *Slow Motion* (London: Virago, 1990), stated that "through dancing, athletic and erotic performance, but most powerfully through music, Black men could express something about the body and its physicality, about emotions and their cosmic reach, rarely found in white culture – least of all in white male culture", p. 191.

76 Moore, *op. cit.*, p. 175.

Chapter seven

Here to stay?
24 hour (post) party people

This open book, yet to be read
This second look – this leap ahead.[1]
New Order, "Here to stay."

Most days, I am disheartened by Cultural Studies. It is either being derisively labelled as (capital T) 'Theory' or wildly and unproblematically celebrating the banal. When reading current Cultural Studies journals, I feel like I have discovered where all the boring people from High School ended up after the term finished. Still wearing bad clothes and now accompanied by worse politics, a paradigm of great potential has stripped into beige-frocked fallacies of radicalism and resistance. The big ideas, once chased with relish and passion, are now replaced with a fascination for 'slow cultures' and ordinariness. If reality television is the source of the next revolution, then we are in serious trouble. Cut to nostalgic interlude. Summon the time tunnel. Cultural Studies was once as cool as Claude Rains.

Rarely does the cultural landscape dislodge my disquiet. Dance music remains dazzling and cinema still offers potential. Michael Winterbottom's *24 Hour Party People* is the only film I have ever seen that is improved by the acquisition of a Cultural Studies education. Not a *Cultural Studies for Beginners*, the script sutures semiotics with postmodernism, situationism with neo-liberalism, to display a (post)industrial explosion of ideas and insights. Even better, traditional film critics have misunderstood and mislabelled its agenda, with enthusiastic fans (invariably) offering the best reviews of this dance-infused masterpiece. Most significantly, the film is grounded and founded in the workings of popular memory. Without an understanding of how times and places morph and shift, the film is unreadable. Within this film, there is a way forward for Cultural Studies. For nearly fifteen years, generic courses in the broad areas of television studies, everyday life and semiotics have taught generations of students to summon the predictable tropes of carnivalesque resistance, hegemonic renegotiation and popular pleasures. The emergence of these easy mantras is not surprising as the radical explorations of the 1970s are collapsing, only to be replaced by a hardening of disciplinary boundaries, seen in Cultural Studies by the domination of semiotic and sociological approaches.

This chapter brings a Cultural Studies film home, providing a relevant and resonant method in which to frame and grasp the visual, aural and temporal bullets fired out of the mise en scene. *24 Hour Party People* is an inspiration, a reminder of what we in Cultural Studies could be doing with our words, imagination and creativity and why the production and analysis of popular knowledges is politically necessary and theoretically innovative.

You really should read more

We assume history is about other people.[2]

Peter Carroll

If you get it, fine. If you don't, that's OK. But maybe you should read more.[3]

Tony Wilson

The disciplinary dialogues between history and Cultural Studies, particularly in (post) youth studies, have been disappointing. As argued in this book, to understand how youth cultures age requires the application of new theories and ideas from Popular Cultural Studies. While history is a method, practice and product, it is also an affirmation of the priority granted to evidence and fact. Tracking disempowered groups requires different skills from the writing of diplomatic or maritime history. The powerful invariably leave many verifications of their victory. Theorists who are interested in 'recovering' disempowered voices and ideas must work harder to find alternative evidence, while also monitoring the metastories in the present that continue to crush alternative views in the past. While historians construct a smooth interpretation formed by the three-tiered rubric of thesis-antithesis-synthesis,[4] many stories and images jut out of this framework. The difficulty in representing multiple viewpoints and dislodging the tendency for insiders to speak on the behalf of outsiders, is a primary problem for those wishing to formulate Popular Memory Studies as a method to track oppositionality and emancipation. The 'whole story' cannot be told. Each day releases a new jigsaw puzzle piece that does not fit within yesterday's pattern.

Many popular memories can never be written, doomed to be pushed beyond prologues and epilogues and unable to be encased in the cardboard covers of books. Popular music in particular suffers the greatest disparity between social impact and critical interest. Dave Hickey ponders this disparity:

> During the nineteen seventies, when I was writing rock criticism and pop songs, and playing music, I used to wonder why there were so many love songs. More specifically, I wondered why ninety percent of the pop songs ever written were love songs, while ninety percent of rock criticism was written about the other ten percent.[5]

Music is a talisman of memory. It offers a way inside an emotion and a quick, sharp jolt back to the past. While most of our lives are socially regulated and mandated, music memories are hot, fiery and creative. Writing is a shopping list of memory, whereas music is a palette of evocative colours and unrealized potential.

We attend school and university to understand facts and ideas not experienced in the rest of our lives. Educational systems are based on a desire to separate experience from knowledge.[6] Living – rather than formal learning – is immersive, visual and tactile. Alternately, scholars are aloof tourists through this past. Such academic journeys not only probe the analysis of the past, but its ownership. Why do some events, like the Final Solution or Nazism, crush the potential for relative interpretations, while popular cultural histories are continually debased, debated, decentred and denied?[7] It is even more difficult to write about an event or an idea that never happened. The consequences of constructing a chronological series of events mean that the disappearances from history, like water draining from a sink, are unnoticed. Greil Marcus recognized the consequences of this loss.

> Today there are dozens upon thousands of people who, only moments ago, lived just this life, but who, because this is a story outside of history, thrown out like a ranting drunk ... from a bar, can barely credit even their own memories, people who are cut off from each other, and isolated even from their own selves, by the shame of stories they cannot tell and that no one would believe if they could.[8]

Dancing is a 'story outside of history.' The revolution in rhythm, the transformation of body shapes and energies, is unspoken and rarely recorded beyond 'shock horror' tabloid ecstasy scares. Lives are changed through dance, but history does not catalogue the transitory moments in dry ice and lasers. Popular Memory Studies has both remedial and medicinal work to accomplish: to bring the beat back to history.

The 'facts' of memory depend not only on the way they are understood, but the judging of value or significance. Only when relevancy is established, is a memory articulated and then perpetuated. Therefore a voice cannot be 'given' to the voiceless. A medium must be established to channel and deliver alternative renderings of the past and present. The New Right markets nostalgia to arch public debates and discourses away from critiques and difficult questions and towards acceptance and agreement. Nostalgia filters out the bad and the unpleasant. It is conservative, imposing order and tradition. Labour and class struggle are removed and capitalist modes of production and consumption are naturalized. In such a context, *24 Hour Party People* is a post-industrial museum of dance culture, summoning an imaginative geography and plurality of past representations.

Popular memory, even one inflected by socialist or democratic principles, perpetuates absences. *24 Hour Party People*, while summoning the aura of punk, Madchester and rave culture for an era which naturalizes J. Lo's third marriage, also perpetuates two major historical gaps. The Hacienda was built and survived on the pink pound through much of its early life. The gay nights in the club, known as 'Flesh,' and the famous Gay Traitor bar, were all excised from the surfaces of the film. Instead, Tony Wilson's heterosexual credentials were established through multiple marriages and hookers performing services in the back of a van. Similarly, the 'story' of Factory became a highly masculinist tale of great men: Martin Hannett, Ian Curtis, Shaun Ryder and Mike Pickering. Gillian Gilbert – one quarter of New Order – was hidden in the corner of one shot during the recreated composition of 'Blue Monday.' Women were written into the familiar roles of wives, girlfriends, prostitutes, cloakroom girls and anonymous mobile bodies in a club. In the contestation of youth and masculinity, women were removed from the dance. Such an absence is of no surprise and has been perpetuated through the critical literature of post-Acid house electronic music. Ten years after the break of House in Britain, Maria Pini stated that "none of the existing academic work on this scene, or on clubbing more generally, seriously addresses the position of girls and women within rave".[9] To make matters worse, *24 Hour Party People* does not explore more generally the position of women in Manchester's popular culture, or in memory. Deborah Curtis, wife of Ian and mother of his child, is shunted to the side of a scene. She is marginalized in the vision of the past. Women are pushed out of (post) youth cultures, Generation X and the popular memories of a supposedly shared past.

Beyond the Master's narrative, popular memory can create a politicized space to attack dominant renderings of the past, both inside and outside history. Popular memory is soaked with multiple modes of representation and expression, defined only against the (un)popular memories that are so disturbing within a dominant discourse that they are erased or censored from media traces. Popular memory may emancipate counter-history, providing the space and sources for marginalized groups. New ways of making memory emerge from the stereo and the screen. Knowledge is shaped through the visual and aural media. As a political project, we must welcome the noise of the past, the traffic jams of sweat, sound, colour and movement. Silence is destructive to radical intellectual work.

Too big for death

When you're dead, you can't remember your name.[10]

Paul Morley

I will never be able to cope with Ian's death. It will affect me now ... forever ... I will never be able to forget it.[11]

Bernard Sumner

The dance between synchrony and diachrony is an embrace of the dead and the living. Every text has a ticking clock within it, bending and attacking the notion that time is objective and linear. Popular memory is never safe and is highly political when demarcated – strongly and clearly – from heritage and nostalgia. While youth has been a topic and trope of myriad films, from Bill Haley, Elvis and Sandra Dee through to the John Hughes series of angst-ridden teen flicks, it is rare that the institutions of youth culture – such as record labels and clubs – are the stars of a narrative. While teen films are marked by a dire fear of leaving high school, *24 Hour Party People* features a (post) youth culture gone to fat. Indeed, it is the Manchester equivalent of a passage from Sun Records Elvis to White Jumpsuit Las Vegas Elvis. There was always something gloriously grotesque about the decline of Presley. Similarly, it is haunting to realize that many of the cultural figures in the film such as Martin Hannett and Rob Gretton, legendary record producer and manager of New Order respectively, died in their late forties. They only just lived longer than Elvis. In creating a popular memory of death and ageing, *24 Hour Party People* assails Andrew Blaikie's thesis that "each of us is engaged in a losing battle against the ravages of time".[12] In the film, narratives twist, plot points are jumbled and disordered and funerals have more screen time than births. Wilson described Hannett as "too big for death".[13]   Indeed, music history is always too big – too important – to fuse into a clean ending. There will either be a fade out or endless sampling through the mix.

Even after the 'discovery' of ginkgo biloba, there is a struggle to remember. The desire to assemble memory maps and trajectories of significance is an attempt to fight redundancy and obsolescence. 'Youth' does not end at 18, 20, 25 or 30 years of age: the past is not jettisoned with the arrival of a particular birthday cake. If particular songs, images and ideas are to survive, then a textual capsule must be created that preserves the beat, the fabric, the dance steps, the living and the dead. To study (post)youth necessitates an understanding of loss. *24 Hour Party People* is the film of Tony Wilson as much as the music and he – like Dorian Gray – does not age in the film, even though it encompasses 15 years of his life. A haircut signals the end of the 1970s. But he does progress through several wives. Indeed, he changes partners more often than he changes hairstyle. We can always judge a middle aged man by the calibre of his last wife. The first wife is a mistake, the second wife is the father of his children and the third wife determines if he has become a grown-up. Tony Wilson ended up in his forties with Miss United Kingdom. She was in her twenties. No comment. It is no coincidence that the brilliant Steve Coogan plays Tony Wilson. He is able to convey charm and self absorption, being both funny and an object of humour. It is a great comedic performance and Wilson's story demanded such a deft touch.

24 Hour Party People is a hard drive of (post)youth cultural experiences, available for retrieval. Many images and ideas are saved to the metaphoric disc, from the Sex Pistols and Iggy Pop, to Joy Division and Durutti Column and the building of the Hacienda to the destruction of Factory Records. The distinction between childhood, youth and adulthood is difficult to manage at any time, but through this film ageing is looped, strung out and jump cut. While the best of drug/dance films such as *Human Traffic* transform a weekend into a life, *24 Hour Party People* does the reverse. Time and significance is sampled in a continuous dance mix that is refreshed through new beats, new haircuts and new clothes. The two great deaths of the film – Ian Curtis and the Hacienda – are the iconographic hooks into the chorus.

Ian Curtis was the lead singer of Joy Division. Such a simple statement does little to capture his long term importance in popular music and popular memory. He killed himself on May 18, 1980, the day before he was to commence a tour in the United States. Again, the banality in the details escapes their significance. As Stephen Morris remembers, "on Sunday night, I was turning up my trousers, on Monday morning, I woke up screaming".[14] Both the Joy Division album and single entered the British charts in the weeks after his death. What makes Curtis significant is what happened after his death. The three remaining members added a woman – Gillian Gilbert – to their ranks and continued to produce music under the name New Order. Few bands survive the death of their lead singer. The Foo Fighters are another important example. The history of New Order is extraordinary and one that *24 Hour Party People* does not tell. For the purposes of Factory Records and Tony Wilson, their innovative input ended with Joy Division. Ian Curtis faded out the thrash of punk and faded in the synthesizer soar. New Order would merely continue a trend, whereas the Happy Mondays would alter the soundscape of music.

24 Hour Party People never recovers from the death of Curtis. Green commented that "when Curtis hangs himself, near the midpoint of the film, the film is unfortunately deprived of its most fascinating character".[15] Sean Harris's performance as the doomed singer is so powerful – so accurate – that it shakes the playful inauthenticity of the film. Steve Coogan moves in and out of Wilson's filmic present to comment on the future distortions of the real. But Harris grabs the screen and resonates with such energy that the funeral sequence shuts down the ironic interpretative space. As one reviewer commented, "there's a sense of urgency hanging about the Joy Division story that the movie doesn't quite recover once it switches to documenting the rise of the more buffoonish Mondays, but the scenes showing the last days of the Hacienda have a nicely elegiac quality".[16] While I disagree with this statement, it does explain the near invisibility of New Order in the second half of the film. New Order (debatably) gained a success far beyond what would have been possible with Curtis – and they entered popular memory because of their persistence and courage. On December 5, 2002, they released a four CD set titled *Retro*. The complexity, sweep and scale of their work and legacy are confirmed through this compilation. New Order is a band where the four members all think that they are the musical leader. The singing basslines of Peter Hook changed not only the complexity of fretwork on the instrument, but the skill, dexterity and strength of plectrum work over the pickups.[17] Hook's bass barks at the beat rather than fulfilling the conventional role of the rhythm section – of keeping it. Bernard Sumner plays intense and souring lead breaks[18] and complex rhythm guitar patterning. Gillian Gilbert's keyboards provide a gleaming path through dance tracks and Stephen Morris's drumming, with his pared down kit and reduced use of cymbals, creates a melodic rhythm, assisted by a digital delay.[19] Before the formation of New Order, it was obvious that Joy Division had only one leader.

Ian Curtis has become so singular and potent in popular memory through a combination of words and vision: Kevin Cummins' photographs and Paul Morley's journalism. A great but underestimated pop writer, certainly comparable to Hunter S. Thompson and Greil Marcus, Morley has written best on Joy Division.[20] In *24 Hour Party People*, the scene featuring Tony Wilson dragging Mick Middles into the viewing of Curtis's body actually happened to Paul Morley. Wilson's words over the body of Curtis were significant: "I want you to write the book … This is where your book should start. That is the musical equivalent of Che Guevara."[21] This viewing of Curtis went on to commence Morley's memoir, *Nothing*. He recorded that "I have only ever seen one dead body in my life."[22] Like the story of Factory, Paul Morley's life is also punctuated by death, the suicides of his father and Curtis and the later demise of Hannett and Gretton. Morley recognized that Gretton "died a relatively young man: perhaps he lived as long a life as the myth of the group demanded from its manager".[23] When the 'natural' order of life and death is disturbed, the volatility of popular memory fetishizes youthful mortality.

Ian Curtis has tragedy tethered to him, encasing all the conventional baggage of heterosexual masculine angst. He was in love with a woman who was not his wife, distanced from his child and suffered an illness – badly. Mick Middles believes that all these factors created an aura around Curtis on stage.

> Ian Curtis allowed his emotions, clouded and confused as they were, to channel into his performance – arguably, and rather disturbingly, the most intense performance of his career. Nervous glances were passed back and forth among the band, as Curtis's dance steps steadily quickened and the band's deep growl staggered to a number of false finishes, before the musicians, unable to stall things any further, finally crashed to a halt. Curtis was dancing still (it was an uneasy, unrhythmic and fairly chilling 30 seconds), by which time he had broken into an uncontrollable spin before crashing into Steve Morris's drum kit, knocking cymbals almost comically on to the floor. With the audience still clapping and blissfully unaware of the drama – Ian Curtis had suffered a fit before their very eyes – the band coldly, silently, carried Curtis from the stage.[24]

Joy Division produced frightening music and Curtis captured the fear. The jagged dancing, terror-filled eyes and melancholic intensity of the lyrics combined to cast a long shadow over Manchester music.[25] *24 Hour Party People* fed off this iconographic influence, from the epileptic little deaths to the grand mal of suicide. Curtis's death was stark amidst the youthful excesses of pop music. Jon Savage remembered that

It was the first time that many of us had had to encounter death: the result was a shock so profound that it has become an unresolved trauma, a rupture in Manchester's social history which has persisted through the city's worldwide promotion as Madchester, and through the continuing success of New Order.[26]

Joy Division's tragic narrative provides one appropriate 'origin' for the Manchester sound. All 'local' scenes or 'sounds' are frameworks that simplify the complexity of the music emerging from the city but does provide a brand name and marketing base.

After the death of Curtis, Manchester could export music as it had once exported textiles. It also became the site of "youth cultural tourism".[27] The Hacienda was a shrine for this journey. Opening in 1982 to little success, New Order and Tony Wilson showed extraordinary vision in their support for the club. A yachting warehouse was transformed into a musical arena and a centre for crime and controversy. In July 1989, Claire Leighton died in the queue outside the front of the club, after taking a tab of Ecstasy. The resultant Entertainments (Increased Penalties) Act of 1990 policed night life and received Margaret Thatcher's full support. With 19th century industries in lingering decline,[28] and the legislative targeting of proto-Creative Industries of Manchester, the Prime Minister confirmed the dominance of southern (and Conservative) sensibilities. In her 1979 cabinet, the majority were Oxbridge educated and none had studied at a provincial university. Through the 1980s, the cities that had been the foundation of the industrial revolution became the crumbled ruin of a post-industrial nation. In difficult times, places like Manchester offer the potential to challenge standards, limitations and boundaries. It was a place where even a Situationist slogan could be built with concrete, steel and glass.

Just no way of knowing[29]

Manchester is one of the birthplaces of the industrial revolution. The scale of inequality, poverty and progress changed labour patterns, the production of textiles and even understandings of time. The factory clock was invented in 1880 and with it the phrase 'clocking on.' Work transformed from task to time orientation, or the passage from toiling until a task is completed to working until stopped by a clock. Industrialization also scarred the landscape, with new towns, transportation systems and water and power stations. Manchester, so integral to theories of commerce, culture and politics, offers a stark reminder of the uneven nature of globalization. Frederick Engels recognized that the pain and anguish facing Manchester's working class was required to ensure the prosperity of the middle class. Manchester, in moving from the 'old' industries to the new creative industries of music, screen, design and tourism, is now in the business of marketing differences, rather than homogeneity.

Like wrinkles on a forehead, a city reveals its past. Manchester's derelict cotton mills are overwritten by the popular music that created a newer vision. These sounds and images – from Take That to 808 State, the Buzzcocks to Simply Red, the Smiths to M-People and New Order to the Happy Mondays – interlinked the histories of music and Manchester. It would be impossible to write of contemporary dance music without a sizeable chapter based in the north of England. The industrial past is part of this gritty present. As Bernard Sumner affirms,

> By the age of twenty-two, I had quite a lot of loss in my life. The place where I used to live, where I had my happiest memories, all that had gone. All that was left was a chemical factory. I realized then that I could never go back to that happiness. So there's this void. For me Joy Division was about the death of my community and my childhood.[30]

The two great escapes of working class men – into football or music – are both avenues of success and fame for Manchester. Music – like architecture – is the grammar of popular memory and a way to carry stories of past loss into the present.

There are few public discussions about place. Architecture journals and design magazines have cramped the imagination, deflecting consideration away from imaginary spaces. Manchester, like all named sites, is a label to frame and control abstract space, determining how people build a social and material identity. These "storied landscapes"[31] provide more than a filmic backdrop. Places are constituted as a multi-media library of shared memories. Such over-reading of difference creates a fragile sense of community. Redhead and Rietveld realized that "these days the history of culture – especially popular culture – tends to be written in terms of buildings and spaces rather than, as it once was, subcultural styles".[32] If the Hacienda was to be built, then Manchester offered it an appropriate (and appropriately transitory) home.

The Hacienda opened on May 21, 1982 at 11/13 Whitworth Street, West Manchester. Membership cards were created by the Factory design guru, Peter Saville, who went on to design a Hacienda model kit for members as a Christmas present in 1983. The Hacienda could be 'built' out of five A4 cardboard pieces, featuring a black and white banderole with the famous

Situationist slogan. This club became more than the physical architecture, but created a web of media images and cultures of consumption. Opening during a time of high youth unemployment, the Hacienda functioned in the space between leisure and work and legitimate and illegitimate pleasures. The limits of social control were patrolled and negotiated. Buildings such as this provide a record of how particular cities organize subjectivity, memory and identity.

There is little sadder than an empty dance floor. The first person to enter this space is rarely granted the heroic status they deserve. The man who – metaphorically – filled many dancefloors is a minor star of *24 Hour Party People*. Bez's role in the Happy Mondays has always been clouded. He supplied the drugs and played the maracas, but most significantly he invented a new way of dancing. His movements educated a generation of clubbers how to interpret – through the body – the changes to rhythm. Like Curtis, Bez's dancing created a new movement. Instead of Ian Curtis's swerves, jerks and fists, Bez jumped, lolled and strutted. Bez's background – of appalling schooling, dysfunctional family life, prison and unemployment – created an obvious inspiration to move beyond the poor, the delinquent and the irrelevant to a new type of work.

> The struggle to provide ourselves with the means to survive led whole armies of young lads like myself to take to the streets in search of the missing ingredients, an (sic) we found it in a happy marriage of music an (sic) drugs ... Everyone knows that if you party all night, the days take care of themselves ... You sleep to avoid the day an (sic) all its depressing reminders that you don't even belong to the category of working class.[33]

Bez is a remarkable cultural figure. He is one of the long-lasting images of the 'baggy' period of music particularly associated with the Hacienda. For Bez, drugs, dancing and music are work and structure his life. With dance steps inspired by Jalen from *Planet of the Apes*, he embodies a musical moment. Urban popular culture is raw: getting drunk, dancing like a corkscrew on active duty and staggering home. In Manchester, boredom and poverty create a necessity to live a life differently. By the late 1980s and moving along with Bez, the Hacienda's dance floor had become the centre of (post) youth culture.

Great dance genres have always needed a great club. Acid House had the Hacienda, providing the venue for soaring piano breaks and screaming divas. Since 1986, house music dominated Friday nights in the Club, DJ-ed by Martin Prendergast and Mike Pickering, creating a distinct musical (and sociological) space from the Gay Traitor bar.

Through much of the early unsuccessful history of the club, it was a venue for live bands. The dance floor became the basis of its fame, altering the grammar of making, playing and dancing to music. Dave Haslam – the DJ who made his reputation at the Hacienda's decks – remembers that from 1988-90, "everybody danced; on the stairs, on the stage, on the balcony and at the bar. They danced in the cloakroom queue".[34] These spaces in the dancing imagination changed allegiances of identity and challenged belonging structures to a city, nation or genre. As a docu-drama, *24 Hour Party People*, like *Bloody Sunday* released in the same year, explored the potential of hybridity in form and frame.[35]

This tale of Manchester captures a narrative arc from the industrial to post-industrial and from textile to creative industries. No longer marked by the act of making and building, marketing and public relations are potent economic strategies. Music and design are the currency of the early twenty-first century, just as cotton and coal were the foundation of the nineteenth. *24 Hour Party People* is a catalogue of the people, events and ideas that created this new economy and the new Manchester. Not surprisingly, it features the mythic Sex Pistols gig at the Lesser Free Trade Hall on June 4, 1976, where a tiny audience witnessed a moment of social change.

> 4 June 1976. The Sex Pistols play Manchester for the very first time. There are only forty-two people in the audience but they are all dazed, in shock and absorbing the energy on which they are all starting to feed; on power, on energy and magic. Inspired, they will go forth and perform wondrous deeds.[36]

At the performance were Steven Morrissey, Peter Hook, Bernard Sumner, Howard Devoto and Tony Wilson. Significantly, Jon the Postman was also present and then featured throughout the early stages of the film. From 1972-1980, he was famous for jumping on stage at the end of gigs to sing Louie Louie. Jon the Postman has a place in the film, as do many other significant figures, rhythms, songs and dance movements.

24 Hour Party People is an intensely stylish and fashionable film. It is able to present a design(er) history of Manchester, while also actively creating a popular memory of music, clothes, people and places. The producers literally (and appropriately) rebuilt the Hacienda dance floor as a film set, while concurrently creating a comedy that broadens the limits of humour, taste and comfort. That critics disliked it so much – and fans adored it in similar quantities – requires some explanation.

Renaissance Florence

Wilson: What's wrong with London Records?

Gretton: Well, the name for a start.[37]

Films occupy semiotic space and at their best lash out to occupy political space. *24 Hour Party People* is important because it raises questions about who owns the past and which memories survive. Directed by Michael Winterbottom and written by Frank Cottrell Boyce, it was released in 2002. Winterbottom is known for extending filmic languages through such films as *Jude, Welcome to Sarajevo* and *9 Songs*. Through *24 Hour Party People*, he has been able to mix Spinal Tap with authentic 'rock' documentaries, while blurring the division between film and television, tragedy and comedy, club and industrial aesthetics. The film focuses on Tony Wilson, who gave the Sex Pistols a television debut and also created Factory Records and the Hacienda. He has the singular distinction of having changed popular music twice: through Joy Division and then the Happy Mondays. The film not only captures these seismic innovations, but extends them. This is, put simply, a film that changes film making. It melts the fourth wall of cinema, cuts up narrative time, corrodes the delineation between sound and vision and provides the strongest application of Cultural Studies theories and ideas on the screen.

This film is self aware. Perhaps this explains my commitment, fascination and belief in it. The economic, social and political structures have changed so much in the last twenty years that we can no longer appreciate or read films in the same way as taught in the old film theory textbooks, which have been through too many reprints and not enough revisions. Yet these old strategies and prejudices of viewing and thinking remain. One reviewer wanted a 'straight' realist presentation of 'the Manchester scene:'

> What the filmmakers fail to understand is that making a based-in-truth film and being self-aware inherently work against each other ... the best movies based on any sort of real-life events/people make us forget we're watching a movie by accurately recreating and sucking us into what feels just like, well, real-life.[38]

This reviewer offers an odd argument. Obviously all films – including documentaries – never present a truth. They are highly edited, mediated representational matrix. From the grainy celluloid of punk gigs to the black and white shades of foreboding that capture Joy Division through to the sharp and stark images of the Hacienda, a realist discourse is subverted. This form is meant to problematize the content. There is honesty in Winterbottom's inauthenticity. He offers a continual reminder that this film is just a film, offering a guidebook to interpret other cinematic visions that take themselves too seriously. Fans of the film who reviewed it for Amazon.com, believed that the direct address to the camera gave the events of the film the feel of reportage.

> The actual style of the editing is more than worth mentioning also, because along with Steve Coogans (sic) occasional comment to the camera, you sometimes feel you to (sic) experience the events as they unfolded for the people involved – it had me glued to the screen.[39]

Winterbottom is one of the most interesting young directors working in the industry, with an astounding imagination and creative vision. To refer to *24 Hour Party People* as "Cult Movie Central"[40] is an attempt to crush its more wide-ranging influence and challenges to narrative structures. Other critics have referred to it as being "a little too clever for its own good".[41] The problem is not the film: the difficulty is that cleverness – in film, music, politics or critical writing – is not valued in our mediocre, dull era.

Two of my favourite reviews – that are radiant in their silliness – are, to quote Coogan/Wilson, "just wrong".[42] They are funny (peculiar *and* ha ha), demonstrating why there are far more good films than reviewers. The first extraordinary review from Ian Birnie could not be more inaccurate and embarrassing if he had called his aunt an uncle.

> Shorn of the usual moralizing and melodrama, this wildly entertaining look back at the Birmingham punk scene trades in verbal wit, inventive editing, and quirky characters.[43]

I hope that film reviewing is not Birnie's day job. At least he may have another career to fall back on, after attempting to write about a film without seeing it. My hope is that he actually never viewed it. If a critic confuses Birmingham for Manchester and punk for rave, *after* having watched *24 Hour Party People*, then I worry about the accuracy of the supposedly smart bombs. The smart critics leave a lot to be desired. Even worse is Thomas Doherty's review for *Cineaste*. After citing the innovative opening of the film and the mention of Icarus, he worries about the references and humour utilized throughout the dialogue.

> Actually, rather than in ancient Greek myth, the viewer, or at least the American viewer, may require orientation, plus the occasional subtitle, in the argot of late twentieth-century British pop. Though a storied tale in the U.K., the glory that was

musical Manchester and the glibness that was Tony Wilson is little known outside the stateside college radio demographic.[44]

The reduction of all audiences into an American national base is stark in its confidence and rationale. Obviously, it is difficult for Doherty to grasp that maybe – just maybe – not all viewers are American. If he has difficulty with the Manchester accent and requires subtitles, then perhaps he should go on the fully anthropological journey to the deepest, darkest north of England: enter cinematic Newcastle and watch *Purely Belter*.[45] The notion that he may *not* be a target market is outside Doherty's thoughts. Those of us who are not derived from either side of the Atlantic find this mode of review arrogant in the extreme. Being a New Zealander, Singaporean, Malaysian or Australian, for example, means that translation and decoding is always required when confronted by a Hollywood-styled or British-derived film. American narratives do not naturally slot into other environments, but require work from the viewer. Winterbottom's film is a reminder that there are many histories, origins and orientations outside of Sun Records and the Fred Astaire musical.

Generations of American film critics have a box in which to insert 'British film,' invoking historical drama, crinoline and crisp Bee-bee-see accents. *24 Hour Party People* provoked the greatest distinction between British fans and American critics that I have seen in response to a film. During an era when anti-Americanism is a weapon of critical destruction, U.S. writers attacked this remarkable cinematic innovator as featuring "thick accents, anonymous bands and blurred identifiers".[46] Ignorance – instead of being an embarrassing attribute to hide from (re)view – is celebrated and an excuse for abuse. If a writer does not know this music, if the writer cannot interpret accents other than American and if visual literacy in important popular culture is lacking, then they should find another hobby and leave film reviewing to others. The McDonaldization of film and film reviewing has shut down spaces for innovative iconic representations and risk-taking cultural inscriptions. For *24 Hour Party People*, London is irrelevant, let alone New York or Los Angeles.

It is rare to release a film about a local scene. It can seldom find financial backing, a distribution mechanism or an audience. In such an environment, encouraging oppositional activity is difficult. The notion that Hollywood film and music history is the Esperanto of and for the world needs to be attacked and often. *24 Hour Party People* should be applauded because it stands for difference. It triggers a reminder that popular memories are locally inflected and are influential beyond a town or a city. One film reviewer believed that "much of this will seem like *Inside Baseball* to folks who don't know Manchester from Liverpool, or who cant (sic) tell the difference between Joy

Division and Durutti Column … For pop mavens, however, it's great, geeky fun – a little slice of heaven".[47]   Comparing a British film to an American sport whose 'World' Series features teams from only one country is probably appropriate for this writer, but not for others. The great difficulty faced by film reviewers has been an inability to grasp the specificity of dance music in the period from Acid house to rave. The point is that this scene and the music within it, disengaged from 'rock.' Dance music – while currently featuring multiple hybrids with varied guitar-based genres – had a distinct trajectory in the late 1980s and early 1990s where it dominated popular music and rendered ridiculous the excessively authenticating nonsense of U2, Bruce Springsteen and Bon Jovi. It was a distinct culture. This was a 'world' where the death of Kurt Cobain did not matter. Named bands and identifiable singers were lost. Instead of capturing these remarkable differences, Green found a different moral from the film.

> I couldn't help but reflect at the current state of rock'n'roll after the picture ended. One of the things that changed in the twenty-odd years that are covered in *24 Hour Party People* is the increasingly ruthless efficacy of advertizers … Personal attachment to a particular group happens in the headphones, often late at night, in reflective moods and with the illusion that the band is addressing you. That illusion is lost when a rock group is sponsored by Budweiser.[48]

Winterbottom's film has no connection with this debate. If Green wished to discuss commercialization and music, he would have been better pondering the punk aesthetic that frames the film, or the Situationist slogans that dominate the design and directives of Factory. Joy Division, New Order and the Happy Mondays are tangentially (at very best) linked to Budweiser rock and roll. Because the film is 'about' the past, Green has assumed that it must be nostalgic. He has then injected his desire for a simpler, DIY rock into the review and grafted it against current commercialism. The film is unfettered by this issue. The desire to willingly erase dance memory and to incorporate Factory's story into the rock discourse is damaging to the texture and complexity of the past. Doherty wonders why "such terrific music should remain so coldly detached from the warm heart of rock and roll".[49] The old binaries of rock and pop, guitars and dance, independent and corporate, slice through such statements. These divisions were not a problem for Factory, Wilson or the film. While sprouting Situationist slogans, Coogan's Tony Wilson never relinquishes his employment at Granada Television. In other words, he waits for the revolution while keeping his options open in the capitalist media. Wilson is not nostalgic for the past. If he was, then Factory would have died with Ian Curtis. It continued for over a decade.

There are always unwanted parts of popular memory. Films such as *24 Hour Party People* confirm that Hollywood tropes and accents for film making can be translated and challenged in local conditions. In the intersection of identity, politics and culture, alternatives can be created. The film industry is not a Fordist formation of mass production and consumption. Instead, new aspects of a social life are being commodified, instigating a greater differentiation of purchasing patterns by different audiences. The use of diverse accents, colours, fashions, sounds and cities is a productive cultural act.

Popular music films are filled with myths and legends. It is impossible to write the truth of Factory Records or the Hacienda. Shaun Ryder, Bez, Rob Gretton, Martin Hannett and Ian Curtis could all have been featured in their own film, each providing a distinct interpretation. But Wilson is an effective core. Such an intricate tragi-comedy could never be structured in a linear way. Jason Parkes suggested it is "a fun post-modern take on history".[50] The film owed little to history: it was a popular memory palette of potentials. For *24 Hour Party People*, with Coogan/Wilson speaking to the camera as in a television news bulletin, narrative time is criss-crossed and sampled. Plot points are circular, such as the early reference to Martin Hannett: "he will later try to kill me."[51] Similarly, the film is peppered by 'real' men and women mentioned in a fictional context. These 'characters' merge into the mockumentary – which is the point. Coogan/Wilson, for example, constructs a revenge narrative where his first wife has sex with Howard Devoto. The 'real' Devoto then spoke to camera, stating "I really don't remember this happening."[52] The myth was printed. In the film though, *both* the myth and its critique survived.

Appropriately, *24 Hour Party People* is multi-modal: a book, screenplay, film, DVD[53] and soundtrack. These cultural artefacts were not created in the accustomed order. Tony Wilson's book was actually produced after – and derived from – the screenplay. Wilson used Coogan's lines and asides and followed the structure of the film. The book even featured stills from the set that mingled with 'real' images of Wilson's television career, family and history. Tony Wilson is simply made more interesting through the eyes and body of Steve Coogan. He is a deft comic and ideal for the unreliable narrator role of the film. After one scene, he reports

I know you have no idea what the hell is going on right now, but by the way I got married to this woman and we had kids and I wasn't a very good father. None of that matters though, because I'm just a minor character – this movie's about the music.[54]

This is provocatively ironic. The film is obviously about Wilson and he is intoxicatingly attractive in his compulsions, failings and weaknesses. His marriages and career in Granada are the fodder for Coogan's monologues to the camera. Tony Wilson as a reporter was a regular feature of television in the north west of England in the late 1970s. His music programme *So it goes* was able to recognize and present the punk explosion as it was happening. Wilson's diversity of television roles also granted him a profile for a larger project – Factory. As Matthew Higgs realized, "Wilson and company ran Factory Records like an avant-garde art movement: with its groundbreaking graphic design and cryptic references to the Situationist International, it would forever change the landscape for independent labels."[55] Appropriately, fact and fiction danced. Archival footage of the Sex Pistols is cut against the film's characters. News events, such as the rise of the National Front, are balanced against the ambivalent success of Joy Division. Also altered is the link between image and music. The soundtrack is able to be far more than a sales device for the film. It is the foundation, core, plot and language. It is not 'background' or incidental to the events or scenes. Clifford described it as the "most original of movies".[56] It claims an ironic, postmodern originality through its form as much as content. Just as the Hacienda changed the music in the mix, so did this film change the mix of sound and vision.

There are problems with *24 Hour Party People*, but these reveal the difficulties in aligning popular memory, localism and cinema. The absence of the Stone Roses – arguably more famous and influential than the Happy Mondays – The Smiths and New Order in the film does create an oddly shaped narrative. It is Tony Wilson and Factory's story. The film fans out from the groups and histories of the company, not those bands outside of it. Great moments emerge from these absences. At the end of the film 'God' – who looks just like Tony Wilson – berates him for not signing The Smiths. These absences can be forgiven for the act of rebuilding the Hacienda once more.

Club films are difficult to shoot. Through outstanding editing and the innovative use of hand-held cameras, *24 Hour Party People* was able to show the dynamism of dancers through long shots, while also entering the crowd by allowing Tony Wilson's monologues to emerge from close-ups of the dance floor. This editing displayed a remarkable confluence of form and content. Ignoring this subtlety, the 'Movie Chicks' attacked the club-focus of the film.

There are too many shots of the nightclub scene with nothing happening but people bouncing around. After a while, the movie starts to feel long and gets more than a little tedious.[57]

Upon reviewing the film after reading this analysis, it is clear that each club scene has a purpose, whether to introduce the birth of rave culture, the role of the DJ, the spaces of the Hacienda, the place of ecstasy or the scale of violence. In other words, there is no connection with this review and the film under discussion. Also, the editing of *24 Hour Party People* is extremely tight: every scene is tightly enmeshed with what comes before and after. Clifford described its structure best: "Winterbottom's film is an exuberant mess which is, in actuality, brilliantly put together. It's a heady rush that defies its audience to keep pace."[58] Importantly too, all the elements of the film come together in the final club scene, where the major players in Tony Wilson's life return to life on the Hacienda's final night. Curtis, Hannett and Gretton all circulate in the crowd, along with Wilson's former wife. The Hacienda transcends life and death, to become a venue for popular memory.

The second act

F. Scott Fitzgerald has this thing about how American lives only have a first act. No comeback stuff. But this is Manchester. We do things differently here. We have second acts. This is the second act.[59]

Tony Wilson

Post-postmodernism, authentic film realism would never be the same or, indeed, what it used to be. The music scene presented through the eyes of Tony Wilson created 'the long 1980s,' from punk in 1976 to the closing of the Hacienda in 1992. The story starts in 1976 with his Granada 'report' of hang-gliding off the Pennines. Breaking away from the temporal landscape of 1976, he then addresses the contemporary filmic audience acknowledging that "obviously it is symbolic – it operates on two levels. I'll just say Icarus".[60] Similarly, Wilson continually asked "Have you never heard of Situationism or postmodernism?"[61] Few film critics hold knowledge of this scale. They really did need to read more.

Coogan's Wilson pontificates near the end that "we are not a record label. We are an experiment in human nature".[62] Similarly, the film is a semiotic laboratory to test the tensile strength of cinematic genre. Cultural Studies theorists have a lesson in media and politics through *24 Hour Party People*. The

157

honest inauthenticity forms a space for questioning the role and place of knowledge and memory in film. There are historical moments where change does not seem possible, where beige blocks the red colours of resistance and difference. Winterbottom's film was released in an era where Blair staggered through a second term, bereft of fresh ideas and Bush defied the United Nations to summon the oddly named Coalition of the Willing (COW). In such a context, creativity and imagination matter. *24 Hour Party People* does not laugh at death. Instead, it laughs at the living.

Notes

1   New Order, "Here to Stay", words and music by B. Sumner, P. Hook, S. Morris and G. Gilbert, *24 Hour Party People* (London Records, 2002), track 17.

2   P. Carroll, *Keeping time: memory, nostalgia, and the art of history* (Athens: University of Georgia Press, 1990), p. 191.

3   T. Wilson, *24 Hour Party People: What the sleeve notes never tell you* (London: Macmillan, 2002), p. 32.

4   Robert Berkhofer stated that "because of their preference for reference over representation, historians possess few and very limited ways of discussing the discursive aspects of the histories they produce", from *Beyond the great story: history as text and discourse* (Cambridge: Harvard University Press, 1995), p. 76.

5   D. Hickey, *Air guitar* (Los Angeles: Art Issues Press, 1997), p. 15.

6   Scientific discourse remains the exception, with experiential experimentation required to verify a hypothesis. For the humanities, culture is frequently severed from the experiential passion and preoccupations of the present.

7   H. White explored the consequences of some events being locked away from the relativity of interpretations in K. Jenkins (ed.), *The postmodern history reader* (London: Routledge, 1997).

8   G. Marcus, *The dustbin of history* (Cambridge: Harvard University Press, 1995), p. 20.

9   M. Pini, "Women and the early British rave scene", in A. McRobbie (ed.), *Back to reality* (Manchester: Manchester University Press, 1997), p. 153. For a full discussion of Pini's reinscription of women in dance culture, please refer to M. Pini, *Club Cultures and Female Subjectivity* (London: Palgrave, 2001).

10   P. Morley, *Nothing* (London: Faber and Faber, 2000), p. 238.

11   B. Sumner, from M. Middles, *From Joy Division to New Order* (London: Virgin, 2002), p. 151.

12   A. Blaikie, *Ageing and popular culture* (Cambridge: Cambridge University Press, 1999), p. 86.

13   *24 Hour Party People* (Revolution Films/Film Consortium, 2002).

14   S. Morris, *The Madchester Scene* (Harpenden: Pocket Essentials, 2002), p. 31.

15   J. Green, "24 Hour Party People", *Film Dissent*, http://www.filmdissent.com/fd_24hourpartypeople.htm, accessed on January 12, 2003.

16 "24 Hour Party People", *Deep Focus*, http://www.deep-focus.com/flicker/24hourpa.html, accessed on January 12, 2003.

17 For example, please refer to the 'lead' bass line in "The Perfect Kiss", from New Order's *Retro* (London Records, 2002), disc four, track eight.

18 An example of the use of 'lead' rhythm guitar is New Order's "Temptation". A version of this song is included on *Retro*, disc one, track two.

19 The use of digital delay on Morris's drum pattern was one of the remarkable innovations in Martin Hannett's production on *Unknown Pleasures* (Factory Records, 1979). His interest in echo and digital delay – and his belief that the drums are the basis of all recordings – created the distinctive drum line and sound of Joy Division's albums.

20 Paul Morley stated that "Joy Division are, in my order of things, which is pretty correct all things considered, the dead centre of the rock universe", from P. Morley, *Nothing* (London: Faber and Faber, 2000).

21 Tony Wilson, *24 Hour Party People*.

22 Morley, *Nothing*, p. 7.

23 *ibid.*, p. 40.

24 M. Middles, *From Joy Division to New Order* (London: Virgin, 2002), p. 141.

25 Mick Middles described Joy Division's last album – *Closer* – as "the record was simply the darkest thing you could own; a close friend perhaps, who understood your deepest moods, your most profound fears. And it was terrifying too", *From Joy Division to New Order*, p. 156.

26 J. Savage, "Foreword", from D. Curtis, *Touching from a distance: Ian Curtis and Joy Division* (London: Faber and Faber, 1995), p. xii.

27 S. Redhead, "The end of the end-of-the-century party", from S. Redhead, *Rave off: politics and deviance in contemporary youth culture* (Aldershot: Ashgate Publishing Limited, 1993), p. 1.

28 The case for this decline is clearly made in post-war Liverpool, where an overdependence on the port for business and employment left the city vulnerable with a skewed economy that lacked a viable manufactory sector and a shortage of skilled labour. John Morton described the city as "in the public consciousness, Liverpool was transformed from the capital of the Sixties to the nightmare of the Eighties", from *Two Tales of One City: A Media Iconography of Liverpool, 1963-1985*, Masters of Philosophy, University of Birmingham, 1986, pp. 182-3.

29 New Order, "True Faith", words and music by B. Sumner, P. Hook, S. Morris, G. Gilbert, S. Hague, *Retro* (London: London Records, 2002), disc one, track three.

30 B. Sumner, from D. Haslam, *Manchester England: the story of the pop cult city* (London: Fourth Estate, 2000: 1999), p. xxiv.

31 B. Osborne, "Landscapes, memory, monuments, and commemorations: putting identity in its place", *Canadian Ethnic Studies*, Vol. 33, No. 3, 2001, p. 49.

32 S. Redhead and H. Rietveld, "Down the club", from J. Savage (ed.), *The Hacienda must be built!* (Woodford Green: International Music Publications, 1992), p. 72.

33 Bez, *Freaky Dancin': Me and the Mondays* (London: Pan, 2000), pp. ix-x.

34 D. Haslam, "DJ Culture", from S. Redhead (ed.), *The Clubcultures Reader* (Oxford: Blackwell, 1997), p. 175.

35 James Parker recognizes the role of the film in revaluing hybrid genres. Please refer to "And the winner is…", *The American Prospect*, January 13, 2003, p. 32.

36 T. Wilson, *24 Hour Party People: What the sleeve notes never tell you* (London: Macmillan, 2002), p. 24.

37 Tony Wilson and Rob Gretton, *24 Hour Party People.*

38 "*24 Hour Party People*", http://www.taredsapolin.com/24hourpartypeople.htm, accessed on January 12, 2003.

39 M. Daly, "Highly enjoyable historical comedy", [17 September 2002], Amazon.co.uk, http://www.amazon.co.uk/exec/obidos/ASIN/B000063W10/026-6273079-8035620, accessed February 9, 2003.

40 T. Merrill, "24 Hour Party People", http://www.filmthreat.com/Reviews.asp?ld=3331, [August 8, 2002], accessed on January 12, 2003.

41 "24 Hour Party People", http://pages.prodigy.net/zvelf/24_hour_party_people.htm, [August 17, 2002], accessed on January 12, 2003.

42 Tony Wilson, *24 Hour Party People.*

43 I. Birnie, "Best of 2002 film", *Artforum*, December 2002, p. 27.

44 T. Doherty, "24 Hour Party People", *Cineaste*, Winter, 2002, pp. 35-6.

45 *Purely Belter* (Film Four, 2000).

46 Mongoose, "24 Hour Party People", http;//www.haro-online.com/movies/24hour_party_people.html, accessed on January 12, 2003.

47 "24 Hour Party People", *Deep Focus*, http://www.deep-focus.com/flicker/24hourpa.html, accessed on January 12, 2003.

48 J. Green, "24 Hour Party People", *Film Dissent*, http://www.filmdissent.com/fd_24hourpartypeople.htm, accessed on January 12, 2003.

49 Doherty, p. 37.

50 J. Parkes, "OK film on the Factory story", [January 11, 2003], http://www.amazon.co.uk/exec/obidos/ASIN/B000063W10/026-6273079-8035620, accessed February 9, 2003.

51 Tony Wilson, *24 Hour Party People.*

52 Howard Devoto, *ibid.*

53 The *24 Hour Party People* DVD is – itself – a remarkable cultural object, also extending the medium. A two-disc set, it features interviews with Peter Saville and an interview with Steve Coogan and Tony Wilson. The lines between fact and fiction, documentary and drama, continue to merge through this package. As Dade Hayes recognized, "Wilson on the commentary track exhibits all of the self-involved-yet-self-deprecating charm of the screen version. He's like the party guest being imitated by a gifted mimic; the more he complains

about the inaccuracies of the imitation, the more accurate the imitation is proven to be", from "Reveler's tale blends beat and street", *Variety*, February 17-22, 2003, p. 47.

54 Tony Wilson, *24 Hour Party People*.

55 M. Higgs, "Rants and Raves", *Artforum*, 2002, p. 36.

56 L. Clifford, "24 hour Party People", *Reeling Reviews*,
    http://reelingreviews.com/24hourpartypeople.htm, accessed on January 12, 2003.

57 Movie Chicks, "24 Hour Party People", http://www.themoviechicks.com/aug2002/mcr24hourparty.html,
    accessed on January 12, 2003.

58 Clifford, *op. cit.*

59 Tony Wilson, *24 Hour Party People*, p. 138. The original statement was derived from the
    incomplete notes of F. Scott Fitzgerald's *The Last Tycoon* (Harmondsworth: Penguin, 1960).
    The statement was, "there are no second acts in American lives", p. 196.

60 Tony Wilson, *24 Hour Party People*.

61 *ibid.*

62 *ibid.*

Chapter eight

Looking through rouge coloured glasses

Christian: Was it an act?
Satine: Of course
Christian: It just felt real.[1]

There is a brilliance to *Moulin Rouge*. Whether this innovation is marked through the dense humour of Kylie Minogue's performance as the absinthe fairy, Nicole Kidman's startling close-ups or Ewan McGregor's emergence as a remarkable leading man, this film – like *24 Hour Party People* – occupies a significant place in the history of the medium. From such cinematic risk taking, critical commentary was mixed. Even *Time*'s critics were split: Richard Corliss voted it in his top three films, while Richard Schickel termed *Moulin Rouge* the worst movie of the year.[2] At Cannes, *Moulin Rouge* did not win any prizes. Scarlet Cheng described this as "an oversight on the jury's part".[3] She appreciated the daring mobilization of popular music, the performance of the two leads and their capacity to sing evocatively and appropriately. The Golden Globes was a more rewarding venue, claiming three awards including best musical or comedy, best original score and best musical actress for Nicole Kidman. Academy Awards were won for costuming. But it was no Lethal Weaponesque blockbuster. Instead, it is a metamovie and talisman: the Dead Sea Scrolls of cinema.

Musicals are pivotal to the history of film. They enact and perform the fashions, desires and disappointments of the era more than dramas, comedies and westerns. As Vincent Porter realized upon the release of the earlier *Moulin Rouge*, produced and directed by John Huston in 1953, "when the Conservatives came to power, austerity started to wane and the need for cross-class fantasies became less pronounced and the successful musicals started to address the values of the new cultural order".[4] With the United States and Australia in the midst of conservative governments and Britain surviving a New Labour third way, *Moulin Rouge* verified Porter's claim.

Musicals soak in politics, sing the dissatisfactions and kick and tap over the cultural paradoxes. Different contexts and styles in the genre are seen in the 1972 release of *Cabaret*, where the musical orchestrations were basic, the band played poorly and the dancers were intentionally dressed in ripped pantyhose, featuring poorly applied make-up and underarm hair on full view. *Cabaret*'s cinematography was stretched out – through the recurrent distorting mirrors – and appeared drugged out. The dancers were filmed at odd angles, creating distinction from the clean long shots and minimal editing cuts customary with Fred Astaire's dance routines. Linda Brengle recognized that "after the murders of Martin Luther King and Bobby Kennedy, after the dissension of the Vietnam War, film audiences were ready for a darker kind of decadence".[5] Musicals – because of their excess – marinate in myriad contextual references. The ambiguous interweaving of aural and visual codes – of sound and vision – grants an expansive vista. *Moulin Rouge* allowed the survival and revival of the genre: without this film, there would have been no *Chicago* and certainly a less willing audience to give it applause.

Moulin Rouge – like every nightclub – is all mise en scene. Every surface is saturated with sparkling jewels, gaudy fabric and puckered lighting. This chapter deploys (only) three visual and ideological grenades lobbed from this remarkable film. By investigating place, time and memory, *Moulin Rouge* is shown to initiate a new visual database and a profoundly appropriate application of visual literacy and popular memory. All the strategies and theories mobilized in *From Revolution to Revelation* swirl through the colours and fabrics of *Moulin Rouge*.

Place

> A night club, a dance hall and a bordello.[6]
>
> Christian

Surprisingly – but perhaps not – the worst review of *Moulin Rouge* came from the home of tea-bag weak Blairism, the *New Statesman*. Philip Kerr maintains the history of supercilious English reviews of the Australian film industry. Devaluing the text as a slightly advanced Barry MacKenzie with a soundtrack, the narrative was described as "a Scotsman on the make meets a tart with a heart and the two fall in love".[7] The colonization of Australia continues through filmic criticism, with Kerr attacking the operatic framework as being caused "because Luhrmann has doubtless seen the reduced Puccini version of La Boheme".[8] To attack the film as a 'reduced Puccini', or the *Reader's Digest* condensed version, is arrogant in any circumstance, but betrays the reviewer's ignorance that Luhrmann has actually directed *La Boheme* for the stage. In other words, Luhrmann has a detailed, directorial relationship with the opera, rather than sampled knowledge of a few arias. The desire to attack Luhrmann as a Dame Edna with a walkman fetish is matched by his ridicule and dismissal of Nicole Kidman.

> A film I can recommend only to those who have an interest in celebrity dentistry, as it affords many cavernous shots of the mouths and back molars of Nicole Kidman … Having seen her take a pee in *Eyes Wide Shut*, I feel I now need only watch her shave her legs, or blow her unimpeachable retrousse nose to know what it might be like to be married to this antipodean angel.[9]

This is wish fulfilment on Kerr's part. The colonial cringe is clear. Baz Luhrmann's great advantage was to cast and capture Nicole Kidman at her most radiant and beautiful. The closest parallel is the cinematography mobilized by Joshua Logan for Marilyn Monroe in *Bus Stop*. The extreme close-up technique, where part of her leading man's – Don Murray – face is obscured and Monroe's face is cropped by the camera, initiates a disturbing intimacy, an intensely feminine space. The attack on this framing strategy was also found in Barbara Ellen's review of *Moulin Rouge* in *The Times*.

> The aural effect is that of a belligerent drunk with an eclectic musical taste and a lot of spare change hogging the jukebox in a Milton Keynes pub on a crowded Sunday lunchtime.[10]

From right and left, from broadsheet to political magazine, English reviewers demeaned the film for its excess and gaudy style. The film is tacky, flashy, crass and loud – basically an English stereotypical rendering of an obnoxious Australian in a London pub. The film, like the archetypal Aussie, is "uncorseted by good taste".[11]

English reviewers are correct in situating *Moulin Rouge* in a tradition of Australian cinema. It conveys a movement away from fetishized outback panoramas and dramas set in the colonial period. While *Proof, Strictly Ballroom, Romper Stomper* and *The Big Steal* transferred the filmic frame into the contemporary, urban environment, *Moulin Rouge* registered an unexpected vectoral shift.

In 1983, Ross Gibson suggested that the post-1970s wave of Australian films "have been about landscape".[12] Gibson's article, which changed the way in which national visuality is considered, is now twenty years old. The divided critical and popular response to *Moulin Rouge* clears the way for an opportunity to rethink national cinematic imaginings and recognize that the passive, timeless and unchanging Australian landscape is the most lavish drag queen of all. By mobilizing the genre of Hollywood musical, *Moulin Rouge* adds spice to debates about Australian content. The task of promoting national identity shifts from the text and towards the reader. As a popular film, *Moulin Rouge* transgresses the ideological and critical demarcations of cultural space. It holds much similarity with *Babe* in this regard. In the earlier case another *New Statesman* critic deflected the Australianness of this film, believing that the Hoggett's farm was situated in Kent.[13] Romney stated that

> *Babe* is set in idyllic countryside, a hyper-kitsch imagining of Enid Blyton England, all rolling hedgerows and skies candy-coloured in orange and yellow.[14]

At such a statement, Mick Dundee would weep into his beer. The review does demonstrate the malleability of the Australian landscape. Silence the broad accent[15] and deflect the camera from Uluru or Bondi and the most adventurous of reviewers can discover the Famous Five darting amid the hedgerows.

Clear obstacles face any non-American national film industry. During its moments of 'revival', Australian cinema has been reflexively (and at times embarrassingly) nationalist. Working against British codes of behaviour, Australian films like *The Adventures of Barry MacKenzie* and *Gallipoli* assembled a unified national ideology, rather than a contradictory amalgam of differences and memories. What makes *Moulin Rouge* different in Australian cinema is the intensely feminine visuality that punctuates the cinematic frame. This is an important shift as the bloke, whether Breaker Morant or Mick Dundee, has been the metonymy for the nation. Only as the industry entered the 'quirky' phase did *Proof* signal the timely arrival of a new iconographic database. Featuring the story of a blind photographer who, in proto-*X Files* fashion, trusts no one, it was made in 1991. The story was based around the Hugo Weaving character, Martin, who is so distrusting of people that he takes photographs to confirm that 'the world' exists. The only problem with this proof is that he needs to find a trusted narrator to explain the photographs and thereby confirm Martin's perceptions. The film verified that Australian cinema could ask complex emotional questions and enact black humour. Similarly *Strictly Ballroom* needs to be reclaimed as one of the most significant films to be made and released in Australia. Featuring an urban, cosmopolitan life, it freely blended pseudo-documentaries and 1950s Hollywood musicals.[16] It performed a critical, rather than celebratory, Australian multiculturalism through a conflictual and consensual blending of Anglo and Spanish cultures. Australian masculinity was further reinscribed and critiqued through *Muriel's Wedding* and *Priscilla: Queen of the Desert*. Muriel's pathetic longing to marry *anyone* and remake herself into a different person positions the film as politically significant. *Priscilla*, too, reshaped masculine ideologies and transformed national narratives.

What actually makes any of these films Australian is an elusive question. With Australian cinema framed as an 'other' to Hollywood releases, internal divisions between the 'local product' seem arbitrary and meaningless. Phillip Adams stated that "our best films are, I reckon, our most culturally specific, the ones that don't attempt to integrate themselves with an audience in Los Angeles or, for that matter, at Cannes".[17] Popular culture transgresses the boundaries of a nation, particularly when networked through electronic transfers of information. Yet debates about Australian culture and content are conducted at a national level. This policy discourse ties local, regional, subcultural, ethnic, indigenous and experimental cultures to the fate of the nation state. It is a defensive framework that evaluates the Australian film industry through the 'accuracy' by which it produces an effective image of the nation and its people/audience. By Adams' evaluation, *Moulin Rouge* is not successful within a national industry. The desire for films to offer an Australian advertizing campaign for world consumption shows an inadequate framing of complex, fluent culture. This form of popular imaging can be socially damaging, narrow and oppressive. Making films national is a complex process of semiotic reclamation. As McKenzie Wark suggested in his assessment of *The Piano*,

> But was this an 'Australian' film? The answer is less interesting than what the question reveals; a New Zealand location, American principal cast, Australian development money, a French co-production with a major American distribution deal. This is 'Australian' cinema in the 1990s; a blend of the local and the international, the subsidized and the market-driven − a set of contradictions that have to be resolved.[18]

It is no coincidence that *Lord of the Rings: The Fellowship of the Ring* was released in the same year as *Moulin Rouge*. Both have a similar relationship with their Antipodal host. New Zealand's diverse and gothic landscape is morphed into Middle Earth, while Fox Studios in Sydney encloses the sets to summon fin de siecle Paris. There is a reason for this parallel production success of the trans-Tasman neighbours. Tony Safford, Vice President of Acquisitions at Miramax Films, has stated that "our ease with Australian cinema ... is knowing that it will be at once familiar (in language and culture) and unique (in character and setting)".[19] Both *Moulin Rouge* and *The Fellowship of the Ring* are placed in this quirky – that is, familiar but comfortably different – niche.

The sheer difference, excess and scale of *Moulin Rouge* is actually a product of Australian cinematic history in the last ten years. As Neil Rattigan has suggested, "Australia has a long history of cultural schizophrenia regarding its national image."[20] *Mad Max* and *Priscilla: Queen of the Desert* imported the American genre of a road movie and re-placed it over the Australian landscape. This form of generic movement transforms the films into sites for semiotic tourism, with little commitment to the ideologies, contradictions and problems of contemporary Australia. The movement from a frontier discourse to touristic consumption is not an apolitical journey.

The land is the primary determinant of nation building. Both *Sunday Too Far Away* and *The Chant of Jimmy Blacksmith* featured opening scenes which starred the landscape. McMahon and Quin have suggested that "the land becomes as powerful a force in the narrative as any of the characters".[21] To situate a community (an audience) into a nationalized imagining involves grazing the surfaces of the landscape, moulding it within the dominant forms of belonging. The increasing invention and proliferation of languages and practices within a territorial frame make any claim for solidifying national boundaries and territories more aggressive, conservative and deliberate. As Turner has offered,

> It is probably fair to say that in most Australian films today, national identity is simply not an issue ... something has happened to the way in which the nation is represented in our cinema and this may be related to the fact that something has happened to the way arguments about the category of the nation are currently framed.[22]

The limits and stories of the nation are changing, as seen through the astonishing *Rabbit Proof Fence*. It is not surprising that the discursive dust from the cinematic landscape is still circulating in the filmic semiosphere through such texts as *Japanese Story*. But even Tom Burlinson's horse could not ride over the contemporary contradictions within Australian nationalism. Between the tortured, brutal imagining of *Mad Max* and the suburban park of *The Sum of Us* lies a web of intertextual networks. Significantly, *Moulin Rouge* withdrew from the rural landscape and into Fox studios: the entire film was shot indoors. Therefore, it could have been shot *anywhere*. What makes it Australian is therefore determined in the realm of acting, production, financing and policy.

While *Moulin Rouge* had mixed success around the world, it was incredibly profitable in Australia. While it has been described as "the most expensive Australian film every made", the film collected A$21 million during the first six weeks of its run.[23] This is an Australian film with no recognizable 'oz-tray-lee-un' accents, no native wildlife or landmarks. There are some significant national interventions in *Moulin Rouge* for an Australian audience. There is a humour and shock of visual recognition. From Kylie Minogue's green fairy, who emerges during an absinthe trip, to Christine Anu's role as a can can girl in fin de siecle Paris, there are touchstones of meaning for those wishing to insert the film into a nationalist discourse. This knowledge system creates a shared reading strategy and understanding for a particular group of Australian viewers and a subtle node of resistance to American cinema. *Moulin Rouge*, through the delicate incorporation of Australianness, provides a few alternative textual crumbs and interests for Australian viewers, even in the midst of an American musical, set in Paris. Such meanings from a place are productive and imaginative, waging a war over surfaces. This ideological exfoliation cannot be cleanly won, but creates productive irritants to globalizing, Americanizing visuality. Continually, Baz Luhrmann has claimed the Australianness of the film. When Fox would not finance the absinthe fairy sequence featuring Minogue, he paid A$300,000 out of his own money to make the scene.[24] Brian McFarlane presented the film's critical problem: "*Moulin Rouge* has been touted as the most ambitious Australian film ever, raising again the question of what constitutes an Australian film."[25] It could not have been made in Hollywood: instead, intellectual distance from the musical tradition was required. This interpretative space creates an opportunity for generic translation. While being set in Paris, filmed in Australia, financed and distributed by Hollywood and styled by Bollywood, *Moulin Rouge* is a metonymy of contemporary film making.

Intimate relationships link space with culture. The material effect of places, like Sydney or Paris, allows the manipulation of cultural symbols and new modes of filmic display. Cosgrove has argued that "we should not scorn the study of imaginative geographies".[26] With no division between the symbolic or the real, the real or the representation, the representation or the simulacrum, the urban imaginary is changing. Every site has both signifying potential and authoritative meanings, as determined by empowered institutions. The relationship between social subjectivity and cultural practices is an ambiguous and contradictory topic and is best explored through a specific textual focus. *Moulin Rouge* is liminally located: between text and context, memory and history, repression and autonomy. It also corrupts the wall between time and space.

Time

I'm paid to make men believe what they want to believe.[27]

Satine

Baz Luhrmann has a history of playing with history. His 1996 rendering of Shakespeare's *Romeo and Juliet* was set on Verona Beach in the 1990s. The soundtrack was inspired, featuring passionate covers of disco tracks and a version of Prince's 'When doves cry'. Even critics who despised *Moulin Rouge* believed that his earlier film possessed "a wildness [that] evoked some of the passion of the original".[28] Notice that there is a desire to decentre the film's innovations, trying to claim the authenticity and credibility of the Shakespearian origin. If Luhrmann's films possess a single characteristic, it is the capacity to restitch the cinematic past in a new way.

Luhrmann was born in 1963 and was thirty-eight years old when *Moulin Rouge* was released. By the customary definition of Generation X, those born between 1961 and 1981, he slots cleanly into the category. He actually embodies the interests and expertise of this imagining community more than most. The marks of the music video decade are clearly found in his work. MTV began on August 1, 1981 and generated a new genre that freely melded art and commerce, popular and avant-garde techniques, realism and abstraction. The music video is a text of colour, shape and substance and excessive in its editing, incorporating thousands of editing cuts within a four-minute track. The genre increased the visuality of music, opening out its spaces and presence through circulation in clubs, television and bars. Music videos have a complex history, splicing through the other histories of film, television, popular music, dance and postmodernism. Music video has also changed the way in which audiences respond to cinema. While film privileges the image over a sound-track, music video is a far more composite form. Further, they unravel the categorical divisions between the aural and the visual, being a highly interdependent medium.

All these music video techniques can be viewed in Luhrmann's work. Generation X is the readership for a three-minute plot line and a promiscuous bleeding between sound and vision. Luhrmann is not working alone in such an intricate cultural field. While Quentin Tarantino was the pin-up director for Generation Xers everywhere, there were Xer films before this group were invented into consciousness. Not just *Ferris Bueller's Day Off*, but *Pretty in Pink*, *St. Elmo's Fire* and *Breakfast Club*. There are attitudes, ideologies and literacies that unify this proto-Xer filmic generation besides lip gloss and hair gel. With *Pump up the volume*, angst was added to the agenda, but accompanied by an apathy which has become an Xer filmic trademark. A fascination with the bizarre, such as *Heathers* and *Shallow Grave*, literally allowed the underdog proto-Xers to kill off their peers. As the 1990s progressed, the pomo gothic horror film became a major subgenre, most famously realized in *Pulp Fiction*. Not only the ideology, but the form and shape of these films is fascinating and owes much to music video. Therefore, Luhrmann's film is situated in a complex web of texts, all feeding into each other and building innovative visual literacies. As Susan Hopkins has suggested,

> Generation Pulp is defined and defines itself by entertainment discourse, in particular, the language of popular culture. What we are witnessing here is the violent play of urban life. Life is perceived as an aesthetic construction and television becomes a shared reality.[29]

This parasitic cultural formation creates not only endless pastiche and parody, but interpretative detachment. More in a narrative can be taken as given and plot points can be skipped or assumed. The strength of music videos is that they teach accelerated editing and plot. The energy and pace of *Moulin Rouge* can therefore be seen as both appropriate and necessary to the literacy of the audience viewing it.

The spaces of the text create many reading options. Hopkins realized that "this ambiguity speaks to a Gen-X audience; a generation which may be, out of necessity, more comfortable with uncertainty in both cultural and personal narratives".[30] The filmic impact on consciousness is clear: identity is being built out of cinematic clichés, pop music rhythms and advertizing jingles. In such an environment, a desire for authenticity is not as ironic as it may appear. This is where critics have been lost in the film: the excess of swirling fabrics surrounds the four catchwords of *Moulin Rouge*: beauty, truth, freedom, love. This nostalgic desire for the real is viewed in a range of films: the intense desire for a passionate encounter with life. *Trainspotting*'s junkies desire to be freed from choice. Bethany loses her *Dogma*, to be replaced by a profound belief in the ideas and debates of religion. *Good Will Hunting* is a dense screenplay, featuring long monologues and intense emotional panoramas. The desire for love grasps a desperation for an authentic, real relationship. This film slots in the space between the representations of romance and the reality of relationships for the audience. Sean counsels Will with a gritty honesty rarely captured on celluloid.

> And if I asked you about women I'm sure you could give me a syllabus of your personal favourites, and maybe you've been laid a few times, too. But you

couldn't tell me how it feels to wake up next to a woman and be truly happy ... And if I asked you about love I'd get a sonnet, but you've never looked at a woman and been truly vulnerable. Known that someone could kill you with a look. That someone could rescue you from your grief. That God had put an angel on earth just for you. And you wouldn't know how it felt to be her angel. To have the love to be there forever. Through anything, through cancer. You wouldn't know about sleeping sitting up in a hospital room for two months holding her hand and not leaving because the doctors could see in your eyes that the term visiting hours didn't apply to you. And you wouldn't know about real loss, because that only occurs when you lose something that you love more than yourself, and you've never dared to love anything that much.[31]

This long speech, delivered by Robin Williams, accesses the train wrecks of a love life. Through a fictionalized counselling session, a desire for authenticity is profound and obvious. Luhrmann's father died on the first day of *Moulin Rouge*'s filming. Kidman's well publicized divorce from Tom Cruise punctuated the publicity for the film. The director hailed and claimed these 'real life', authenticating synergies, by stating that

The story of the film and our lives are very parallel. It's about coming to terms with the moment when you grew up. Oh, you mean people die? Oh, there are relationships that cannot be?[32]

As Kidman emerged from the chrysalis of Mrs Tom Cruise and walked the red carpet in her own right, she bounced freely between the real, representation and simulacrum of self and identity.

The greater question remains how Generation X can manage the media to transform political life. The topographies of consumption allow a mapping of the social and the opening of spaces of reception – including memory spaces. *Moulin Rouge* is, as Brian McFarlane has stated, "a kind of movie museum".[33] He is suggesting that this film is an amalgamation of disparate objects, ideas, films and fashions. The film floats through genre and time. As a platform for cultural display, it transforms viewers into tourists, dipping into a past situated between expectations and lived reality. These stylistic and musical references are not ephemeral or 'clever clever' film making, but significant building blocks of plot, character and effect.

For viewers, *Moulin Rouge* activates postmodern filmic tourism, or what MacCannell described as a "theory that, like the Western tourist, can imagine roaming widely without losing its place or identity".[34] Tourism is a framework that stresses some elements of a landscape – and some parts of a history – over others. The most important ideology located in this discourse of tourism is authenticity. The economies of tourism drive a wedge between the modern world and the past, with the latter becoming what we have lost, a retreat from the present. *Moulin Rouge* establishes such an effective representational logic because it, like *24 Hour Party People*, fetishizes that which is different, yet situates it within a familiar knowledge system. Therefore the past – whether 1899 Paris or the 1950s American musical – is both exotic and familiar. Such a journey is nostalgic, what Lowenthal described as "a growing rebellion against the present".[35] *Moulin Rouge* performs this principle to excess, raising a 1899 Paris from the digital bits and bytes. The music too confirms a retreat to the past. Both sound and vision are reframed and recut in the present. Just as the tourist part is the artificial preservation of the non-modern world in the midst of modern society, *Moulin Rouge* creates a manufactured Paris that is unsteadily positioned in time. The film industry has always made shallow connections between present lives and history. When history is a surface to be read, films perform the multiple representations and paths through the past.[36]

Moulin Rouge is a museum film, capturing and preserving a century of popular culture. National museums act as storehouses of a society's treasures, aligning the past and present and relying on the functional ideology of progress. Museums circulate a culture's rules in a controlled environment. That means, whatever happened in the past can be explained (away) by focussing on present accomplishments. *Moulin Rouge* plays with time, with the story starting in a dark present, with a bereaved Christian writing his love story and his loss. Time moves, ducks and weaves. Christian is the museum guide through this pastiched past, framing and limiting reading potentials. *Moulin Rouge* wrestles with the past, summoning a reading community with a remarkable range of literacies, building a community around a specific filmic text. The blending of profound and trivial in *Moulin Rouge* has created the basis for cult status. Actually, the film confirms Eco's maxim that "these are 'postmodern' movies, where the quotation of the topos is recognized as the only way to cope with the burden of our filmic encyclopaedic expertise".[37] The organic textuality of the film transforms viewers into mobile semioticians. The role and reason for this range of cultural references is to open the text out to other songs, movies and narratives, capturing the multiple experiences of popular memory.

Memory

The woman I love is dead.[38]
>
> Christian

Luhrmann's trademark is sampling filmic styles. *Strictly Ballroom* fused Spanish rhythms within the most formal of ballroom dancing structures. Politically, it grasped a sample of multiculturalism and mixed it with an emerging urban Australianness. *Moulin Rouge*'s entire plot is based on an act of memory, regret and retrospect, where Christian declares at the start of the film, "the woman I love is dead". *Moulin Rouge* blends high and pop culture, with parallel narratives woven through the film. Christian's desire to rescue Satine mirrors Orpheus' relationship with Eurydice. Satine's Parisian consumption hails Mimi's coughing contagion in *La Boheme*, while her death at the denouement echoes from *West Side Story*. The mistaken identity ruse, where Christian is mistaken for the Duke, is pure French farce. The emotional and cinematic continuities are startling and offer a profound translation of the Hollywood musical. Kidman is diva-fied, amalgamating Rita Hayworth, Marlene Dietrich, Marilyn Monroe and Madonna.

The most savage critics of the film believe that Luhrmann "is manipulating us".[39] Kauffmann dismisses the notion that the audience for this film is intelligent enough to read it on many levels, through the ironic distance required for a meta-movie experience. This ironic inauthenticity welcomes an emotional investment in an image that does not link to realist codes. He does not grasp that it is possible to be playfully ironic and emotionally sincere, trashily pastiching the past, while simultaneously constructing a monument to cinematic history. To view this linear mode of filmic analysis, ponder Kauffmann's final blistering attack:

> The net result of all this cinematic whirling, of the 'wrong' music and of the parodic plot, is that nothing at all in the film moves us ... He wants us to be unmoved. He wants us to see the emotional climaxes as trickeries, disclosed here by a caustic postmodernist. With near-Brechtian brutality, swathed though it is in silks and frills, he is scoffing at the fabrications of romance.[40]

Obviously, there are many possible interpretations of *Moulin Rouge*. A reading of the film which argues that it is anti-romantic and against an expression of love is highly aberrant. The film is ironic certainly, but it affirms and performs a deep commitment to love and desire. Luhrmann has answered the charges of manipulation and reflectivity. He has also explained the rationale behind his motifs and motives.

> You're constantly awaking the audience so they participate ... Just when you think, 'this is so cheesy, I'm going to throw up', I'm going to kick you in the stomach. In that state, there's an agreement that they know they are going to be emotionally manipulated, and they surrender to it. The audience does not come and pay $8 to watch someone else be really careful.[41]

Luhrmann is actually demanding interest and activity from his audience, rather than accepting it as formed by dull, poorly educated cultural dupes.

Because Kauffmann has a poor sense of the role and place of cinematic music, he cannot move beyond a chronological positioning of popular music's back catalogue. But songs move through time and are changed by the journey. To understand *Moulin Rouge* and its audience, there must be a realization of pop music's function in the personal experiences of viewers and in popular memory. *Moulin Rouge* is a musical and that genre has been misunderstood and misinterpreted. It has always been a genre of heightened reality, of banal repetition and groundbreaking surprise. Dominic Strinati – although hostile to postmodernism – offers a clear answer to those critics attempting to distance *Moulin Rouge* from the cinematic history of the musical.

> From the postmodern point of view, contemporary cinema is seen to be indulging in nostalgia, living off its past, ransacking it for ideas, recycling its images and plots and cleverly citing it in self-conscious postmodern parodies ... Yet again, this exaggerates the novelty of these kinds of developments and misconstrues their character and their history. The repeat and the sequel have been part of the way cinema has worked from its earliest stages.[42]

Musicals have always recycled songs, characters and scripts. Using rock music in 1899 Paris is not a violation of the genre. The musical has always bent time. Ponder the contextual appropriateness of 'Have yourself a merry little Christmas' in 1904 St Louis.

So much of popular music's joy involves sharing a *feeling*. Kauffmann denies the power of this collectivity, by the throwaway argument that the "musical incongruity leads to easy laughs".[43] Again, there is no sense of the function of music for an audience. A moment of brilliance, where popular memory is used as a scalpel to cut through time, space and plot, is the first scene in the *Moulin Rouge* where the male 'punters' sing Nirvana's 'Smells like teen spirit' – with the breathtakingly appropriate lyric, "Here we are now, entertain us." This melody becomes woven through as a harmony line to the courtesans' siren call of 'Lady Marmalade', one of the most explicit and sexualized lyrics of the disco era. These two dance lines of prostitutes and paying customers also duel the histories of disco and grunge, empowered women and scrawny white boys with bad hair and personal hygiene issues. Importantly, LaBelle did outlast Cobain, just as disco outlived grunge. Through the choice of music, women are granted strength and autonomy, riding on the back of disco's feminized, empowered history. Beyond words, music, vision or dancing, *Moulin Rouge* is a site for a dazzling interplay between colours and costuming, sound and beat, that blurs the analytical sense of seeing, hearing and writing.[44] As Timothy Gray and Dade Hayes recognized, "it's audacious and entertaining and those who like it *really* like it".[45] The world summoned in the film is complete, complex and detailed.

Luhrmann revels in the temporal dialogue of popular music, by believing that Moulin Rouge was "the greatest rave there ever was. The first rave".[46] This paradox is not as bizarre as it appears. The film maker uses music to create a community and guide them through an emotional landscape. Popular music *matters* for its complexity, inter-textuality and its accessibility. What makes it such an important source is its capacity to be 'pop' – to capture a moment and experience. While critics have abused *Moulin Rouge*'s musical references, discussing the 'manipulative' mixing of the libretto for *La Traviata* with Elton John, Phil Collins and Nirvana songs, actually the film honours popular music. Excess is not always ironic.

It is remarkable how often *Moulin Rouge* was described as postmodern. David Ansen created a melody of slick adjectives, describing the film as a "deliriously energetic, promiscuously postmodern, tragicomical musical".[47] It seems reviewers use the word postmodern to describe any film with an interesting soundtrack and that does not star Meryl Streep or Jeremy Irons. Too many conservative film critics, schooled in Postmodernism 101, see an investment in surfaces as cold, calculating and artificial. They desire depth and original meanings. *Moulin Rouge* is so powerful, because it realizes *it is a text*: an open mesh of reading possibilities. Like the best of cinema, *Moulin Rouge*'s references, fashions, songs and characters do not stand alone, but hook out of the filmic fabric and into the experiences of viewers. For *Casablanca* to work at its best requires the viewer to remember the Bogart persona, the crumpled man who moved from gangster roles to the ambivalent hero of *The Maltese Falcon*. *Casablanca* has survived and prospered – not because it is a perfect film with a seamless narrative. Instead it is the holes, gaps, paradoxes and incompleteness that creates satisfaction for the viewer. The work conducted by an audience in interpretation allows a film to be grafted onto personal experience. *Moulin Rouge* instigates this project so effectively because musical affectivity provides the bridge between a text and the memories of a readership.

Musical and filmic popular memory frames *Moulin Rouge*. Actually the narrative, characters, setting and songs rely on the viewer's knowledge. Luhrmann stated this tactic overtly: "it's an audience participation film."[48] His creation of new cinematic languages is being read actively and engagingly. As a "karaoke musical",[49] the soundtrack aligns affective communication between the screen and audience. The medley in the elephant building of the Moulin Rouge captures the spark of myriad memory traces. Splicing 'All you need is love' by the Beatles with McCartney's 'Silly love songs', 'One more night' by Phil Collins and (incredibly) Dolly Parton's 'I will always love you', enfolds a short history of love songs in four minutes of footage. The affectivity of this sonic conversation serves to wither the critical function. Ansen described McGregor's serenade of Kidman with Elton John's 'Your Song' as "that moment that my fears melted away and I was swept up in the moonstruck lunacy of Luhrmann's vision".[50] Musicals – particularly those that stretch and probe the genre – are frequently earnest and passionate in their humour and commitment. *Strictly Ballroom*, the first in Luhrmann's 'Red Curtain trilogy', was excessive, garish in its make-up and clothes, with lighting as subtle as a fluorescent light in an escalator, but it was a pivotal moment in Australian cultural history. Musicals are serious in their playfulness. *Band Wagon*, surely the best of musicals, is so celebrated because it carries the trace of Fred Astaire's persona and re-presents it in a narrative about an ageing tap dancer whose best days are in the past. This film was then pillaged in *Moulin Rouge*, with the 'Spectacular Spectacular' production number, which owed more than a glance to the backstage musical.

Journalists have attacked *Moulin Rouge* as "a blatantly artificial story".[51] Such a judgement is forgetting that all film is artificial. Simply because Meryl Streep has a death scene or Julia Roberts weeps at another failed romance does not suggest that cinema captures real life. Realist codes in cinematography mask highly ideological, politicized functions. Artifice is a filmic strategy that permits an audience to probe, question and unravel the colours, sounds and narratives propelling the action. *Moulin Rouge*, as a meta-musical, displays the scaffolding of the cinema, the underwear under the petticoats. Todd McCarthy demeaned the film as "dealing broadly with archetypes and conventions [that] restricts the picture's effectiveness to its brilliant surface".[52] The best directors – Fellini and Lynch – construct a commentary on the genre in which their films are read and placed. A few critics have realized the passionate blurring of fact and fiction, realism and artifice. Kent Jones confirmed that

> The film is at once historically grounded and 150% fantastical, immersed in film history yet giddily unconcerned with its traditionalist solemnities, culturally sophisticated yet destined to become the new favourite movie of 14-year-olds in Topeka.[53]

While films like *Pleasantville* awkwardly and inconsistently rallied popular cultural references, there is an intense discipline to *Moulin Rouge*'s intertexuality. The visual detail and the dancing camera work are enhanced by surprising editing cuts.

Moulin Rouge is not located in a single event or moment. It plays with time, place and memory. One of the few historical fixtures is the presence and role of Henri de Toulouse-Lautrec. His studio in the Montmartre quarter of Paris offered a context for the coming of age story of Christian. The form and style of his paintings provided the palette for the colours, textures and excesses of the film. Lautrec's 1891 poster for *Moulin Rouge* was part of what Howard Lay termed "the commercialization of 'popular' culture in Montmartre".[54] It is appropriate that Luhrmann has continued this thread of meaning through the film. Just as Lautrec lived life as a spectator of decadence, caused through his genetic bone disorder, *Moulin Rouge* transforms his paintings into mobile, chattering museums that can be viewed and walked through. But the nightclub too is excized from history. It takes colour and energy from the past, but uses the music to move through time.

Perhaps more effectively than all other films set in fin de siecle Paris, *Moulin Rouge* captures the spirit and fire of Lautrec's famous 1891 poster of La Goulue's muscular leg encircled by ruched petticoats. Lay believed that

> Lautrec's image quite simply spoke to two publics at the same time: the first, those spectators who wanted little more than to savour the cut-rate glamour and staged irreverence of the place or to take a peek up La Goulue's skirts; and the second, the more privileged audience that went to the Moulin Rouge in order to partake of what they knew quite well was an entirely exploitative form of pleasure, and for whom the exquisite vulgarity of the manufactured 'popular' spectacle accordingly held considerable fascination.[55]

Lay has also captured what makes *Moulin Rouge* function as a film and popular culture. There is an audience who is captivated by the romance, music, skirts and songs. Further, there are viewers who are passionate about the 'exquisite vulgarity' of the film and its tight packaging of cinematic and musical history. Through a bordello red lens and singing through open wound red lipstick, *Moulin Rouge* takes viewers on an emotional bungee jump. This is a film where audiences bring their experiences and realities to the screen. As Eco realized of *Casablanca*, "it is not one movie. It is 'movies'. And that is the reason it works".[56] Below the foaming petticoats is cinematic history.

Notes

1. Christian and Satine, *Moulin Rouge* (Twentieth Century Fox, 2001).

2. For a discussion of this critical reception, please refer to Jonathan Taylor's "Oscar race at a gallop", *Variety*, December 24 2001-January 6, 2001, pp. 34-35.

3. S. Cheng, "Slim pickings in Cannes", *World and I*, Vol. 16, No. 9, September 2001, p. 82.

4. V. Porter, "The Robert Clark Account: films released in Britain by Associated British Pictures, British Lion, MGM, and Warner Bros., 1946-1957", *Historical Journal of Film, Radio and Television*, Vol. 20, No. 4, 2000, p. 479.

5. L. Brengle, "Divine decadence, Darling! The sixty-year history of the Kit Kat Klub", *Journal of Popular Culture*, Vol. 34, September 2000, p. 152.

6. Christian, *Moulin Rouge*.

7. P. Kerr, "Molar rouge", *New Statesman*, September 3, 2001, p. 30.

8. Kerr, *op. cit.*, p. 30.

9. Kerr, *op. cit.*, p. 29.

10. B. Ellen, "Moulin Rouge" (London) *The Times*, September 6, 2001.

11. B. McFarlane, "The movie as museum", *Meanjin*, Vol. 60, No. 7, December 2001, Expanded Academic Database [full-text article].

12. R. Gibson, "Formative landscapes", in S. Murry (ed.), *Australian Cinema* (St Leonards: Allen and Unwin, 1993), p. 45.

13. R. Romney, "Pigs swill be pigs", *New Statesman and Society*, December 15/29, 1995, p. 55.

14. *ibid.*, p. 55.

15. The issue of accent is one that is increasingly common to Australian Popular/Cultural Studies. John Fiske, Graeme Turner and Bob Hodge dedicated a chapter to accent in *Myths of Oz* (St. Leonards: Allen and Unwin, 1987). In this chapter, they argued that "the Australian accent is one of the clearest markers of Australianness", p. 163. Similarly Ian Craven, in his "Introduction" to the edited collection *Australian Popular Culture* (Cambridge: Cambridge University Press, 1994) stated that "one of the most noticeable phenomena evident to students of popular culture in the past ten years has been the increasing ability of an Australian 'accent' amongst the languages and discourse that compose the field of their studies", p. 1.

16 The near-contemporary British rendering of urbanity is in a contradictory form to *Strictly Ballroom*. *Sammy and Rosie Get Laid* is a site where Geoff Eley believed "the urban environment and its traditional class certainties are shown completely disordered", in "Distant voices, still lives", in R. Rosenstone (ed.), *Revisioning History: Film and the construction of a new past* (Chicester, Princeton University Press, 1995), p. 23.

17 P. Adams, "Introduction", from J. Sabine (ed.), *A century of Australian cinema* (Port Melbourne: William Heinemann, 1995), p. x.

18 M. Wark, "Cinema II: the next hundred years", from Sabine, p. 202.

19 T. Safford, "Two or three things I know about Australian Cinema", *Media Information Australia*, No. 76, May 1995, p. 27.

20 N. Rattigan, "Crocodile Dundee: Apotheosis of the Ocker", *Journal of Popular Film and Television*, Vol. 15, Winter 1988, p. 151.

21 B. McMahon and R. Quin, *Australian images* (Marrickille: Science Press, 1990), p. 33.

22 G. Turner, "Whatever happened to national identity? Film and the nation in the 1990s", *Metro*, No. 100, Summer 1994-5, p. 33.

23 S. George, "Around the Globe", *Film Journal International*, August 2001, p. 143.

24 J. Horn, "The Land of Baz: from filling gas tanks to making *Moulin Rouge*, Aussie showman Baz Luhrmann has always been over the top", *Newsweek*, May 28, 2001, p. 58.

25 McFarlane, *op. cit.*

26 D. Cosgrove, "Geography is everywhere: culture and symbolism in human landscapes", in D. Gregory and Walford (eds), *New Horizons in Human Geography* (New Jersey: Barnes and Noble: 1989), p. 133.

27 Satine, *Moulin Rouge.*

28 S. Kauffman, "On films – seeing is disbelieving", *The New Republic*, June 11, 2001, p. 28.

29 S. Hopkins, "Generation Pulp", *Youth Studies Australia*, Spring 1995, p. 16.

30 *ibid.*, p. 17.

31 M. Damon and B. Affleck, *Good Will Hunting: a screenplay* (New York: Hyperion, 1997), pp. 71-72.

32 B. Luhrmann, quoted in B. Johnson "Cannes Cancan", *Maclean's*, May 21, 2001, p. 80.

33 McFarlane, *op. cit.*

34 D. MacCannell, *Empty Meeting Grounds* (London: Routledge, 1992), p. 2.

35 D. Lowenthal, *The past is a foreign country* (Cambridge: Cambridge University Press, 1985), p. 11.

36 For a discussion of tourism, authenticity, inauthenticity and postmodernism, please refer to John Frow's "Tourism and the semiotics of Nostalgia", *October*, Vol. 51, 1991.

37 U. Eco, *Travels in Hyperreality* (London: Secker and Warburg, 1987), p. 209.

38 Christian, *Moulin Rouge.*

39 Kauffmann, *op. cit.*, p. 28.

40 *ibid.*

41 B. Luhrmann, from Horn, *op. cit.*, p. 58.

42 D. Strinati, *An introduction to theories of popular culture* (London: Routledge, 1995), p. 243.

43 *ibid.*

44 The significance of *Moulin Rouge*'s costuming and design is well revealed in Lori Kaye's "Clothes that cancan", *The Advocate*, June 5, 2001 p. 59. She realized that "for the film's overall aesthetic, *Moulin Rouge*'s creative team draws a parallel between Montmartre at the end of the 19th century and modern club culture. Like *Studio 54*, the Moulin Rouge – a combination of dance hall and theater – brought people from all walks of life together". The remarkable work of Catherine Martin's costuming demonstrates how profoundly important clothes are to musical and dancing performances within film.

45 T. Gray and D. Hayes, "Case of the Cuckoo Kudos", *Variety*, December 24-January 6, 2002, p. 40.

46 B. Luhrmann, "The nightclub of your dreams, the making of *Moulin Rouge*", *Moulin Rouge* (Twentieth Century Fox, 2001).

47 D. Ansen, "Yes, 'rouge' Can, Can, Can: not since *Cabaret* has a musical had such a kick", *Newsweek*, May 28, 2001, p. 61.

48 B. Luhrmann, quoted in S. Swart, "La vie en 'Rouge'", *Variety*, May 7-13, 2001, p. 10.

49 K. Jones, "Real artifice", *Film Comment*, Vol. 37, No. 3, May 2001, p. 22.

50 Ansen, *op. cit.*, p. 61.

51 T. McCarthy, "High-kicking 'Rouge' brings razzle-dazzle to Croisette", *Variety*, May 14-20, 2001, p. 21.

52 McCarthy, p. 21. Similarly, Julia Klein, in "Live, laugh, love", *The American Prospect*, July 30, 2001, p. 31, states that "his central characters ... are all painted surface, and their passions remain unconvincing".

53 K. Jones, "Read Artifice", *Film Comment*, p. 22.

54 H. Lay, "Toulouse-Lautrec", *The Art Bulletin*, Vol. 76, No. 1, March 1994, fulltext.

55 Lay, *op. cit.*, fulltext.

56 Eco, *op. cit.*, p. 208.

Conclusion

Save Ferris

It all started normally. I was writing a lecture about how the Beatles are positioned within modern memory. The aim of the week's teaching was to assess how the Beatles' *Anthology* documentary re-inscribed the past. Well, that was the official justification. In pre-mediated fashion, it was an opportunity for a (then) 27-year old media lecturer to explain to the assembled 18-year-olds how much she despised the Beatles specifically and their boomer audience generally. Even the most polemic of lectures requires some evidence, so I investigated my video collection for traces of post-1960s Beatles' iconography. It was during this process that I rediscovered an old, loving media friend.

How could I have forgotten Ferris? I was seventeen years old when *Ferris Bueller's Day Off* was released in 1986. It was *my* film, about *my* friends. We all wanted to be as cool as the smooth dressing, extroverted, socially successful Ferris. The image of the young Matthew Broderick, lip-synching The Beatles' 'Twist and Shout' on a float in the middle of a Chicago street, remains transfixed in my iconographic database. Everything was *right* about that film. It was radically intertextual, anti-establishment, anti-school, pro-love and friendship and hipper than a year's subscription to *The Face* during the decade when that meant something.

All these emotions came cascading back, so that even trashing the boomers seemed less important. I remembered a moment of my life when nothing seemed more significant than owning a pair of Raybans. I remembered finally buying the shades and wearing them constantly for two weeks. This was a simpler me without all the anti-boomer angst to weigh down my affectivity.

The lecture passed, including the clip of Ferris singing 'Twist and Shout', but my disquiet remained. As I continued to read Xer theorists and theorizing, I realized that we – that is Xers who claim the term – have lost something: our recent past. We have absorbed the criticisms of the eighties as 'a bad time' and been trapped by discourses of sexual repression (the AIDS virus), economic depression (youth unemployment) and poor taste (Madonna). Contemporary reviews of XerTV (XTV), like *Buffy* and films, like *Pulp Fiction*, have focused on the darkness of the texts.[1]

Julie Burchill once asked of the 1980s, "is this decade the end of the world, or just another excuse for a party?"[2] On a 1990 album, Katrin Quinol, the lead singer of Blackbox, belted out the words "I don't know, I don't know, I don't know when the party ends."[3] It seems the long eighties is over: the dressing up, the dancing, the laughing has ceased. Perhaps – now – the popular memory party (of the party) can commence. More seriously, though, Douglas Coupland may be right. In *Life after God* he stated

> I believe that you've had most of your important memories by the time you're thirty. After that, memory becomes water overflowing into an already full cup. New experiences just don't register in the same way or with the same impact. I could be shooting heroin with the Princess of Wales, naked in a crashing jet, and the experience still couldn't compare to the time the cops chased us after we threw the Taylor's patio furniture into their pool in the eleventh grade. You know what I mean.[4]

Generation X, as the archetypal (post)youth culture and media citizens, has learnt its televisual lessons well. Yet Max Headroom, Ren, Stimpy and Pee Wee Herman will not age. Xers have to discover a pathway that television could never teach us: how do we grow old? Again, Coupland provides us with the answer.

> When you are young, you always expect that the world is going to end. And then you get older and the world still chugs along and you are forced to re-evaluate your stance on the apocalypse as well as your own relationship to time and death. You realize that the world will indeed continue, with or without you, and the pictures you see in your head. So you try to understand the pictures instead.[5]

The world will indeed continue without Generation X. We will still wear Raybans, laugh with Ferris and sing along – quietly at first – with Wham's 'Wake me up before you go go.' By *understanding* these sounds and visions – and that means constructing a popular memory – these media citizens will continue to be reflexive and, therefore, elusive.

Popular memory is a tantalizing, elusive subject: tough to discuss and intensely complex to theorize. Therefore, *how* this book has been written is part of the argument. Each chapter has built on that which preceded it. Summoned from the same moment, but with different impulses and impetuses, the chapters have moved history, Popular/Cultural Studies and (post) youth culture into a new theatre of debate: popular memory. Each part has looked through one angle of the intellectual crystal. Kevin Smith's films, Robbie Williams, Tony Wilson, *Moulin Rouge* and the Hacienda Club in 'Madchester' form overnight stops, but other curious visions spiral into view. *From Revolution to Revelation* provides a trace of (con)textual struggles waged during the decade when Cultural Studies 'made it big'. It also tells the truth – and some interesting lies – about a group of style victims who can make a Brandy Alexander faster than scrambled eggs.

Popular memory is not only an object of study for Cultural Studies. It can create a new path for an interdisciplinary humanities education. Generation X has been such an intoxicating media invention because it offered a simple answer to difficult cultural questions. As a community, audience or readership with advanced cultural literacies and a story of light, colour and humour, they offer Cultural Studies a new agenda, a way to link text with context, media with history. Irvine Welsh grasped this tight embrace between politics and pleasure.

> It was the party: he felt that you had to party, you had to party harder than ever. It was the only way. It was your duty to show that you were still alive. Political sloganeering and posturing meant nothing; you had to celebrate the joy of life in the face of all those grey forces and dead spirits that controlled everything.[6]

There are many mornings when I agree with Welsh: surviving the last fifteen years with humour and integrity is a noteworthy achievement. Therefore, this book has not only revelled in the party. It has explored the function of the party long after the hangover and clean-up. The political rigidity of the post-cold war environment and the evaporation of Keynesian notions of public good and public funding, has disconnected people from the experiences of their own life. Commonsense and good sense are seemingly never more disparate. When we champion both popular culture and popular memory, these playful textual movements create spaces outside officially sanctioned sites, histories and meanings. By claiming the potential of revelation through popular memory in a time when revolutionary change has lost its appeal, repair work to shrunken social structures can commence.

At its ironic, profound best, *Trainspotting* demanded that we 'Choose life … But why would I want to do a thing like that?'[7] With a hyper-capitalism shaped by post-Fordism, what is required is not choice, but a freedom *from* choice. (Post) youth culture, throughout their archaeology, has been labelled as either lost, or having innovatively found a resistive pod outside of capitalism. In choosing not to choose life – in choosing not to choose

185

capitalism – the filmic mantras of *Moulin Rouge, 24 Hour Party People, Trainspotting, Fight Club, Clerks* and *Dogma* hold a teaching function, presenting alternative lives when few options seem available. These films have built on other landmark memory sites, such as the *Star Wars* Trilogy. While the force is with us, spirituality becomes a commodity to be bought and sold. Therapy, bonding and spiritual epiphanies are as everyday as an *Oprah Show*. We need more meaning and politics than Dr Phil can provide. Indeed, as Tyler Durden from *Fight Club* reminded us, "how much do you know about yourself if you've never been in a fight?"[8] In mapping the cultural landscape, inversion, irony, reflexivity and nostalgia jut out of popular culture. Now, we require a methodology to understand them.

The aim of *From Revolution to Revelation* is to enact disciplinary repair work. I have returned to a minor debate, published in a minor book by the Birmingham Centre at the turn of the 1980s. In this context, popular memory is shorthand for destiny, the possible, the past, loss or critique. The passionate possibilities of Popular Memory Studies seem ideally suited to the rebuilding of community-based politics. It provides an affective way to reclaim and repair the organic intellectual in us all. While research at universities is defined as that which attracts grants from 'industry', and teaching becomes a series of generic skills and competency boxes to tick, a Cultural Studies education must demand and achieve more. It is time to follow the lead of Noel Gallagher. Singing from the nest of Oasis, he is "gonna start a revolution from my bed".[9] It is time for Cultural Studies writers to start a revelation – in the head.

Notes

1   A provoking and impressive review of these texts and the ideologies that underpin them is Susan Hopkins' article "Generation Pulp: Entertainment and the postmodern generation", *Youth Studies Australia*, Vol. 14, No. 3, Spring 1995.

2   J. Burchill, "Apocalypse now (please)", *The Face*, May 1985, p. 14.

3   "I don't know anybody else", written by M. Limoni, D. Davoli and V. Semplici, from Blackbox's *Dreamland* (Liverpool: Deconstruction, 1990), track two.

4   D. Coupland, *Life after God* (New York: Pocket Books, 1993), p. 48.

5   *ibid.*, p. 108.

6   I. Welsh, *Ecstasy* (London: Vintage, 1996), pp. 26-7.

7   *Trainspotting*, directed by Danny Boyle (Miramax, 1996).

8   Tyler Durden, *Fight Club* (Twentieth Century Fox, 1999).

9   Oasis, "Don't look back in anger", *(What's the story) Morning Glory* (Big Brother, 2000), track four.

Select Bibliography

Blaikie, A., *Ageing and popular culture* (Cambridge: Cambridge University Press, 1999).

Bull, M. and Back, L. (eds), *The Auditory Culture Reader* (Oxford: Berg, 2004).

Carroll, P., *Keeping time* (Athens: University of Georgia Press, 1990).

Chambers, I., *Popular culture* (London: Methuen, 1986).

Collin, M., *Altered state* (London: Serpent's Tail, 1997).

Coupland, D., *Generation X* (London: Abacus, 1992).

Coupland, D., *Microserfs* (New York: Regan Books, 1995).

Davis, M., *Gangland* (Sydney: Allen and Unwin, 1997).

Eshun, K., *More brilliant than the sun* (London: Quartet, 1998).

Grossberg, L., *Dancing in spite of myself* (Durham: Duke University Press, 1997).

Hall, S. et al., *Policing the crisis* (London: Macmillan, 1978).

Haslam, D., *Manchester England* (London: Fourth Estate, 2000).

Heath, C., *Feel* (London: Ebury, 2004).

Hebdige, D., *Subculture: the meaning of style* (London: Routledge, 1979).

Hebdige, D., *Hiding in the light* (London: Routledge, 1988).

Hobsbawm, E., *On history* (London: Weidenfeld and Nicholson, 1997).

Jenkins, K. (ed.), *The postmodern history reader* (London: Routledge, 1997).

Johnson, R et al. (eds), *Making histories* (Minneapolis: University of Minnesota Press, 1982).

Lipsitz, G., *Time passages* (Minneapolis: University of Minnesota Press, 1990).

Marcus, G., *Lipstick traces* (London: Secker and Warburg, 1989).

Marcus, G., *The dustbin of history* (Cambridge: Harvard University Press, 1995).

Martin, A., *Phantasms* (Harmondsworth: Penguin, 1994).

Morley, P., *Words and music: a history of pop in the shape of the city* (London: Bloomsbury, 2003).

Morris, M., *Too soon too late* (Bloomington: Indiana University Press, 1998).

Pickering, M., *History, experience and cultural studies* (Houndmills: Macmillan Press, 1997).

Redhead, S., *The end of the century party* (Manchester: Manchester University Press, 1990).

Redhead, S., *Rave off* (Aldershot: Ashgate, 1993).

Redhead, S., *Paul Virilio – theorist for an accelerated culture* (Edinburgh: Edinburgh University Press, 2004).

Reynolds, S., *Energy flash* (London: Macmillan, 1998).

Samuel, R., *Theatres of memory* (London: Verso, 1994).

Savage, J., *England's dreaming* (London: Faber, 1990).

Savage, J., *Time travel* (London: Chatto and Windus, 1996).

Smith, K., *Clerks and Chasing Amy: two screenplays* (New York: Hyperion, 1997).

Smith, K., *Dogma* (New York: Grove Press, 1999).

Thompson, E., *The Making of the English Working Class* (Harmondsworth: Penguin, 1968).

Toop, D., *Exotica: fabricated soundscapes in a real world* (London: Serpent's Tail, 1999).

Toop, D., *Haunted weather: music, silence and memory* (London: Serpent's Tail, 2004).

Turner, G., *British cultural studies* (London: Routledge, 1996).

Wilson, T., *24 hour party people* (London: Macmillan, 2002).

Windschuttle, K., *The killing of history* (Paddington: Macleay Press, 1994).

Index